'Midorikawa and Sweeney have  of literary espionage. English lit
– *Financial Times*

'[A] medley of vivid narratives.' – *The Atlantic*

'Glorious insights into female rivalry and female solidarity and the delicate balancing act required to ensure one doesn't override the other.' – *The Herald*

'[An] evocative and well-researched ode to female solidarity.'
– *Publishers Weekly*

'Rich and revealing ... these forgotten friendships, from illicit and scandalous to radical and inspiring, are revelations.' – *Kirkus*

'As friends, fellow teachers and kindred scholars, [Emily Midorikawa and Emma Claire Sweeney] carry the torch of feminist cultural criticism. Meticulous researchers, they leave no manuscript unturned.' – *New York Journal of Books*

'Extraordinary detective work... Readers interested in women writers and these authors in particular will find this work enlightening.' – *Library Journal*

'Enthralling, illuminating, and a treat for fans of any of the writers who are covered.' – *Booklist*

'In digging up the forgotten friendships chronicled in *A Secret Sisterhood*, Emily Midorikawa and Emma Claire Sweeney have done much service to literary history.' – **Margaret Atwood**, Booker Prize winner and author of *The Handmaid's Tale*

'*A Secret Sisterhood* offers a clever new perspective on established literary figures. While we may inherit family and circumstances, we get to choose our friends; and those these famous women writers have chosen reveal much that is fresh and fascinating about their lives and their work.' – **Tracy Chevalier**, author of *Girl with a Pearl Earring* and editor of *Reader, I Married Him*

'*A Secret Sisterhood* is a marvel. On the strength of a hunch, two friends embark on a research mission that winds up becoming a vital and necessary contribution to women's history, literary history, and the literature of friendship. Beautifully written, rich with insight and feeling, this book is a must-read for anyone who knows that behind every great woman stands a great female friend.' – **Kate Bolick**, author of *Spinster: Making a Life of One's Own*

'Genuine scholarship that reads like a detective novel... My nonfiction book of the year.' – **Amanda Craig**, reviewer and author of *A Vicious Circle*

'*A Secret Sisterhood* will help make women's literary friendships of the past relevant to the present.' – **Michèle Roberts**, author of *Daughters of the House*

'*A Secret Sisterhood* ... helps to redress the marginalisation of serious non-fiction by and about women.' – **Karen Maitland**, author of *Company of Liars*

'Such an important, neglected topic: friendships between women writers and their influence on one another. It has long been downplayed – at last Emily Midorikawa and Emma Claire Sweeney are challenging this, with many fascinating revelations.' – **Jill Dawson**, author of *The Great Lover*

'Wise and exhilarating.' – **Samantha Ellis**, author of *How to Be a Heroine: Or, What I've Learned from Reading Too Much* and *Take Courage: Anne Brontë and the Art of Life*

'Brilliantly researched and eminently accessible.' – **Emma Henderson**, author of *Grace Williams Says it Loud*

A
SECRET
SISTERHOOD

The Hidden Friendships of
Austen, Brontë, Eliot and Woolf

EMILY MIDORIKAWA AND
EMMA CLAIRE SWEENEY

Brimming with creative inspiration, how-to projects and useful information to enrich your everyday life, Quarto Knows is a favourite destination for those pursuing their interests and passions. Visit our site and dig deeper with our books into your area of interest: Quarto Creates, Quarto Cooks, Quarto Homes, Quarto Lives, Quarto Drives, Quarto Explores, Quarto Gifts, or Quarto Kids.

First published in 2017 by Aurum Press
an imprint of The Quarto Group
The Old Brewery
6 Blundell Street
London N7 9BH
United Kingdom

www.QuartoKnows.com

This paperback edition first published in 2018 by Aurum Press

A catalogue record for this book is available from the British Library.

ISBN 978-1-78131-786-0
Ebook ISBN 978-1-78131-725-9

10 9 8 7 6 5 4 3 2 1

2022 2021 2020 2019 2018

Typeset in Garamond by Jayne Martin-Kaye

Printed by CPI Group (UK) Ltd, Croydon, CR0 4YY

CONTENTS

To Jack and Jonathan,
for support from the wings of the stage.

FOREWORD
BY MARGARET ATWOOD

'Lasting joys the man attend, Who has a faithful female friend,' said the Victorian poetaster Cornelius Whur. The role of the female friend, for a male writer, was to soothe, to sympathise, and to admire; if more than a friend, to be beautiful, and perhaps to play the Muse by inspiring. And to refrain from turning writer herself: competition from such a direction might be crippling to the male ego.

And damaging to the woman herself, since it was a received opinion throughout the last two millennia, up to and including much of the twentieth century, that women, if they were to write at all, should not attempt anything heavier than an etiquette guide. They were naturally without talent, since all their energy was channelled into their reproductive organs, not their tiny brains, and they lacked the larger experience that men could easily acquire. To write seriously was immodest for a woman, and even if she did manage to squeeze out a literary effusion, it was bound to be stunted and inferior. If, against all odds, she managed to enter the literary world, she would be deemed abnormal. Female writers were reclusive, tormented, neurotic, even morbid. Best not to try.

But many women did try, and many succeeded. In the eighteenth and nineteenth centuries they turned out quantities of light verse, patriotic songs, social and Gothic novels, histories and biographies. They could sell their work more easily if they remained anonymous or wrote under a male pseudonym – no publisher need meet them face to face – and the prospect of making some money of their own was a not inconsiderable motive. Unlike other means of earning a livelihood, writing was something they could do at home.

Some of these female writers became very popular. Nathaniel Hawthorne wrote resentfully about 'that damned mob of scribbling women' who were taking up market space that should rightfully have been his. George Eliot wrote an acidic essay, 'Silly Novels by Lady Novelists', denouncing the frivolity of such novels, of which by 1856 there were many. A woman writer with higher standards would have to write very well indeed to overcome the belief that she couldn't do it, that she shouldn't do it, and even if she did do it, she could not do it well.

This book is about four women who did overcome: Jane Austen, Charlotte Brontë, George Eliot and Virginia Woolf. Where could a great talent – if female – turn for support? A man might play a sustaining role – George Henry Lewes for George Eliot, Leonard Woolf for Virginia – but for Charlotte Brontë and Jane Austen such a figure was lacking. There might be sympathetic siblings – her sister Cassandra for Jane Austen, Emily and Anne for Charlotte Brontë – but there might not.

In accounts of the lives of male writers, peer-to-peer friendships, not unmixed with rivalry, often loom large – Byron and Shelley, Charles Dickens and Wilkie Collins, Hemingway and Fitzgerald. But female literary friendships have been overlooked, partly because they were actively suppressed by surviving relatives, as with Jane Austen, or overshadowed by better-known family bonds, as with Charlotte Brontë, or passed over by biographers, as with George Eliot and Harriet Beecher Stowe, or interpreted as merely spiteful hissy-fights by commentators, as with Woolf and Mansfield.

In digging up the forgotten friendships chronicled in *A Secret Sisterhood*, Emily Midorikawa and Emma Claire Sweeney have done much service to literary history. We are reminded how hard it was for two of these writers to make their way when they were young and as yet unpublished. The physical privation, lack of status and financial desperation endured by Charlotte Brontë, and the shrunken circumstances in which Jane Austen found herself after the death of her father, are recounted here in painful detail. But for each of these writers there was a secret sharer. The energetic Mary Taylor – an aspiring writer herself – pushed the diffident Charlotte Brontë to exploit her talent; Anne Sharp, a nascent playwright, shared Jane Austen's passion for writing in a way that her sister Cassandra could not.

George Eliot and Harriet Beecher Stowe, and Virginia Woolf and Katherine Mansfield are somewhat different, as all four were published and already part of the literary world when the friendships began. These friendships were trickier, as matters of relative literary success and thus resentment were bound to intrude.

In all four of these friendships, there were cooling periods, misunderstandings, perceived slights, hurt feelings and silences. A betrayal by a female writing friend must have seemed a triple betrayal – of friendship, of female solidarity in the face of a powerful society dominated by men and of writing itself. Many readers will recognise the delicate dances these writers perform through their letters to one another: complimenting here, hinting there, ignoring subjects that they can't comment on without causing pain. How much should be expected of a friend – how much tact, how much empathy, how much honesty, how much praise? It's still an open question.

Once people become famous their images tend to congeal. They become engravings of themselves, and we think of them as always having been grown-up and respectable. *A Secret Sisterhood* reminds us that this is not the case. Sweeney and Midorikawa take us back to formative years, retrace forgotten footsteps, and tap into emotional undercurrents in these writers that we had not suspected. These four women, however iconic they have now become, were not two-dimensional icons, nor were they plaster angels: they were real people, with all the neediness, anxiety, ardour, and complexity that come with the territory.

INTRODUCTION
IN SEARCH OF
A SECRET SISTERHOOD

Literary friendships are the stuff of legend. The image of Samuel Taylor Coleridge and William Wordsworth tramping the Lakeland Fells has long been entwined with their joint collection of ground-breaking poems. The tangled sexual escapades of later Romantics Lord Byron and Percy Bysshe Shelley fuelled gossip in their own time, and remain a source of endless fascination. By the mid-nineteenth century, Charles Dickens was taking Wilkie Collins under his wing: publishing the younger writer's stories, acting in his household theatricals, initiating excursions to bawdy music halls. And the memoirs of Ernest Hemingway offer readers a ringside view of his riotous drinking sprees with F. Scott Fitzgerald, thereby securing the pair's Jazz Age friendship its place in literary lore.

But, while these male duos have gone down in history, the world's most celebrated female authors are mythologised as solitary eccentrics or isolated geniuses. The Jane Austen of popular imagination is a genteel spinster, modestly covering her manuscript with blotting paper when anyone enters the room. Charlotte Brontë is cast as one of three long-suffering sisters, scribbling away in a draughty parsonage on the edge of the windswept moors. George Eliot is remembered as an aloof intellectual, who shunned conventional Victorian ladies. And Virginia Woolf haunts the collective memory as a depressive, loading her pockets with stones before stepping into the River Ouse.

Our own experiences, as writer friends, led us to question these accounts of extreme seclusion. We met in the summer of 2001, when we were in our early twenties – part of a group of several hundred graduates who would soon be taking up teaching posts in Japan. On the surface, back then, we had little in common. Emily's razor-slashed dark hair had recently been streaked blonde and she wore a T-shirt and cropped trousers bought while visiting relatives in Tokyo. Emma's fair locks, in contrast, flowed down her back and she was dressed in a long skirt and sandals. We had both been allocated jobs in the rural prefecture of Ehime. Emma positively embraced the prospect of a year in the remote village to which she had been assigned. But Emily, despite having been placed in the region's capital, fretted about returning to 'small-town' life after her university years in London. And while Emily remembers that, of all the people she encountered that day, the young woman in the long skirt and sandals was the one with whom she felt an instant connection, Emma's feelings were less certain. She couldn't decide whether our differences would always loom large, or whether we'd end up the best of friends.

Looking back, we laugh about this, and wonder how we managed to detect in each other a hidden similarity that would eventually draw us together. Though we both kept it secret, we shared the same ambition: to write books and see them published.

We settled into our new lives in Japan and it wasn't long before we were regularly making the 90-minute drive along the mountain highway that divided our homes, and planning weekend road trips far and wide. At parties held by other English teachers, we'd frequently find ourselves drifting off from the group, sipping Asahi beers in the corner, happily engrossed in our own conversation.

After almost a year of friendship, we had not yet shared our hopes of becoming published writers. Emma had decided by then to leave her mountain village, while Emily – who'd enjoyed life in her 'small town' after all – would be remaining for another twelve months.

When we arranged to meet for a farewell dinner, we had no idea that we'd come to look back on this evening as a key moment in our friendship. We chose a garlic-themed restaurant in Emily's local shopping mall, which had become by then an eccentric favourite of ours. Seated at a table covered in a chequered plastic cloth, we talked about news from home, plans for the future, the books we loved. And then, over the course of the next hour, while twisting strands of spaghetti around our forks, we 'came out' to each other as aspiring authors. Neither of us had much to show for these aims just yet: diaries kept this past year, a few short stories. We understood next to nothing about the book industry either. But nonetheless, by the time we laid our cutlery down, we had something perhaps more precious: we knew that we had a friend with the same dream, and that by supporting each other, we could follow it together.

During the years ahead, we would come to rely on each other: critiquing early drafts, passing on news of writing courses and contests, exchanging details of literary agents. As we trod our joint path, sharing moments of both celebration and consolation, we found ourselves wondering whether some of our favourite female authors of the past had enjoyed this kind of support.

The research we'd end up undertaking would offer us sustenance during our long years of striving to become published

authors. We had, by our thirties, found jobs as lecturers at the
same university, but we'd never studied together. And so, now
spending much of our free time scouring library archives, we
relished this second stab at studenthood. This joint work would
lead us – via bundles of letters, yellowing with age; neglected
wartime diaries; and personal mementoes stored in temperature-
controlled rooms – to a treasure trove of hidden alliances.

We would make the surprise discovery that, in the early 1800s
– the era of Wordsworth's treks with Coleridge, and Byron's
adventures with Shelley – Jane Austen forged a rather more
unlikely bond. Ignoring the raised eyebrows of her relatives,
she befriended one of the family's servants. Anne Sharp, the
governess of Jane's niece, penned household plays in between
teaching lessons. Though separated by the mighty class divide,
the pair shared the status of amateur writer and this acted, for a
time, as an important social leveller. Yet the differences in their
circumstances always threatened to open up a gulf between
them. The audacity of these two intelligent single women, who
built their relationship against the odds, upturns the well-worn
version of Jane as a conservative maiden aunt, devoted above all
else to kith and kin.

Charlotte Brontë is rarely imagined outside the world of her
Yorkshire village, where she dwelt with her literary siblings. But
we'd learn that she enjoyed a lively friendship with the pioneering
feminist writer Mary Taylor, whom she had met at boarding
school in 1831. From frictions during these early days, to daring
adventures as young women, to a shock announcement from
Mary: these two weathered many storms. Their relationship
paints a picture of two courageous individuals, groping to find
a space for themselves in the rapidly changing Victorian world.

Unlike Jane and Anne, and Charlotte and Mary – writer
friends who enjoyed vastly different levels of recognition –
George Eliot and Harriet Beecher Stowe shared the unique
status of being the most famous female authors of their day.

In the mid-nineteenth century – as Dickens was fêting the work of Collins – Eliot heaped public praise on this far-off American author who had written *Uncle Tom's Cabin*, the era's great anti-slavery novel. And so, in 1869, Eliot felt delighted to receive an unexpected letter from Harriet's Florida orange-grove home. She thrilled to her correspondent's ebullient personality, and – overcoming vast differences in character, opposing views on religion and the social stigma of Eliot 'living in sin' – they would soon form a deeply personal attachment. But, somehow, despite the enduring fame of both women, this compelling friendship remains little known.

Of all the historical collaborations that we have explored, the most complex, perhaps, is that of Virginia Woolf and Katherine Mansfield, who met during the dark days of the First World War, not long before Fitzgerald and Hemingway became friends. Unlike the pairs who came before them, the relationship between Virginia and Bloomsbury-group outsider Katherine, *has* gone down in history. But for all the wrong reasons. Despite the many affectionate letters and thoughtful gifts they exchanged, their simmering creative rivalry frequently threatened to boil over. And so – while Hemingway and Fitzgerald have been remembered as combative friends – these women are too often regarded solely as bitter foes. Yet Katherine and Virginia in fact enjoyed a powerful partnership that would profoundly influence the course of English literature.

When the two of us began searching out details of these female friendships, we had very little light to guide us and no clear destination. As we uncovered more and more facts about these four relationships, we gradually came to realise that each of these stories presented its own challenges.

Although many references to her friend crop up in the correspondence of Jane Austen, only one letter from her to Anne Sharp survives. We were able, however, to catch glimpses of their creative collaboration from a rich variety of archival sources. Chief among these were the unpublished diaries and letters of Jane's beloved niece. As the pupil of Anne, the family governess, Fanny Austen was a regular observer of exchanges between her teacher and her aunt. Invaluable though her diary entries are, they remain the words of a child, watching the comings and goings of the adults not from the bright-lit heart of the action, but from the darkened wings of the stage. We have often had to read between the lines of Fanny's childish scrawl to decipher the obscured truths that exist there. Sometimes this has meant questioning received wisdoms about Jane's life, some of which have become so entrenched that they seem almost impossible to dispute.

Correspondence between Charlotte Brontë and Mary Taylor is similarly limited, since Mary destroyed almost all missives from her friend 'in a fit of caution' to protect the women's reputations. But mentions of Mary litter Charlotte's wider communications, and that of other individuals close to this pair. Rather than being overwhelmed by a wealth of reliable information, though, we soon grew used to dealing with the inevitable contradictions and inconsistencies of opinions given to different people at different times. To work out the most likely versions of events, we had to weigh one clue against another, careful not to take sources at face value.

Willingness to look beyond first impressions was important, too, when we considered the transatlantic ties that united George Eliot and Harriet Beecher Stowe. Too many critics have written them off as mere acquaintances, supposedly lacking genuine closeness since they never met – and, unbelievably, given the reputation of each woman, a significant proportion of their correspondence remains unpublished. But once we had read all the letters and placed them within the framework of the authors' lives, a startlingly different picture emerged.

Reams of Virginia Woolf's and Katherine Mansfield's diary jottings and correspondence have survived, and these women were part of a self-mythologising milieu that prized conversational candour. But instead of finding this the most frank of the four pairs, the more we read, the more we learnt to be wary of each woman's inclination towards performance. If we wanted to enter into Katherine and Virginia's private sphere, we'd have to avoid jumping to hasty conclusions. Rather than fixating solely on each woman's much-quoted insults, we needed to view their words – both kind and cruel – within the context of their literary game of cat-and-mouse.

As writers today, we have always known that we owe a great debt to the lives and works of female authors of the past. In setting out to discover more about the friendships of Jane Austen, Charlotte Brontë, George Eliot and Virginia Woolf, we hoped to learn valuable lessons about how we, too, could sustain our friendship in the years to come. We'd always considered ourselves fortunate to have met at the start of our careers, which allowed us to celebrate early achievements together, and also to commiserate with someone who understood as publishers' rejection slips stacked up. It had long been a nagging worry, however, that it could be the success of one of us before the other that could end up driving us apart. From our research, we have witnessed just such moments from the past, gleaning warnings about these kinds of pitfalls, as well as heartening examples of trust.

In their own lifetimes, these women overcame differences in worldly success and social class, personal schisms and public scandal. But they could not fight against the march of history that would miss, ignore or even wilfully cover up their treasured collaborations.

In piecing together the lost stories of these four trailblazing pairs, we have found tales of hidden alliances that were sometimes illicit, scandalous and volatile; sometimes supportive, radical or inspiring; but, until now, tantalisingly consigned to the shadows.

PART 1

JANE AUSTEN AND ANNE SHARP

~ The men think us incapable of real friendship, you know, and I am determined to show them the difference

Northanger Abbey, Jane Austen

~

CHAPTER 1

A CIRCLE OF SINGLE WOMEN

In the most famous portrait of Jane Austen, she wears a gauzy dress and frilled cap, and sits demurely, gazing into the middle distance. In 1869, half a century after her death, her nephew James Edward Austen-Leigh commissioned this romanticised watercolour for his commemorative biography of Jane. The posthumous image took inspiration from a sketch, drawn by her sister Cassandra in around 1810, when the novelist was in her mid-thirties. Her plain dress in this informal portrait is a far cry from the blue ribbons and diaphanous fabric of the painting used to create the frontispiece to *A Memoir of Jane Austen*. And the woman who stares from this original conveys an uncompromising demeanour: a wry look in her eyes, her lips pursed and arms defiantly crossed.

Like the later picture favoured by her nephew, his sanitised book, written with the assistance of siblings and one of his cousins, scoured Jane's personality of all its grittier qualities. Conveniently ignoring their aunt's sharp tongue, they preferred to emphasise the neatness of her handwriting, the precision with which she dropped sealing wax onto her letters, the matchless nature of her needlework.

Not only was this younger generation keen to appeal to high-minded Victorian ideals about propriety, they were also hampered by fading childhood recollections and a dearth of surviving documentation. Here, Cassandra must take some blame. In the 1840s, the elderly woman read each letter she'd received from her sister one last time. Whenever she came across anything particularly intimate or revealing, she paused, committed Jane's words to memory and then fed the pages into the parlour's blazing fire. And so, their most private confidences curled and flared and finally darkened to ash.

Cassandra's eldest niece, Fanny, followed her aunt's example. She refused to collaborate with her cousins on the memoir and failed to preserve the letters that her father had received from Jane, as well as the vast majority of her own. This stealth begs the question: what secrets could Fanny and Cassandra have been at such pains to hide?

In 1926 *The Times* published two previously unseen letters, one from Jane and one from Cassandra, both addressed to a woman little known to fans and critics alike. Subtitled 'Devoted Friends', the article introduced readers to 'a shadowy figure' named Anne Sharp 'for whom Jane Austen had no ordinary affection'. That this woman had not appeared, even fleetingly, in the authorised version of Jane's life would have seemed strange to readers. From Jane's opening greeting of 'my dearest Anne' to the warmth of the private jokes, family gossip and heartfelt confidences that followed, it is clear that the recipient was a most treasured confidante.

It might seem curious that the Austen family had been so keen to exclude a figure like Anne on whose 'tender' feelings Jane had come to depend and to whom she considered herself forever 'attached'. After all, by the Georgian era, the British had moved so far from the Classical ideal of friendship as an exclusively male domain that they especially prized such bonds between women. But Jane's letter, passed down by acquaintances of Anne through their female descendants, calls into question the Austen family's genteel portrayal of their famous aunt. For Anne was employed as the governess of Jane's niece, Fanny. Here was a relationship that belied the *Memoir*'s image of a woman content solely with the company of her family, and whose refined acquaintances 'constituted the very class from which she took her imaginary characters'.

The uptight tone of Cassandra's letter to this same Anne Sharp hints at another reason for family disapproval. She accused Anne of 'ardent feelings' and made a point of asserting her own greater claim on Jane. Cassandra's possessiveness and the younger generation's snobbery speak volumes about why this correspondent appears to us today only as a ghostly apparition, absent from official portraits of the novelist's life.

But unpublished papers stowed deep in library archives still whisper of this woman and the bond she shared with Jane. To understand why Anne has been so excluded from histories of her close friend, we must turn to the words of Jane's niece. Keen as Fanny was to get rid of her father's documents, her own crimson pocket diaries – in which she'd made meticulous entries from the tender age of ten – have been passed down to us unscathed.

These unpublished notebooks and letters, largely unmined by literary critics, shed light on what must have lain at the heart of the deep affection between her governess and aunt: like Jane, Anne was a writer.

The child's entry for a Saturday early in 1804 transports us to a time before Fanny knew anything of Anne's literary bent. On 21 January, the governess was on her way to Godmersham Park, the grand home of Jane's far wealthier brother, to take up employment teaching Fanny. Anne's overnight journey took her through neat Kent villages, and land scarred by freshly dug ditches that divided up commons and heaths – these regimented fields worlds away from the bustle of London where she had been born thirty-one years earlier.

History has shown such scant interest in Anne that, until we discovered her name in an old baptismal ledger, even the year of her birth was unknown. And, as with most working women of her generation, no portrait nor direct record of her words has ever been unearthed. Despite the wealth of information we have found, our reconstruction of Anne's life must largely rely on Austen family papers, most notably the account of Fanny, a privileged child born into the landed gentry, trained to regard household staff with kindly condescension.

Fanny's letters show that she awaited the arrival of her new teacher with both eagerness and nerves – mixed feelings that Anne surely shared. As the coach carrying the governess reached Godmersham Park, it would have halted at the boundary of the Austens' estate, its driver dismounting with his key before leading the horses onto the driveway, the towering iron gates closing behind them. As the carriage continued through the estate's deer park, a break in the trees offered Anne a glimpse of the red-bricked façade of the house, a place already so familiar to Jane: the hatching across its countless windows; the decorative masonry above the pillared entrance; the pleasing symmetry of its flanking pavilions that had been so fashionably added just twenty-five years before.

On approaching the coach-turning circle, it became clear that one of the new pavilions housed a huge reading room – surely a cheering sight for a woman who penned theatricals. This library, where Jane enjoyed many an hour of solitude during her lengthy but occasional visits, dwarfed the size of the entrance hall and rivalled the ballroom, creating the impression, at least, that its owners were great lovers of literature. Beyond its chequered windows stood floor-to-ceiling bookshelves whose volumes would have offered something of a sanctuary to the intellectually curious.

From the moment Anne's feet touched Godmersham's black-and-white marble flagstones, all eyes would have been upon her, the brood of children trying to get the measure of her, while the footmen and lady's maids sized her up for signs of haughtiness – a characteristic considered common in governesses, who, though gentlewomen, were often paid little more than other household staff. *The Times*, whose later interest in Anne would stem only from her connection with Jane, would compare such a role to 'a kind of shuttlecock between servants and mistresses, and the butt of both'.

Unbeknown to Anne at this stage, Jane, too, had never felt at ease during her stays at Godmersham, despite it being the home of her brother. The employees could tell she was a poor relation, the housemaids learning not to expect much in the way of tips and the visiting hairdresser offering her a discounted rate. Even the family of the house could at times be disparaging, sneering at Jane's unfashionable attire. She and Cassandra tended to dress dowdily, in matching clogs and bonnets. And on those occasions when they marked a bereavement, they had to soak in black dye the bombazine and crêpe of their old pelisses before resewing them into gowns. In the sisters of a landowner, such lack of refinement was cause for embarrassment. But no one would raise an eyebrow at the new governess showing up in makeshift mourning garb, her air that of genteel impoverishment.

Anne's engagement with the Austens had likely been necessitated by a misfortune to have befallen the Sharp family. Fanny recorded that her new governess had suffered a bereavement, but failed to mention for whom she grieved. 'I think Miss Sharpe pretty but not strikingly so,' she noted, before adding: 'she is in mourning & I think it becomes her'. With the era's casual disregard for consistent spelling, the girl had added an 'e' to her new teacher's surname – a mistake that Jane would also make throughout her long friendship with Anne. A woman of Anne's mother's name, Elizabeth Sharpe, had been buried in London in April 1803, and so it appears that the governess had lost a parent. In the early nineteenth century, a single woman in her position, without affluent male relatives to support her, would have faced the unenviable task of securing a respectable way to earn her keep.

Anne's employment had got off to a poor start. She should have taken up her role as governess to young Fanny some months earlier, but a dangerous bout of ill health – perhaps exacerbated by her recent bereavement – had forced her to delay her departure. Her new home would hardly prove a suitable place for convalescing, and she would soon realise, too, that the hectic frivolity of Edward Austen's huge household allowed little time for solitary hours in the library. Her pupil, Fanny, was the eldest of five boys and four girls – the youngest a sweet-natured but noisy newborn – and the stuccoed ceiling of the entrance hall forever rang with the sounds of Edward's and Elizabeth's many relatives being welcomed in or waved back off.

Both master and mistress hailed from large families, and each was one of eight siblings. In all other ways, however, their backgrounds contrasted. Edward had been brought up with Jane in a Hampshire rectory, where their father supplemented his modest clergyman's income by running a farm and taking paying pupils into his home. Elizabeth, on the other hand, had been raised at Goodnestone Park – an estate almost as grand as her current home, the neighbouring Godmersham. This unlikely match had come about due to Edward's adoption as an adolescent by the Austen family's landlord and distant cousin, Thomas Knight, who owned grand homes in Hampshire and Kent. Such an arrangement suited all concerned. The wealthy couple gained a longed-for child while their tenants, who negotiated to continue educating Edward at home with his siblings, saw their third-born rise from a mere rector's son to the inheritor of three lucrative estates. By 1804, when Anne joined the staff at Godmersham, Edward had become firmly entrenched in the landed gentry, his lifestyle a far cry from that of his sister Jane, who could count hardly a penny to her name.

Edward enjoyed his fortune, taking his children to extravagant firework displays; treating his guests to delicacies such as French wine, lobster and ices; and encouraging his wife and daughters to purchase coloured Persian silks, muslin neckerchiefs and hats stylishly ornamented with artificial fruit. But he was also keenly aware of the responsibilities incumbent on a landowner to preserve his assets for the next generation. Encouraged by his wife, it would appear, his generosity fell short at times when it came to his less fortunate sisters – strait-laced Cassandra and sharp-tongued Jane.

Anne's early days at Godmersham Park boded well, however, since the first Monday of her employment fell on her pupil's eleventh birthday, and the lady of the house invited the governess to join the family for the exchange of gifts, special meals and games of cards. And so, at ten o'clock in the morning on 23 January 1804, Anne sat down with her master, mistress and Fanny in a wood-panelled parlour, where a table was set with fine china.

During her own visits, Jane would marvel at this leisurely lifestyle, describing such lazy days as '*a la* Godmersham'. But on this particular morning, the 28-year-old was 150 miles away with her parents and sister in Bath. It was her custom to rise early, preparing a breakfast of tea and toast for her family before taking up her quill. She had been writing since childhood, when she used to read aloud her stories and plays to the high-spirited glee of her household audience. By now, just shy of 30, she had produced reams of such entertainments, and even three full-length novels – books that sent up the kind of snobbery and entitlement she'd witnessed as an outsider looking on at the 'happy Indifference of East Kent wealth'. But, like the governess who was about to enter her life, Jane had not experienced the pleasure of seeing her words in print.

On the morning of her pupil's birthday, Anne was about to witness the kind of seemingly trivial incident that would provide fodder for Jane's works-in-progress. Following the manifold pleasures of a gourmet breakfast – treats at the time included ginger-spiced plum cake, buttered brioche and hot chocolate poured from a silver-spouted pot – the mistress of the house offered her daughter a gift of a pretty sandalwood box containing toothpicks. Readers of *Sense and Sensibility* would one day encounter just such a decorative object: a symbol in the novel for the extravagance and conceit of those with surplus wealth. Jane had embarked on the story some years earlier but she would continue to revise it for several more, the final version bearing the influence of Godmersham in far more significant ways.

If Jane raised a wry smile at the expense of her brother's family, the suspicion seems to have been mutual – at least in the case of her sister-in-law. Elizabeth did not take kindly to intellectual conversation, her main interests ranging between her beloved children and cherished mare, to the dress patterns and rolls of muslin that she liked to order from travelling salesmen or through friends in town. At Godmersham, Jane's talk fell all too often on unappreciative ears. As one of her nieces would recall in later life, Elizabeth – for whom 'a little talent went a long way … & much must have gone a long way too far' – was not overly fond of her bookish sister-in-law.

During the months that followed Anne's arrival, the illusion of scholarship conveyed by the lofty library was swiftly dispelled. Elizabeth cancelled lessons with such frequency that it appeared she did not want her eldest daughter to receive much of an education, and Edward spent his days hunting and fishing and settling neighbourhood disputes. It was also his responsibility to inspect the troop of volunteer soldiers whom he'd given permission to exercise at the top of his parkland, for rumours abounded that Napoleon Bonaparte's French forces were planning to invade English shores via the local Kentish coastline.

Such grave worries were thrown into relief by the cheerfulness of family life. Anne would have quickly got to know the younger children, who still came under the nursemaid's care: William, a six-year-old, who loved to practise shuttlecock for hours on end; Lizzy, a bright little thing already taken to needlework at just four years of age; Marianne, a toddler, easily identifiable by the traces of a mark on her neck (the causes of which Fanny would later white out from her letters during the more squeamish Victorian era); Charles, a curly-haired child, who carried with him a doll that he called his wife; and the youngest, Louisa, a black-eyed infant with a loud cry and an infectious smile. In time, Anne would also meet the elder boys who boarded at Eltham School: Henry, Edward and George.

Anne and Fanny soon fell into a pleasing routine. They usually met in the schoolroom at ten, where they began the working day by breakfasting à deux. The governess then heard her charge recite her lessons, testing Fanny's knowledge of French conjugations, picking out distant lands on the globe and discussing the books Anne had selected from Godmersham's library. They punctuated their studies with strolls along the lane to take tea with the child's great-aunt, or more boisterous expeditions into 'the Wilderness' – an overgrown area made treacherous by exposed roots and low-hanging boughs. On fine days, they sometimes allowed themselves to be lured from their studies by the entreaties of Fanny's brothers, or even her mama and papa, to join them on cross-country rides, or fishing for pike in the serpentine – a bend in the river at the south-easterly edge of the park.

Almost six months passed by in this manner, the sharp frost of January giving way to sunbursts of daffodils in spring. And, just as the plants shrugged off the darkness of previous months, so

Anne too must have felt revived. What bliss, after the hardships of the previous year, to find her health returned to an even keel.

While Anne gamely threw herself into the fun and frolics, she had less time alone than she might have preferred. Even nightfall failed to bring with it a few solitary hours. She could hardly read or write by candlelight lest she disturb Fanny, for her role as governess involved sharing her bed most nights with her pupil – a common practice during this era, although one that Anne might well have hoped to avoid when she secured employment in a house of such a respectable size.

But, over the coming year, she must have managed to steal some time for herself, perhaps rising early while the housemaid was still pumping bellows to reignite the embers in the kitchen's hearth. With the dawn light climbing up the library walls, Anne may have dipped her quill in ink to work secretly on her play scripts, instead of turning to the correspondence that ladies ordinarily dealt with during the quiet, pre-breakfast hours. In the same vast, empty room where Jane also holed herself away during visits, Anne could have taken her pick of the five library tables and the room's twenty-eight chairs. She had surely heard by now of her young pupil's paternal aunts: Cassandra, the favourite, such a help with the children, and Jane, who thought herself so very clever with her own made-up stories and plays.

Over in Bath, Jane was finding it difficult to carve out the time and solitude she required for her literary work, because, like Anne, she had endured an upheaval from home. Three years earlier, her clergyman father had announced his intention to retire from Steventon Rectory in Hampshire. It had occurred to neither Reverend nor Mrs Austen to consult with their unmarried daughters, both of whom still resided with them, about their intention to relocate to a spa town over 50 miles away. No thought was given to the effect of wrenching Jane and Cassandra from their female friends, the Bigg-Withers and Lloyds, nor was the disruption of their longstanding creative and domestic routines taken into account. The expectation that Jane should accompany her family to fashionable tea rooms, opulent bathhouses and chandeliered balls kept her from writing as much as she might have liked. Despite the enjoyment of such distractions, she longed for her former Hampshire hillside.

Though forcing such a move on his daughters had cost Jane her creative haven, her father had always been a staunch supporter of her work. Back in 1797, when she was 21, the Reverend George Austen had sent one of her manuscripts to Cadell and Davies, a leading London bookseller. He clearly paid no heed to those who deemed it improper for women to publish, and neither was he browbeaten by the repressive tendencies of Britain's wartime rule – an era of great paranoia about any writing that criticised the status quo. It was a charge that could have been levelled against Jane. *First Impressions*, the novel that she would later rename *Pride and Prejudice*, dared to criticise the behaviour of the king's soldiers, and it also called into question women's lack of economic clout. Whether or not Thomas Cadell found such subject matter troubling, he certainly failed to predict that this book would become one of the world's most beloved works. He turned it down by return of post.

Jane held her nerve, though, and in 1803 – the year Anne had agreed to join the large household staff at Godmersham – she'd sought publication of another of her novels, known today as *Northanger Abbey*. On this occasion, she had cause for celebration. Benjamin Crosby of Crosby & Co. in London purchased her satirical story's copyright, albeit for just £10 – a sum with which Jane could have purchased a fur-trimmed shawl or two along with a velvet cloak and bonnet. The paltry nature of the fee aside, she must have felt overjoyed when she learnt that this great man of letters had advertised her book's forthcoming publication in his annual catalogue of Gothic romances. After a decade and a half of writing, she would finally see one of her novels ushered into the world.

Throughout 1804, while Jane was anticipating her first publication, her home life had taken a downward turn. When the lease expired on their house in Bath's fashionable Sydney Place, overlooking the pleasure gardens, the Austens were forced to move to quarters in the far less desirable western fringe of town. Just three years earlier, they had rejected this low-lying area close to slum housing on account of the dampness of the buildings and 'reports of discontented families & putrid fevers'.

Anne was experiencing difficulties too. By the early summer, her ill health had reared up once more. On 19 June, the children of Godmersham were in fine fettle, the kitchen garden having yielded the season's first strawberries, for which the cook had whipped up vast quantities of the dairy's fresh cream. But, despite the good cheer bestowed by these early summer gifts, Anne could not hide from Fanny the fact that she was 'not quite well'.

The next day, the two met in the schoolroom. Anne was hopeful that she had endured the worst, but soon she began to feel faint. As she gradually lost track of the lesson, shadows cast the light from her eyes, her legs gave way beneath her and she fell to the floor.

When she stirred she found herself in the arms of Susannah Sackree, Godmersham's nursemaid, who helped the governess to her feet and then guided her slowly upstairs. On entering her room, Anne flung herself onto the bed, her energy entirely spent. Here, she was administered a draught of laudanum before being left alone for slumber to descend. But, despite the sedation, Anne found herself unable to sleep.

The hours passed in a haze until the house came alive with the tell-tale sounds of dinner. Before too long, the rap of a knock intruded into her sick chamber, and then little Fanny appeared in the doorway, proffering a bowl of whipped syllabub. Its sickly scents of sugar, sherry and cream made Anne's stomach turn, but she took the curative dessert from the child and gathered all her strength to get up so that the maid could change her bedding. Try as she might, though, she couldn't so much as raise a spoonful of syllabub to her mouth.

During this period, Anne received sympathetic treatment from her employers and fellow staff. But, as the months wore on and she kept suffering intermittently from similar spells of ill health, she must have grown anxious about retaining her position. After all, the Godmersham Austens were known for their high turnover of household staff. It could only be a matter of time before Edward and Elizabeth dismissed a governess who so frequently took to her sickbed.

This period was ridden with trepidation, not only for Anne but also for Jane. Having waited in vain for two years to see *Northanger Abbey* go to print, the eager writer could only speculate that Crosby & Co. might have had second thoughts about bringing to press a satire that sent up the Gothic genre in which the firm specialised. In fact, the publishing company had simply run into financial trouble. Regardless, Jane's disappointment at the lack of progress must have been crushing. She'd prioritised her writing over courtship and domestic responsibilities, turning down at least one proposal of marriage, eschewing invitations whenever possible and allowing her sister to take on more than her fair share of family duties. Now Jane had to suffer the ignominy of yet another rejection of her work. Ultimately, though, she was undeterred. She simply picked up her quill and continued drafting a new novel, provisionally entitled *The Watsons*.

But then a catastrophe befell the Austen household, which would fracture every aspect of the life Jane knew. Ever since moving into the damp-ridden house in Green Park Buildings, her father had been suffering from weakness and fevers. On 19 January 1805, he endured a violent seizure, and, within days, he passed away.

His death robbed the Austen women of an affectionate father and husband, and Jane of an enthusiastic admirer of her work. Since women could not inherit church pensions,

Mrs Austen and her daughters also lost their main source of income. The only wellspring of hope that Jane could have drawn from these saddest of circumstances was the possibility that she might now return to surroundings more conducive to her creativity. Thank goodness for her brother Edward's adoption by the wealthy Knights. His estates in Hampshire and Kent each comprised dozens of properties, and his inherited fortune would surely stretch to subsidising his mother and sisters for the loss of Reverend Austen's retirement fund. And yet, perhaps Jane always harboured some doubt about her brother and sister-in-law's generosity. *Sense and Sensibility* would later portray a buffoonish brother and his self-serving wife who cruelly neglect a mother and her daughters after the death of the family patriarch.

Neither Jane nor any of her books' heroines faced the prospect of fending for themselves. But, like Anne, she was now similarly reliant on the purse of Godmersham's owner – a man who guarded his wealth.

Edward and the rest of Jane's brothers consulted on their womenfolk's financial affairs and presented their mother with a fait accompli: between the six of them, they would pool a sufficient annual income to allow her and her daughters to winter in serviceable lodgings in Bath and summer between the abodes of more affluent relations, such as themselves. This plan seemed to suit Mrs Austen well enough, but, once again, no one gave a thought to the wishes of her daughters. Despite Edward's own vast fortune, he promised his mother and sisters a yearly stipend of only £100 – no more than that offered by one of his younger brothers, Frank, a less prosperous naval man recently engaged to a penniless girl. Jane put a brave face on it, but her exploration of fraternal betrayal in *Sense and Sensibility* suggests that she felt badly let down.

The Austen women soon came to realise that their modest finances could not cover the rent for Green Park Buildings. And so, just two months after her father's death, Jane and her grieving sister and mother were forced to relocate to still cheaper lodgings, 10 minutes' walk away at 25 Gay Street.

It was during this period, in April 1805, that a governess friend named 'Miss Sharpe' first crops up in Jane's surviving correspondence. Within four months, she would be writing warmly of Fanny's teacher 'Miss Sharpe' in her letters, and, throughout the rest of her life, references to this governess friend would litter Jane's missives. But, surprisingly, an annotation tucked away at the back of the authoritative edition of Jane Austen's letters insists that the Miss Sharpe first mentioned in April 1805 could not possibly be the same woman to whom Jane would grow so attached. *This* governess friend cannot be Anne, so the story goes, because she and Jane could not yet have met. There's no evidence that Jane had paid a visit to her Kentish relatives during the fifteen months of Anne's employment. And Anne must have been holed away in Godmersham throughout that time.

But this, in fact, was not the case. Young Fanny's metal-clasped diaries and wax-sealed letters reveal that, during that spring of 1805, her teacher *was* away from home. These unpublished manuscripts show that Anne's month-long absence coincides with the same period of Jane's removal from Green Park Buildings to the poky rented rooms of her new abode.

Fanny waved off her governess during the week commencing 18 March and Anne didn't return for almost a month. So it seems possible that Edward sent her to assist the Austen women with their move, and that Jane and Anne grew fond of each other far from the watchful eyes of the owners of Godmersham.

If so, this would not have been the first time that Anne had been told to cancel lessons and fit herself around the family's other plans. She was regularly instructed to work outside the schoolroom: sent to drop off the boys at their boarding schools at the beginning of term and pick them up at its close, and called on at times to chaperone her employer's guests on their journeys too. But any inconvenience must have been outweighed by Edward's promise to stop in London en route so that Anne could consult a doctor about her eyes, which had been troubling her ever since her collapse.

Within the spacious drawing room of Green Park Building East, Anne would have been greeted by Cassandra, Jane and their mother all dressed in mourning garb, only slightly less shabby than the outfit she herself had worn when she began her employment at Godmersham. Cassandra was a polite woman, outwardly reserved. But the younger sister, like her mother, was a much more spirited character, whose love of literature sustained her through difficult times. Packing up the household together, she and Anne would have found plenty of opportunity to exchange thoughts on favourite books by the likes of Maria Edgeworth and Frances Burney, their newfound, literary conversation brightening each other's lives.

This flicker of friendship would have ignited to flame, their difficulties giving each woman a reason for trading confidences. Anne's persistent headaches and eye problems must have hampered her attempts at devising plays, and Jane had not been able to concentrate on her new novel during the months since her father's death. In the years to come, these women would find all sorts of ways to support each other's endeavours, but, on this occasion, the pair could no sooner have become acquainted than they would have been forced to part ways – Anne returning to Godmersham and Jane remaining in Bath.

At the right moment on 9 April 1805, Jane would have been easy to spot, picking her way between the crowds that thronged Gay Street – her parasol, dyed dark for mourning, out of tempo with the cheerful hubbub in this part of town. Sedan chairs, shouldered by one man at the front and another at the rear, carried visitors down the steep hill to take the waters in the Grand Pump Room. In this spa town, Jane was surrounded by holidaymakers and husband hunters, with whom she found little in common. While *she* had to call Bath home, most women of her age and class were just passing through.

When Jane stepped inside 25 Gay Street that morning, she would have found the rooms especially quiet, since her sister had gone to Hampshire to help nurse the terminally ill mother of their old friend Martha Lloyd. Jane soon settled down to continue a letter to Cassandra that she'd started the day before. Dipping her quill into homemade ink, she began with a wish that the mercy of death might come to Mrs Lloyd as swiftly as it had settled on their father. Just as she succumbed to the flow of her words, the arrival of a visitor was announced: a Miss Colbourne, the lady who owned the school on Lansdown Crescent.

As Jane would admit when she resumed her letter, this interruption made her hackles rise. She knew that her dark rooms were a world apart from Miss Colbourne's grand institution on a hill above town. And Jane had, in fact, long harboured negative feelings about schools. At seven years old, she'd been sent to Oxford to board along with her sister and cousin. All three girls had contracted a dangerous fever, and their lives hung in the balance. They'd managed to get word out to Jane's aunt, who fetched them immediately and eventually nursed them back to health. But, in the process of saving the girls, she'd caught the disease herself, and, for her, it proved fatal. Despite this trauma, after a year at home Jane had been sent off to another school – this time her life was not endangered but she received little in the way of learning.

Miss Colbourne had come to enquire after the character of one of the Austen women's former maids, whom – thanks to Edward's parsimony – they could no longer afford to keep on. The brothers had decided among themselves that their mother could 'reduce her establishment to one female domestic' instead of the three she had previously employed. Jane had no choice in the matter and now she felt she was being subjected to this school owner's condescension. These days, it couldn't escape

Jane's notice that guests often seemed to look down on her – though, she drolly noted, they were more than happy to partake of her precious supplies of tea leaves and sugar.

And yet both Jane and her sister saw some opportunities in their new impoverishment. In her next surviving letter, she would discuss with Cassandra the intention to invite their childhood friend Martha to join their new household. The sisters had been keeping this plan from their family, but now that Mrs Lloyd's death was imminent, the time had come, Jane wrote, to let others know of these hopes. Martha's meagre finances could supplement theirs and her skills as an amateur cook and apothecary would come as welcome indeed. But, more than anything, it was her friendship they held dear.

A line buried in this very same letter suggests that friendship was also at the heart of another of Jane's schemes. Her note to Cassandra gives the impression that she had been looking for work on Anne's behalf – an endeavour that would have involved going behind her brother's back, prioritising the bond she shared with his governess over the loyalty owing to him. And now her efforts had met with success. The daughter of one of her acquaintances, she revealed, was soon 'to take lessons of Miss Sharpe' – surely the same governess whose company Jane would prize in the years to come. For all her pleasure at the prospect of establishing a close female circle in Bath, she nonetheless knew to proceed with caution. 'Among so many friends,' she mused, 'it will be well if I do not get into a scrape.'

Scrapes aplenty did indeed await Jane as she tried to embrace the keen playwright into her group of intelligent single women – the others all avid readers of her novels in draft, but none of them able to offer quite the creative solidarity of a fellow writer such as Anne.

CHAPTER 2

REBELLION BEHIND CLOSED DOORS

In June 1805, two months after Jane Austen sought employment for Anne Sharp in Bath, the pair were indeed together. But they were not among the crowds of women at one of the city's circulating libraries, laden with conduct books, sermons and popular novels. Nor were they huddled over the fire in the parlour at the Austen women's new quarters in Gay Street, discussing their writing over tea and Bath buns covered with sugar-coated caraway seeds. For reasons lost to history, Jane's plan to include Anne in her circle in Bath had clearly not come to pass. The unlikely friends had to resort to meeting up within the walls of the Godmersham Park estate in East Kent, for, despite Jane's efforts to secure Anne a new post, the governess remained an employee of Edward Austen.

On 19 June, the diary of Anne's pupil, Fanny, mentions the arrival at six o'clock in the evening of 'Grandmama Austen, Aunts Cassandra & Jane', along with two of Fanny's favourite cousins, both 12 years old, like herself. As the women's carriage came into view, the sun still high in the sky, Anne would have had the perfect excuse to join her charge at the coach-turning circle. But it would hardly have been the done thing for Jane to greet her brother's employee with affection, and even her mother and sister might have raised their eyebrows at such intimacy – particularly given Anne's humble roots.

In later years, the governess would keep quiet about her past, a decision made understandable in light of evidence in that neglected baptismal ledger. London ecclesiastical records show that only one baby to share a name with the governess was christened in the city during the weeks following her birth. The father is noted as a gardener, and, while street addresses are included for the other infants christened in February 1773 at St Paul's Church in Deptford, this baby is simply recorded as 'from WH' – a common abbreviation for the workhouse. Such an institution might have offered Anne an unusual level of education for a girl of her modest background, but this proximity to urban paupers was worlds away from the rural parsonage upbringing of the Austen siblings. And yet, with hardly a penny to her name, Jane's current situation was in some ways comparable to Anne's.

Jane, who had come to stay at Godmersham for the whole summer, was deeply in need of a friend. Her situation had gone from bad to worse in the two months since her removal to Gay Street. Still grieving for their husband and father, the Austen women had now discovered that even their modest new dwelling was rather beyond their means. They had been left with no choice but to withdraw their tenancy and impose on the hospitality of their relations while they worked out what they could afford to rent in Bath on their return. The disruption of one house move and the prospect of yet another, not to mention the melancholy brought on by the loss of her father, had sapped Jane of her creative vigour. And with one book rejected and another having languished for two years in a publisher's drawer, she had no reason to believe that her writing would ever reach a readership beyond her close family and friends – especially since she'd arrived at Godmersham having made the decision to abandon her novel-in-progress, *The Watsons*.

The activities of the next few days must have lifted Jane's spirits: gathering around the brand-new pianoforte; trips in the chaise to Canterbury; pony rides around the estate; inspections of the canary's freshly laid eggs. What's more, Jane sometimes got to enjoy these escapades with Anne. The governess cancelled lessons the day after the Austen women's arrival. Instead, the three cousins and their aunts all exuberantly baptised one of Fanny's dolls by anointing its forehead with water and staging grand entertainments to celebrate its christening.

Such diversions could offer a temporary balm, but they would hardly cure Jane's unaccustomed artistic lethargy. As a writer herself, Anne was better placed to help even than Cassandra. But the governess and the houseguest couldn't have risked spending too much time engaging in literary conversations without becoming a source of irritation for Godmersham's mistress, Elizabeth.

The pair would cement their bond within the unthreatening environs of the schoolroom, the one place where Anne held sway. Fanny's entry in her lady's pocket diary on 26 June 1805 escapes into the columns usually reserved for records of money received or spent. Her account of the day fizzes with joy at the memory of dressing up and playing at school along with her governess, aunts, mother and grandmother and her cousins Fanny Cage and Anna Austen. Such games of make-believe were just what the visiting girls needed, since they must have been craving affection. During the previous six months, Fanny Cage had lost both her father and her mother, and Anna faced further exclusion at home now that her stepmother was expecting a second child.

These forlorn girls decked themselves out in costume, and, to their delight, the adults joined in too. In her cross-dressing role as sergeant, Anne issued orders to those who usually held rank over her. Jane and Cassandra were assigned characters strikingly similar to her own real-life role – Jane playing the part of Miss Popham, the teacher, and her elder sister Mrs Teachum, the governess. They needn't have looked far for props; Anne's own chalk and slate would do. Their mother and sister-in-law took on characters even lower down the Georgian social scale: Betty Jones, the piewoman, and a nameless seaside bathing attendant.

Roles assigned, Anne moved between the part of the sergeant and that of the dancing master. This would have appealed to Jane's taste, for she loved cotillions and Scotch reels, and her nimble footwork had long inspired admiration. Jane had inherited her fun-loving, satirical bent from her mother, and so it's easy to picture the 66-year-old widow throwing herself into a country dance, an apron swaying in time with her steps or a rolling pin held aloft. Anne's mistress, too, never shied away from play-acting so long as it was all just fun and games. And Cassandra, far more reserved than the rest, could not deny her nieces the pleasure of seeing all the adults make a show of themselves.

Later in the day, Anne managed with military precision to manoeuvre the party from playing school to acting in a drama that she herself had secretly penned. The maids clearing away the dessert dishes from the wood-panelled dining room would have been privy to her suggestion that the children put on a play. Its title, *Virtue Rewarded*, could have given no cause for alarm. This sketch – like most of the era's theatricals for youngsters – would provide moral instruction, the title cried out; there could be nothing clever or troubling here! Perhaps on account of her mistress's distrust of talented women, Anne did not admit that she was the author of this play. And she couldn't even have counted on support from Jane – a woman who had a tendency towards ridicule, and who, in any case, could only offer encouragement with the greatest of discretion.

Anne turned her attention to the children – the one interest she could legitimately share with Jane. The orphaned Fanny Cage was appointed Duchess of St Albans; Anna Austen, black sheep of her family, transformed into Shepherdess Flora; and the daughter of the house became Fairy Serena.

It would be easy to write all this off as no more than a bit of fun, just as the mistress of Godmersham must have done over two centuries ago. Certainly, most biographers have deemed it unworthy of scholarly attention that the great Jane Austen shared a rapport with a scribbler of children's entertainments, whose scripts no one thought to save. But the events of the coming months and years reveal that Jane treated Anne as her most trusted literary friend, understanding both the value of the governess's playwriting and the constraints under which she laboured due to the demands of her teaching work.

During the fortnight following the impromptu theatricals, the usual restrictions on Anne's freedom eased off. Now that Fanny had her cousins to keep her company, the governess could pack off the children for adventures in Godmersham's grounds. One day, she allowed them each to choose a Gothic novel and then sent them to climb up to the artificial ruin, decoratively situated in the parkland. Here they could devour their stories in a suitably mysterious location. Later that week, loading a basket with books, paper and pencils so that they could complete their schoolwork wherever they chose, she encouraged them to pretend to be gypsies for the day. And she added a large bottle of water, as well as a loaf and a hunk of cheese so that the girls could stay out as long as they pleased.

But the next day, Fanny was taken ill with a cold and fever. She lost her voice and couldn't say her lessons. Anne must have felt concerned that the adventures she'd devised to get her pupil out of the house had proven too much for the girl's constitution. Soon afterwards, Fanny's mother caught the same complaint – suffering more seriously still – and was also confined for two weeks to her bed. Thankfully, nobody in the family seemed to cast blame on the governess, but it was a worrying time since reliance on the rudimentary medicine of the early nineteenth century meant that even the common cold could turn nasty.

Anxieties aside, with both employer and charge laid up in the sickroom, the governess could escape her usual duties and steal time with her friend. Jane would certainly look back on this summer with Anne as a period of great animation. And the events of the coming months suggest that she did all she could to prolong their shared seclusion.

As soon as her sister-in-law rallied, however, Jane was whisked off for dinners at local manor houses, balls in nearby Canterbury and Ashford, and mercy missions to the homes of Elizabeth's ailing relatives. Anne's duties also kept the pair apart throughout much of August and the early weeks of September. She accompanied Fanny on a short break to Canterbury, where they visited the cathedral, feasted on pastries and listened to the music of travelling bands. Here, she shared a few moments with her friend, who was there simply to switch carriages with Cassandra. Jane was on her way to Goodnestone to take over family nursing duties from her sister, so that Cassandra – always Elizabeth's favourite – could return to Godmersham. It may have been a brief exchange, but Anne made quite an impression on Jane's two companions: Edward's wealthy benefactress, the kindly Catherine Knight, and Molly Milles, a single woman who could empathise with Jane's itinerant lifestyle, since she, too, had been forced to move from one set of rented quarters to another. Unlike Fanny's first impression of her governess as 'pretty but not strikingly so', these women were much struck by Anne's beauty as well as her style of conversation. 'Pray say everything kind for us to Miss Sharpe, who could not regret the shortness of our meeting in Canterbury more than we did', wrote Jane in her next letter to Cassandra. 'I hope she returned to Godmersham as much pleased with Mrs. Knight's beauty and

Miss Milles's judicious remarks as those ladies respectively were with hers.'

A plan was already afoot for Jane and Anne to spend the autumn of 1805 together by the sea – and not at the nearby Kent coast but on the far side of the Downs in Worthing. The odds of success, however, did not look good. Who would pay for their accommodation? And they had no means of transport. Moreover, how could Jane's brother and his wife be persuaded to do without their daughter's governess for weeks on end – not to mention the issue of convincing Jane's mother and sister, who wouldn't necessarily be expected to share her enthusiasm for including Anne in their holiday plans.

The benefits of a family holiday at the seaside might not have taken much urging, but Jane faced a far more difficult challenge when it came to convincing her brother to allow his governess to stay on for a further six weeks. Such a discussion must have taken all Jane's powers of persuasion. The coastal air would do Miss Sharpe the world of good; she would return to Godmersham in the best of health, her debilitating headaches a thing of the past. These were the reasons Fanny cited in her letters to account for the prolonged absence of her governess. Yet it hardly seems sufficient to have led Edward to acquiesce to the six-week loss of an important member of household staff – especially since Anne's migraines and eyestrain hadn't seemed to trouble her quite so much of late.

The homeless Austen women had to spend their autumn somewhere, Jane may have reminded her brother, and they could hardly impose themselves much longer at Godmersham. Such an argument would have assuaged any lingering guilt on his part at leaving his mother and sisters so ill-provided for after the death of his father. With so many properties at his disposal, it hardly reflected well on Edward that his female relatives were currently without a place to call home. Anne, as a Godmersham employee, could offer the women invaluable help.

What's more, this was the kind of assistance that Edward could grant without risking the wrath of his wife. After all, she hardly wanted Fanny to grow overly learned, and it must have been rather trying to share one's home with a good-looking woman of quick wit – a quality noted even by James Edward Austen-Leigh, Jane's nephew and first biographer, who would later leave Anne out of his account of his aunt's life. In a note to his half-sister, Anna, dated 1820 – 15 years after she had played the role of Shepherdess Flora in Anne's play – he described the governess as 'horridly affected'. But even he couldn't deny that she was also 'rather amusing'.

Although the seaside plan had succeeded, the group's initial enthusiasm had begun to wane by the time the convoy of coaches made its way from Kent to Worthing. Unable to find accommodation to house the entire travelling party at their intended stop-off point near the abbey at Battle, they were forced to ride on to Horsebridge, a further 15 miles across the South Downs. Fortunately, here they secured rooms before darkness descended. And it turned out that a good night's sleep was all they needed to revive their spirits for the final leg of their trip.

The knocks and bumps of the journey paled into insignificance at the first sight of the sea. They had made good time, and the September sun shone sufficiently bright to afford a pleasant afternoon in Brighton. Here they would have noticed the vast riding school and stables being constructed in Indian style around the pavilion, where the Prince of Wales, later to become George IV, was reputed to indulge in hedonistic pursuits. Jane, in particular, found such extravagance distasteful. Any investment in coastal towns should fund fortifications against invasion. How could the Prince justify constructing a pleasure palace, when the Napoleonic Wars had inflated the price of bread to an all-time high, and the British fleet under Admiral Lord Nelson was preparing for battle against the combined forces of France and Spain?

The weather held up, and, after arriving in Worthing and settling into their rental property, the whole party took an evening walk on the sands. The group consisted of Fanny, her parents and grandmother, her two aunts and her governess. They were also joined by the Austens' childhood friend Martha Lloyd. She was a cheery woman, ten years Jane's senior, and the pair had long enjoyed conversing late into the night. Summer may have been fading to autumn, but hope was abloom: at least temporarily, the household of intelligent women of which Jane had dreamed was about to come to pass.

Once her brother and sister-in-law had departed, there would be plenty of time for creative work: early mornings of writing; strolls with Anne; lamp-lit hours poring over books. Here, the pair could bask in dawn trips to the beach to make purchases from the fishermen's freshly caught haul; experience the invigorating shock of the waves when the attendant lowered them by rope from their mobile hut; spend afternoons lounging in the town's warm salt baths and evenings at the raffle, where Jane won 17 shillings – enough to buy as many four-pound loaves.

It's tempting to imagine that, in circumstances so conducive to creativity, Jane put pen to paper once more. She may well have written up a clean copy of one of her early novellas, *Lady Susan*, a story about a scheming widow, since the manuscript is on paper watermarked with the date 1805. Such an exercise would have eased her back into her work. She could trick herself that she was simply transcribing, but no writer with as much stamina for revision as Jane could possibly have resisted making changes as she went along. Anne, too, seems to have put her time to good use because it wasn't long before she had in her possession a revised version of her play.

They must have felt that these weeks of writing and creative companionship resembled nothing short of a coup. And yet

Jane's removal of Anne from Godmersham bordered on the kind of meddlesomeness of her future heroine, Emma, who takes it upon herself to 'improve' the lot of a less fortunate friend. In real life, Jane was gambling with Anne's future to secure this short-term gain. While they revelled in their freedom in Worthing, Anne's employment at Godmersham had moved onto shaky ground.

Fanny had invited her former governess, Dorothy Chapman, to leave the home of her married sister, where she now resided, to return to her old workplace for a sojourn. Fanny was encouraged by her mother in this scheme – a self-serving act of hospitality if ever there was one. While Fanny breakfasted with her parents over the coming weeks, and was permitted to sleep downstairs in the closet adjoining her mother's boudoir, Miss Chapman's presence meant that the absence of Anne from the schoolroom needn't cause much inconvenience. The master and mistress of the house could go out riding whenever they chose, leaving their daughter in the hands of her dear former governess. And what capable hands they were! Far from stealing solitary hours in the library or taking to her bed with recurring headaches, Miss Chapman roped Fanny and the younger children into gardening duties, showed them how to make pets of dormice, took them off to gather nuts from the estate's trees, and even managed to chivvy on her former charge to complete more needlework than ever before.

But Anne had not been entirely forgotten – at least not by Fanny, who spent her governess's six-week holiday stitching an elaborately embroidered neckerchief to present to her upon her return. It was 1 November by the time Anne went back to Godmersham, the crisp leaves of autumn dampening into mulch.

After the novelty of her time away with Jane, Anne returned to find that not much had changed. Lessons were still punctuated by visits from travelling salesmen, the writing of letters and walks in the parkland – where they had to take good care since

Edward's regiment of volunteer soldiers continued to use the grounds as a firing range in preparation for an attack by France. But small alterations soon emerged: Fanny's garden looked far neater, and a dormouse now resided in a box in the schoolroom. Someone as astute as Anne might even have sensed the rising tension among Edward and his troop, for word had it that a great sea battle would soon commence. If the navy failed to hold back the French ships, the people of Kent expected to feel the full force of a Gallic invasion – an assault that could come any day.

While great tensions were playing out on the national stage, Anne's extended time away appeared to have cured her from the pressures that had been afflicting her body. According to Fanny's diary, her governess seemed to her 'uncommonly well', and Anne assured the child that she thought herself 'better for her stay at Worthing'. The pair soon fell back into their usual routine of breakfasting together in the schoolroom – a far cry from the quiet mornings enjoyed by Jane, who rose before the rest of her household.

Within days of Anne's return, further news from the outside world made its way through the gates of Godmersham. The British had won a great victory, but Nelson had been fatally wounded. It had taken a fortnight for the outcome of the Battle of Trafalgar to reach the householders of Kent, who could now sleep easy in the knowledge that, at least for now, the threat of a French invasion had passed.

But, as it turned out, Anne was only to be graced with three days free of worry. During this brief reprieve, Miss Crow – a professional 'paintress' as Fanny would refer to her within the covers of her pocketbook – arrived at Godmersham to make portraits of the household. With the wintry light streaming in through the floor-to-ceiling windows, Miss Crow's eyes moved from Anne to the page and back to Anne as she sketched the contours of the governess's face. Miss Crow's current task required her to study her subject intently, and she could afford to take her time since she'd be staying at Godmersham for a few days.

Fanny and Anne ended up exchanging their finished portraits as keepsakes, but they do not seem to have survived. Neither has ever turned up in an auction catalogue or a jumble sale. But just like the famous watercolour of Jane, it seems that Anne's likeness conveyed little sense of her true appearance. 'We are all quite *sick* of Miss Crow's pictures,' Fanny complained. 'They are no more like than, *the man in the moon*; mine was the most like but that Miss Sharpe has got. I have hers which might as well be called mine, for Miss S. has not such a very *silly* countenance as Miss C. has chosen to give her, neither such *sleepy eyes*, such a *mumped up* mouth, in short they are all detestable, & fit for nothing but to be *thrown in the fire.*'

But Miss Crow's watchful gaze may have spotted something in the governess's face that had passed her employers and pupil by. The beginnings of one of Anne's headaches was brewing, perhaps drawing the life from her eyes and causing tension around her mouth. During the following days, her migraine reached its peak, the pain that bore through her far worse than any she had known before. On the day of the visiting painter's departure, a specialist doctor had to be called to Godmersham and he advised the governess to take drastic measures – so drastic that he would remain here with the family for the next seven days.

It was mid-November 1805 by now, and the fires roaring in the grates at Godmersham could not quite mask the chill in the air. Fanny had removed herself from the bedroom she shared with her governess, returning temporarily to her mother's downstairs closet. The 12-year-old had been told the undiluted truth about the operation that the doctor, Mr Lascelles, had recommended: a suture to the nape of the neck. But it isn't known whether word of the ordeal had reached Trim Street in

Bath, where, insufficiently supported by Edward, the Austen women were making do in dark quarters in an especially noisy and polluted part of town.

In Anne's room at Godmersham, the doctor ground ingredients such as extract of Spanish fly and mustard seeds, before stirring the powder with plaster until it became a smooth paste. Once the ointment was to Mr Lascelles's liking, he applied it to Anne's exposed nape, her hair pinned out of the way. The dampness of the lotion was swiftly followed by a burning sensation, and then the pain of the needle piercing the freshly formed blister. The sore was then stitched with a suture in the hope that the constriction here might result in the release of pressure elsewhere.

During the days that followed, the mistress of the house ate breakfast with her children and stepped in for Anne by hearing Fanny's lessons. The high spirits occasioned by the baby's first steps, so soon before her first birthday, must have been tempered by the knowledge that Anne writhed in agony upstairs. The governess had to keep the seton stitch in her neck for as long as she could endure it. But, as Fanny wrote to Miss Chapman a week after the operation, the stitch was giving Anne such 'exquisite torture' that it seemed unlikely she could bear to keep it in for many days more.

As time dragged on, Anne continued to be dogged by pain. But, at the end of the doctor's planned week of treatment, she emerged from her room to take dinner downstairs for the first time since the beginning of the attack. Within two days, she was expected to resume her full duties, sharing her bed with Fanny once more. Edward and Elizabeth even left their eldest daughter with Anne while they went off for a week's stay with relations in another part of Kent. Throughout all this, Anne stoically kept the seton stitch in her blistered nape, insisting, as she told Fanny, 'her eyes much benefitted by it'.

Throughout December's cycle of snow and melt, Anne recovered sufficiently to rehearse a series of plays and monologues with the children. In between carol singing, treats of Spanish liquorice, and games of snap dragon, duck apple, and blind man's buff, she prepared the Austen children for a festive performance. The theatricals stood out to Fanny as the highlight of 1805. Not only did she mention them in one of her letters, a jotting in her diary on 20 December referred to her participation in 'a delightful play & several pieces'. But, claiming that 'they were too long to be detailed here', she revealed that she had 'given the account of them as a piece of paper to be found in the pocket of this book'.

Although the diaries themselves have been carefully catalogued, this paper is absent from any library records because archivists assumed it had been lost. But, in fact, hidden within Fanny's tiny calfskin books, we discovered cardboard pouches as brittle as late-autumn leaves. The glue that had originally attached them to the inside covers had long lost its grip, but the fragile pocket of Fanny's 1805 diary still contained her detailed account of Anne's theatricals – just as it had done for well over two hundred years.

According to the child's report, the production went off with aplomb. At six o'clock in the evening, seven-year-old William rounded up the family servants, and then positioned himself at the door, passing out programmes to those who entered and crying out their contents for all to hear. The children acted in a play entitled *Alfred*, which they'd found within the marbled covers of the schoolroom's copy of *Evenings at Home* – a compendium 'consisting of a variety of miscellaneous pieces for the instruction and amusement of young persons'. This patriotic drama about Alfred the Great's successful defence of his kingdom against the Viking invasion was timely indeed, given Britain's recent victory at Trafalgar. They then performed a scene from *Douglas*, a popular blank-verse tragedy, which, years later,

Jane would archly cite in *Mansfield Park* as an appropriate play for household performance. The entertainments culminated in recitations from poetry annuals, and then afterwards Elizabeth treated the children to sips of tea and games of lottery. Fanny went to bed happy, believing that the 'pieces were performed *uncommonly well* as we were afterwards told'.

In the aftermath of the evening's success, Anne grew more ambitious for the children's theatricals. By the Twelfth Night of Christmas, Fanny was penning letters about another evening of entertainments, and, again, she wrote up a detailed account and tucked it into her still pristine copy of the Daily Lady's Companion, recently purchased for her record of 1806. And, yet again, the document has survived.

Anne – whom Fanny now referred to interchangeably as Miss Sharpe and Anny – created great anticipation for the performance on 4 January 1806. Keep it a secret, she told the children, from everyone other than your parents. She stage-managed the whole affair, as well as embroidering the costumes. Elizabeth and her sisters agreed to play the musical accompaniment, and Anne rustled up an audience of servants and guests. The spectators who congregated in the breakfast parlour found the actors positioned in front of a curtain. The nursemaid and cook, footman and lady's maid were subjected to repeats of the pre-Christmas recitations, but, towards the end of the evening, the children went on to act out a redrafted version of the drama they had staged with Jane and Cassandra the previous summer. By now Anne had revised this play of hers, not least by changing its name from *Virtue Rewarded* to *Pride Punished or Innocence Rewarded* – a title later echoed by that of Jane's most famous novel, *Pride and Prejudice*, which, at this stage, was still called *First Impressions*.

According to Fanny, the evening was a great success. No doubt encouraged by this, Anne owned up to being its author – a mistake, perhaps, given what would happen next.

Before the week was out, Anne's employment at Godmersham had come to an end. Fanny was distraught. As she put it in a letter to her former governess, Miss Chapman, 'I *assure* you I regard it as much more than a *disagreeable ceremony*, for I hardly know how I shall bear it, she has been so long with us, & uncommonly kind to me!'

Despite the admirable way Anne had coped after her excruciating operation, the Kentish Austens cited ill health as the official reason for the cessation of her employment. Whatever the truth, she would have had to find new work as a matter of urgency, since the ongoing war had inflated the costs of both food and rent. There was no way Jane could come to Anne's rescue with another attempt to relocate her to Bath. By now, the Austen women's own hold on the city was diminishing. Their cramped rooms in Trim Street – an area they'd categorically ruled out of their house search just five years earlier – could not even accommodate their family friend Martha. So much for Jane's dream of an intelligent circle of single women.

And so in 1806 Jane was living an ignominious existence, still unpublished, her one writer friend sundered from her. Despite her lack of worldly success, Jane's literary ambitions were at least supported by her doting sister and storytelling mother. Their keenness to offer opinions on her work and their willingness to relieve her of all but the most undemanding of household tasks allowed her to keep writing the novels that would finally make her name.

Unlike Jane, Anne received no support for her artistic leanings, and the demands of earning her keep meant that writing could never play a central role in her life. While Jane, through her novels, still speaks loud and clear, Anne's voice has been forever stifled. Her plays appear never to have been put on outside the schoolroom, her scripts, diaries and letters never discovered. In this way, the story of Jane's most important literary friendship has been all but forgotten.

Surely filled with anxiety, Anne left Godmersham for the last time on 18 January 1806, just three days after her thirty-third birthday. Her departure took her away from the schoolroom and library, where she'd enjoyed such animated times, along the avenue of limes that led through the deer park, finally passing between the tall iron gates that closed behind her, shutting her even further away from Jane.

CHAPTER 3

CLOSING RANKS

Within two months of leaving Godmersham Park, Anne Sharp was working once more, this time employed by a Mrs Raikes to teach her six-year-old daughter. But before the spring of 1806 was out, the governess would have to leave this job as well, required to work as the paid companion of her mistress's frail, unmarried sister. Anne now moved in with her new employer Miss Bailey, who lived in Hinckley, a bustling market town in the Midlands.

Jane likewise had little say over where she lived, reliant as she was on the goodwill of her brothers. The Austen sisters had recently relocated to Southampton – almost 150 miles from Hinckley – where they were now sharing the marital home of one of their sailor brothers. Frank's removal of them from Bath's squalid Trim Street further emphasised the neglect of their elder and far wealthier brother, Edward, who had failed to offer the women accommodation on any of his vast estates. The forces that separated Jane and Anne could so easily have triumphed during this time, but the two amateur writers managed to sustain their friendship in the way they knew best: by putting pen to paper.

Almost three years into the correspondence that the pair established following Anne's departure from Godmersham, Jane found herself forced to write a most unexpected letter. Anne's former mistress, Elizabeth Austen, had dropped dead on 10 October 1808, just three days after the safe delivery of her eleventh child. The poor eldest daughter, Fanny, at just 15 years of age, now bore the responsibility of mothering the newborn and consoling her bereft father. Knowing that the girl's former governess would be well placed to offer comfort, Jane wrote to Anne with the sad news. She also exchanged a series of letters with Cassandra, who had been staying at Godmersham to help with the confinement, but she made a point of refusing to dwell for too long on the late Elizabeth's qualities or to write a 'Panegyric on the Departed', as she put it. Beyond enquiring about the state of the corpse, her focus was less on her late sister-in-law and more on the recently bereaved children. Even if no love had been lost between Jane and Elizabeth, she felt shocked by the suddenness of the death. By all accounts, the 35-year-old had recovered well from the birth, and had been tucking into a hearty meal just half an hour before her fatal collapse.

Fanny's loss likely led to a surprising upturn in Jane's luck. Tellingly, less than a fortnight after his wife's death, Edward suddenly found it in himself to offer the Austen women lifelong residence in one of the many properties on his land. They chose the former bailiff's cottage at Chawton, which offered them the opportunity to return to their Hampshire roots and was big enough also to accommodate their childhood friend, Martha Lloyd.

Renovations were completed by the summer of 1809, and the women wasted no time in making the move. Here, Mrs Austen enjoyed watering the shrubbery of sweet williams and columbines, picking apricots in the orchard and even donning a labourer's green outfit to dig up potatoes from the kitchen garden. But, now approaching 70, she let the younger generation take over most of the domestic management. In an extraordinary act of generosity and faith in Jane's writing, her sister Cassandra and friend Martha exempted her from the more onerous household chores. Jane did take responsibility for the tea caddy, however, which she kept under lock and key, eking out the leaves and sugar – ever expensive commodities during those long years of war. She continued to rise early, practising the piano before spearing slices of bread with a fork and holding them close to the glowing embers until the smell of toast drew the others downstairs. But, for the most part, Jane was free to work at her tiny walnut table, poring over the manuscript of *Sense and Sensibility* – the novel about a neglectful brother and sister-in-law that she had begun almost fifteen years earlier. Absorbed in her redrafting, she could be wrenched from her fictional world only by the creak of the parlour door.

In such conducive conditions, Jane began to enjoy a period of creative industry as intensive and enjoyable as that which she had known before the upheaval to Bath. But Anne continued to endure a litany of troubles. She confided in Jane about the strained state of relations with her mistress, whose physical impairments required the ministrations of a full-time companion. It couldn't have helped that, while attending to Miss Bailey, Anne's own symptoms had flared up once more. The seton stitch in the nape of her neck having failed to achieve any lasting improvement to her headaches and eyestrain, Anne sought more newfangled cures. Her hair shorn and electrodes attached to her skull, she bore an early form of electrotherapy. As Fanny would report, Anne's 'eyes have been worse than ever, & she had all her hair cut off, & continual blisters on her head all to no purpose.'

Knowing that the deterioration in Anne's health made writing difficult and that the shift from teaching to hired help robbed her of a ready-made cast and audience for her plays, Jane must have braced herself to share her own good news. With the help of her favourite brother, Henry, a military man turned banker, she had secured her first publishing deal. After fifteen years of intermittent work on *Sense and Sensibility*, such news, which she received as the year of 1810 drew to a close, was cause indeed for celebration. But Jane's achievement represented only a modest success. As its name would suggest, the Military Library, Whitehall, specialised in books about warfare. Such a publisher was hardly the ideal choice for a love story exploring the injustice of primogeniture. To make matters worse, Jane had to agree to a contract that forced her to take all the financial risk yet granted the publisher a share of any profits, and so she was faced with the daunting prospect of making a loss as well as the delightful anticipation of possible success. 'I can no more forget it,' she wrote to Cassandra of *Sense and Sensibility*, 'than a mother can forget her sucking child.'

While Jane was apprehensively awaiting the book's publication, she pulled out another early manuscript, the novel she would rename *Pride and Prejudice*. Among all this literary endeavour, she yearned to converse in person once again with her long-distance friend. And so, when a set of prospective houseguests cancelled their visit to Chawton Cottage at the end of May 1811, Jane spotted the opportunity to welcome Anne for an extended stay instead. First she had to convince the rest of the household to agree to this 'magnificent project', as she referred to it in her letter to her sister. Brimming with excitement, she set out the logistical reasons for extending the invitation: Anne had already scheduled holiday leave for right around this time; they could host her here at Chawton for a lengthy duration before the arrival of the next party of guests; she could share transportation with Cassandra and Martha, their own comings and goings set to coincide with the former governess's prospective travel plans. Time was of the essence, so Jane contacted both her sister and childhood friend, telling them to 'write by return of post if you have any reason for not wishing it done'. To be on the safe side, in a postscript, she added, 'I shall consider Silence as Consent.'

But neither woman held her tongue, each raising objections to the proposal. Jane's frustration simmered beneath the politeness of her reply: 'I have given up all idea of Miss Sharpe's travelling with you & Martha, for tho' you are both all compliance with my scheme, yet as *you* knock off a week from the end of her visit, & *Martha* rather more from the beginning, the thing is out of the question.'

Cassandra and Martha would have had grounds to feel aggrieved by the strength of Jane's admiration for her fellow writer. After all, through their efficient household management, they did more than anyone else to facilitate Jane's creative work. But the soon-to-be-published novelist, never one to give up without a fight, would win them round before long. A throwaway line in the pocketbook of Mary Lloyd – the sister of Martha and the wife of Jane's eldest brother, James – reveals that Anne came to stay in the August of 1811.

Every day, Collyer's public stagecoach, drawn by six horses, passed so close to Chawton Cottage that it caused the windows to rattle, the spectacle offering Mrs Austen a never-ending source of entertainment and the travellers a glimpse of the women's parlour. It was here that Anne descended from the carriage to the idyllic sight of the reed pond opposite the Austens' new home, Edward's Great House towering over the village in the distance, roofs of thatch all around. Once inside the modest dwelling, how glorious the set-up must have seemed: a pianoforte in the large sitting room; books from the local circulating library; the tiny twelve-sided walnut table at which her friend wrote beside the parlour's fire.

While Jane looked forward to finally seeing her name in print, Anne had some good news of her own. She had secured a new position as a governess to the four daughters of the recently widowed Lady Pilkington, and would be relocating to Chevet

Hall, a Yorkshire estate of even higher status than Godmersham. It was perhaps no coincidence that Jane's fellow inhabitants of Chawton Cottage welcomed Anne just when she was about to take up employment at the home of an aristocrat. Whatever the reason, this reacceptance of the amateur playwright allowed Jane to enjoy her last months as an unpublished author alongside all four of the women who'd shaped her work.

When *Sense and Sensibility* came out in October 1811 it was to little fanfare. Jane herself only stumbled across an advertisement for the work a month after it had been published. Still, she was thrilled to see the title of her book listed side by side with that of one of her favourite authors, Maria Edgeworth, whose novels explored issues as taboo then as interracial relationships, women's rights and same-sex desire. Jane's own name did not feature in either the announcement or the cover of her book. She had opted to publish anonymously, including only the words 'By a Lady'. Although the book had not been entirely ignored, reviewers expressed their praise in a rather subdued manner. It took until February 1812 for an article to appear in the *Critical Review*, which concluded that 'the characters are in genteel life, naturally drawn, and judiciously supported'. By now, however, the novel was beginning to be passed around among members of the upper classes, and, although the print run had been small – likely a thousand or so copies – it eventually sold out. Jane made a profit of £140, and, through Henry, secured a £110 advance for the publication of *Pride and Prejudice* – albeit still with the same small military press.

Enjoying the unaccustomed feeling of her own earnings in her purse, in May 1813, a few months after the publication of *Pride and Prejudice*, the 37-year-old author indulged in a trip to London – the like of which Anne could only dream. En route, she treated herself to a new pair of gloves, picking them up at a bargain price. And once she arrived in the nation's capital, she dashed from linen drapers to jewellers on errands for her relatives: fine silk sarsenet for the lining of her mother's gown; a hardwearing, striped dimity cotton for the motherless Fanny; a plain gold locket for her sister at a higher cost than either of them had expected.

When Jane did manage to steal some time for herself, she headed to an art exhibition at Somerset House, indulging in an unusual literary quest. Speeding along the Strand in Henry's barouche, its top concertinaed open, she felt on the verge of laughter, amused to find herself riding in a low-slung carriage on this personal victory parade about town.

She'd decided to entertain herself by searching the great galleries of London for a portrait that might resemble Elizabeth Bennet of *Pride and Prejudice*. Although Jane had scoured the watercolours and oils on display in both Spring Gardens and at the British Institution in Pall Mall, she'd failed to find an image that might resemble her heroine, whom the author herself remarked was 'as delightful a creature as ever appeared in print'.

She *did* have every right to feel proud of herself. Some critics had compared the anonymous author to William Shakespeare, and such compliments must have been fresh in Jane's mind as she rushed about town. The *Critical Review* had proclaimed her book 'very superior to any novel we have lately met with' and the famed dramatist, Richard Sheridan, urged a friend to purchase a copy immediately, describing it as 'one of the cleverest things' he had ever read. Jane must have felt buoyed up by the enthusiasm for a novel that had been turned down out of hand sixteen years earlier and, even now, had been brought out by a little-known press. She was determined to look on the bright side, squeezing every bit of pleasure from her modest triumph.

When Jane stepped from the barouche onto the vast courtyard of the newly built Somerset House, its Grecian-style columns towering above her, she had still to come across a portrait of anyone who bore much resemblance to Elizabeth Bennet. In the first gallery she'd visited that day, she had come across a small painting that looked just like the image in her mind's eye of her heroine's elder sister. That evening, in a letter to her own sister, Jane would marvel that in 'size, shaped face, features & sweetness; there never was a greater likeness'. The young woman in the picture, she explained, was dressed 'in a white gown with green ornaments, which convinces me of what I had always supposed, that green was a favourite colour with her'. Since these fictional characters had inhabited Jane's mind for over seventeen years, it was hardly surprising that they had taken on such a life of their own.

It was perhaps as she paused at one of the decorated landings of the staircase that wound up to the Royal Academy Exhibition Room that she resolved to search for a painting of a woman in yellow. Unlike the green clothing suited to the demure eldest Miss Bennet, her creator felt that Elizabeth would be drawn to something buttercup bright. Walking beneath the ornate painted ceiling, Jane's eyes flitted from one portrait to the next – so many canvasses packed on the walls. Her search was, once more, in vain. Although disappointed, she consoled herself with the notion that 'Mr D. prizes any Picture of her too much to like it should be exposed to the public eye'. Yes, that would be his feeling, she later wrote to Cassandra, 'that mixture of Love, Pride & Delicacy'.

Although she published anonymously, Jane revelled in the opportunity to share her children – as she continued to think of her novels – with doting friends and strangers alike. Anne was in on the secret, of course, and she felt delighted to see Jane's words in print. Their affection burned as strong as ever, with no hint of envy from the unpublished writer, who was still toiling in the schoolroom. She, of course, did not have a land-owning brother to provide a roof over her head or female relatives to help her carve out time to write. And yet, she rejoiced in Jane's achievements. The letter Anne sent in November 1813 following the publication of *Pride and Prejudice* caused the novelist to swell with pride: '– Oh! I have more of such sweet flattery from Miss Sharpe! – She is an excellent kind friend.'

Ever one for a scheme, Jane dreamed that Anne might receive a proposal of marriage from Sir William Pilkington, her employer's wealthy brother-in-law. 'Oh! Sir Wm,' Jane joked in a letter to Cassandra, 'how I will love you, if you will love Miss Sharp!' Such were the lack of opportunities for a woman like Anne to pull herself from impoverishment that her friend had to resort to these outlandish matchmaking fantasies.

But, by 1813, Jane's own dreams were coming true. She'd begun to feel more confident about her status as a novelist. By now, most of Chawton knew that the creator of *Sense and Sensibility* and *Pride and Prejudice* lived among them – a fact that she treated with characteristic levity. Before Cassandra returned from a trip to Kent, her sister felt obliged to warn her that the secret had got out. 'I know your starched Notions,' Jane teased, 'but you must be prepared for the Neighbourhood being perhaps already informed of there being such a Work in the World, & in the Chawton World!' This disclosure offered some simple amusements, such as a letter from Fanny, which mischievously addressed her aunt as if she were Mr Darcy's sister. And Jane rather enjoyed the fact that her identity was also beginning to reach readers far and wide: the daughter of a wealthy gentleman known for his radical politics, the wife of an Irish judge, an elderly lady whom the novelist imagined as clever and good.

After some positive responses to *Sense and Sensibility* and great interest in *Pride and Prejudice* – both revisions of novels she'd begun in her youth – the 37-year-old nurtured high hopes for her third book. Bringing all her mature powers to bear on this work, which she'd begun to write at Chawton, she felt that *Mansfield Park* was her best yet. But, when it came out in the spring of 1814, it did not receive a single review. Presumably finding the silence unbearable, Jane begged Anne to give her an honest assessment. The response, which the novelist later jotted down, is as close as history comes to recording Anne's voice. She praised 'its good sense & moral Tendency' as well as singling out the 'natural & just' characterisation. But the pair's bond was strong enough to cope with criticism too. 'As you beg me to be perfectly honest,' Anne ventured, 'I confess I prefer P. & P.' Never again would she offer the kind of bounteous praise she'd served up on *Pride and Prejudice*. But the published author continued to value the creative support she received from the amateur playwright, who could assess both her work's strengths and weaknesses. After all, despite Jane's modicum of fame, Anne remained her only writer friend.

Such a collaboration – unlike those of the male Lake Poets, for instance – could only go on behind closed doors. At least Anne was now welcome at Chawton Cottage, where she may have had this conversation with Jane about *Mansfield Park* during a visit in June 1815. While she was staying with the Austen women, official intelligence travelled all the way from the battlefields at Waterloo to the woodlands and footpaths of Hampshire: the Duke of Wellington's forces had triumphed. At last, twenty-two years after war was waged with France, these women could look forward to the simple pleasures and privileges of peace: an end to the ever-increasing price of food; a release from the threat of invasion; a relaxing of the authoritarian tendency to regard as sedition any criticism of the state.

Amid the celebrations, Jane was charting her own plan of attack, which she would implement soon after her friend bade her farewell. In an attempt to revitalise her literary career, Jane turned once more to Henry. This same brother would later feel obliged to memorialise his sister as an unassuming lady scribbler concerned with neither 'fame nor profit'. But, in fact, he helped her to carry out a plan to achieve both recognition and remuneration. As the summer of 1815 seeped into autumn, Henry agreed to send out his sister's fourth novel, *Emma*. This time, they submitted it to John Murray, one of the most influential publishers of the day, renowned for bringing out work by writers as celebrated as Lord Byron and Sir Walter Scott. The siblings' audacity paid off, for the publisher got back to them swiftly, proposing to purchase not only Jane's new novel, *Emma*, but also the copyrights for *Mansfield Park* and *Sense and Sensibility*, which, unlike *Pride and Prejudice*, she had not ceded to the military press.

Jane did have some bargaining power by now, since her novels had begun to draw the attention of London's high society. And so it came to pass that, just weeks after these successful negotiations, she found herself back on Pall Mall, that street along which she'd ridden in her brother's barouche two years earlier. It was 13 November 1815, and she was now stepping inside the Prince Regent's royal residence, no less.

Here was a relationship that her successors would be happy to explore. Jane's correspondence with the Prince's Librarian, James Stanier Clarke, has been passed down the generations, as has his Friendship Book, an album in which he painted watercolours of his acquaintances, including one portrait that some claim is of Jane Austen. Along with extant presentation copies of *Emma*, this image of a strikingly fashionable woman, her black hat festooned with flowers and feathers, is among the artefacts that shed light on Jane's visit to Carlton House and its aftermath.

On arrival at the royal residence, this cottage-dwelling daughter of a country clergyman did not convey any sense of awe. The invitation by royal command to roam these decadent chambers of Carlton House – plush Persian carpets underfoot and crystal chandeliers overhead – had, in fact, caused her great anguish. She could not abide the Prince Regent, who had failed to steer the country with care during his father's bout of insanity. It was ten years now since Jane and Anne had seen the Prince's pleasure palace being constructed when they stopped in Brighton en route to their seaside holiday. There, as here, the future George IV had indulged his love of ornate furnishings, decorating cornices and pillars with gilt and displaying his vast collections of lacquered chinoiserie. Not only was he profligate with the nation's dwindling wealth, he was careless in his marital affairs too – something about which Jane was privately livid. In a letter to Martha, she had taken the side of his estranged wife, 'because she *is* a woman, & because I hate her Husband'. But Jane could not risk spurning this man she so despised, and, thus summoned, she was left with little choice but to accept his sumptuous hospitality and hold her sharp tongue.

Jane must have been relieved to discover that the librarian would show her around in place of the Prince. And so, here she was, in a scarlet-curtained ante room, greeting this rather obsequious courtier. The Prince, the librarian told her, had left instructions for him to pass on his admiration for all her novels, sets of which he kept in each of his residences. The librarian was also a particular fan. 'Your late Works, Madam, and in particular Mansfield Park reflect the highest honour on your Genius and your Principles,' he would insist by letter a few days later; 'in every new work your mind seems to increase in energy and powers of discrimination.'

If the portrait in the courtier's Friendship Book is anything to go by, Jane's white gauze gown would have whispered down the elegant double staircase as he escorted her in the direction of the library. She may not have been feeling particularly comfortable in her unaccustomed finery, but she would enter home territory on setting foot among the bookshelves.

Here, with the landscaped gardens visible through the French doors, St James's Park and the towers of Westminster Abbey beyond, the librarian had an important piece of information to impart. He told Jane that she should feel at liberty to dedicate any future work to the Prince. There would be no necessity to seek His Royal Highness's approval.

This proposal nagged at Jane over the coming days. Was it 'incumbent' on her to inscribe her new novel to the Prince, she wrote to ask the librarian. His reassurance that 'It is certainly not *incumbent* on you' did little to persuade Jane that she was off the hook, especially since he went on to add that 'if you wish to do the Regent that honour, either now or at any future period, I am happy to send you that permission which need not require any more trouble or solicitation on your Part.'

Anyone would be reluctant to risk making an enemy of the Prince. And however hateful to her personally, Jane was also shrewd enough to understand that such a dedication could give her leverage with her publisher and printer, thereby increasing her public acclaim. So, with mixed feelings, she acquiesced, contacting her editor to request the simplest of inscriptions on the title page: 'Dedicated by Permission to H.R.H. The Prince Regent'. John Murray informed her that protocol required something rather more elaborate, insisting on devoting an entire page to the dedication and including the assurance that the author was His Royal Highness's 'most dutiful and obedient humble servant'. To add insult to injury, Jane was required to purchase from her own pocket a bound presentation copy of *Emma* to furnish the library at Carlton House. At great personal expense, she had the three volumes of her novel bound in red morocco, the goatskin decorated with gold gilding and embossed with the Regent's hallmark badge of feathers.

At least Jane could divert herself with the more pleasurable task of devising a list of recipients to whom she genuinely desired to send the remaining eleven presentation copies. These gifts, though delivered with real affection, she could not afford to bind. She set aside most of them for family members, but kept two of her dozen copies for fellow female writers. Yet her reasons for wishing to share her work with each of these women couldn't have been more different.

An endorsement from the bestselling writer Maria Edgeworth could have propelled Jane to much greater literary acclaim and financial success. 'The authoress of Pride and

Prejudice has been so good as to send me a new novel just published, *Emma*', wrote Edgeworth in January 1816. But she did not feel at all inclined to extend the hand of friendship, failing even to acknowledge receipt of the gift. She did find time, however, to complain to a friend that she found *Emma* unbearably dull. Two years later, she would outline to her aunt what she considered the failings of the finally published *Northanger Abbey*, making no comment on the fact that it contained an extremely complimentary reference to her own most controversial book. *Belinda*, the narrator of Jane's novel insists, is written in 'best-chosen language', and conveys 'the greatest powers of the mind' and 'the liveliest effusions of wit and humour'.

The failure of Jane's attempts to woo the celebrated author might be explained away by unfortunate timing, or perhaps Edgeworth was guarding her space at the top. For, although she did not care for *Northanger Abbey*, in that same letter to her aunt of 1818, she admitted to a deep admiration for Jane's final completed novel *Persuasion*. In contrast to Jane, though, she would never publicly praise her literary peer.

Unlike the presentation copy sent to Edgeworth, the one Jane set aside for Anne would be given without any self-serving designs. The governess and amateur playwright, whom she'd favoured over her brother Edward when choosing her twelve recipients, clearly couldn't help her to achieve the fame and fortune she so desired. Here was a gesture that spoke simply of Jane's gratitude for Anne's consolation during those long years when she too had been unpublished, as well as the celebrations they'd since enjoyed.

Appreciating the value of this gift, Anne must have scrimped and saved to pay for the binding of the three-volume novel with enough calfskin to cover the spines and corners, the covers more economically protected with marbled card. And yet her gratitude did not make her obsequious. Far from it. Of *Emma*,

Anne admitted that she liked it 'better than M.P. — but not so well as P. & P.' Jane recorded her friend's responses to some of the characters as: 'pleased with the Heroine for her Originality, delighted with Mr. K – & called Mrs. Elton beyond praise'. Yet Anne was not convinced by the portrait of Jane Fairfax, who dreads the future mapped out for her as a governess. It's a telling criticism, since Anne was so well placed to judge. In *Emma*, the inhabitants of the village feel aghast that one of the most elegant and accomplished among them should be destined to labour in the schoolroom, the shackles of the governess's 'human intellect' being likened almost to the sale of 'human flesh'. While such comparisons demonstrate Jane's sympathy for the likes of Anne, they also underscore the vast gulf between them.

In September 1816, only nine months after Anne received one of the precious presentation copies, Jane unexpectedly allowed her tongue to turn against her longstanding friend. Gossiping in a letter to her sister, who was taking the waters in Cheltenham, Jane complained about Anne having sent 'quite one of her Letters'. The governess had been plagued once more by ill health, but her account of her treatment had irked Jane, who wrote off such complaints as hypochondria. Cruelly sending up Anne's suffering, she sarcastically summarised it to Cassandra thus: 'she has been again obliged to exert herself more than ever – in a more distressing, more harassed state – & has met with another excellent old Physician & his wife with every virtue under Heaven, who takes to her & cures her from pure Love and Benevolence'.

Forty-year-old Jane was suffering herself – in her case, from backache – but she was taking a very different approach. While Anne put her faith in physicians, she was attempting to regulate her own health, assuring Cassandra that she was 'nursing myself up now into as beautiful a state as I can' and insisting that 'my Back has given me scarcely any pain for many days'. But, in reality, Jane's self-administered regimen of moonlit walks and curative doses of rhubarb was failing to have the desired effect.

As the autumn of 1816 progressed, the lilacs in the garden at Chawton hanging on their spent flower heads, Jane continued to be tormented by ill health. In addition to the backache, she was experiencing nausea, diarrhoea, muscle weakness and fatigue. Her illness worsening, she began to reassess her recent attitude towards Anne: fellow spinster, fellow sufferer, and, most of all, fellow writer, whose astute literary opinions she'd so often sought.

By 22 May 1817, Jane had been bedridden for at least a month and Anne was still very much on her mind. Pleased to have regained sufficient strength to prop herself up with bolster pillows, she resolved to write a letter to the friend she had come to take for granted. Candour had formed such a central part of their relationship that, sharpened quill in hand, she was left with a conundrum: how honest should she be about the state of her health? Curled up behind the bed's floor-length curtains, she put nib to paper to address Miss Sharp as 'my dearest Anne', admitting to the severity of the recent 'attack of my sad complaint', but thanking the Almighty that 'My head was always clear, & I had scarcely any pain; my cheif sufferings were from feverish nights, weakness & Languor'. Jane reassured her friend that her health was improving, while, at the same time, writing to her what was clearly a prolonged adieu.

This would prove to be the last letter Jane ever sent from Chawton Cottage. Within two days, she would travel in her sister-in-law's carriage to the cathedral town of Winchester, each jolt on the 15-mile journey surely causing her much discomfort. Here, under the specialist care of a local apothecary and surgeon, Jane would end up seeing out her final twenty-five days.

Notified of the death of her dear friend, Anne asked Cassandra to send a lock of Jane's hair. Just four days after the funeral, the devoted sister took the time to fulfil Anne's wish, adding a pair of Jane's belt clasps into the package along with her silver needle. Although these humble mementoes speak of the tenderness shared between women of modest means, Cassandra's accompanying note contains a barbed quality. On her deathbed, Jane may have seen the error of her ways, but her sister by birth continued to distrust the friend who had been singled out. Jane had loved and been loved by both these intelligent women, who, in their different ways, had supported her literary endeavours, but Cassandra couldn't help but assert her greater claim to intimacy. 'What I have lost,' she reminded the governess, 'no one but myself can know.' She did bring herself to acknowledge that Anne too was 'not ignorant of her merits' but asserted that no one else could possibly 'judge how I estimated them'. Worse still, she insisted that 'I am much more tranquil than with your ardent feelings you could suppose possible.'

If only Anne's letter to Cassandra had also survived we could have measured for ourselves the friend's 'ardent feelings' against the sister's 'starched Notions', as Jane had once referred to Cassandra's stoicism.

Cassandra's words were freighted with conflicting emotions, her desire to honour her sister's highly valued relationship competing with a touch of snobbery and envy. She felt compelled to offer to see the woman Jane so loved: 'If any thing should ever bring you into attainable distance from me we must meet my dear Miss Sharp.' But she did not go out of her way to visit the friend her sister called 'my dearest Anne', nor did she offer any specific hospitality.

How surprising, then, to discover that Anne returned to Chawton Cottage for several weeks, three years later, in 1820, and that she and Cassandra remained connected for many decades to come. In 1843, twenty-six years after Jane's death, at about the same time that a 70-year-old Cassandra destroyed most of her late sister's letters, she also left £30 in her Will to the elderly Anne. How did the pair move from competition to compassion?

What took them from a half-hearted offer to meet to staying under the same roof? How did their relationship develop and change during this time? All these tantalising questions remain and more, not only because the lives of working women were seen as unworthy of record, but because Jane's family actively whitewashed this friendship from the official version of her life.

Anne, too, must take some of the blame. By 1823, perhaps through assistance from her former employer Lady Pilkington, she had come into sufficient funds to give up her post as a governess and to establish her own boarding school on York Terrace – a prosperous street, perched wind-whistlingly high above the city of Liverpool with views across the River Mersey to Birkenhead beyond. According to the 1841 census, Anne employed three teachers by this stage and as many family servants, and the school was attended by eleven girls. Over the years, she would come to be considered one of the area's wisest and most formidable of inhabitants. As Mrs Creaghe-Howard of Ottery St Mary wrote of Miss Sharp in *The Times*, following the publication of Jane's deathbed letter to Anne: 'She was very reticent about her early life before coming to Liverpool, and also made a mystery of her age.'

Such a reluctance to share the experiences of her governessing days must have contributed to the secrecy that has built up around this literary friendship. But as Anne accumulated far greater wealth and worldly chattels than her novelist friend could ever have dreamed, she continued to cherish the private memories that she'd pass down, albeit obliquely, through arranging for her presentation copy of *Emma* and Jane's deathbed letter to be left to two of her most reliable friends. Through two centuries, these treasured items would be bequeathed from one pair of hands to the next, reaching today's generation intact, allowing these long-silenced tales finally to be deciphered.

PART 2

CHARLOTTE BRONTË AND MARY TAYLOR

~ *No one understood them as they understood each other.*

Miss Miles, Mary Taylor

CHAPTER 4

THREE'S A CROWD

The route from Haworth to Mirfield is about 20 miles, a daunting day's slog for an anxious 14-year-old in a horse-drawn carrier cart. One chill morning in January 1831, the young Charlotte Brontë set off from her father's parsonage, bound for Roe Head School. She was leaving behind a small Yorkshire mill town on the edge of the moors – a cluster of soot-blackened buildings around a steep central street, its tilted gutters flowing with waste from the shops and the nearest outdoor privies.

Once away from these unsanitary yet comfortingly familiar surroundings, the girl's extreme short-sightedness intensified her inevitable bewilderment. The rugged hills that gradually gave way to green valleys and woods all passed her by as a blur. The wagon's cover could protect her from rain and the worst of the wind, but not the jolts of the wheels over the rough ground. Each bump along the country lanes must have brought with it new discomforts to a frail body already overcome with nerves and cold.

This wouldn't be her first experience of formal education. Six years earlier, she'd spent some ten months at the Clergy

Daughters' School at Cowan Bridge – the future model of the nightmarish Lowood Institution in her most famous book, *Jane Eyre*. Charlotte would always remain haunted by the harsh conditions she'd endured: the school's overbearing discipline, its dirty kitchen and careless cook's servings of disgusting food, the feverish agonies of sickly fellow boarders. Her own older sisters, Maria and Elizabeth, had both died of pulmonary tuberculosis after a serious outbreak of illness at the school. Having brought each girl back to Haworth to die, their grieving father had then rushed to collect Charlotte and little Emily before the consumptive disease could lodge itself inside them too.

After such trauma, it might seem strange that the Reverend Patrick Brontë would put his eldest surviving daughter through another potentially similar ordeal. But, now a widower in his fifties, he could no longer avoid the fact that, on his death, his parsonage would fall into the hands of another clergyman and his children might be left unsupported. It must have been some comfort to know that, if she received the right sort of learning, Charlotte would soon be able to earn her own living – although in the early nineteenth century, as in Anne Sharp's day, job prospects for impoverished young women of their class remained few and far between. Charlotte's best hope, of course, was to 'marry up', which becoming more accomplished might allow. Failing that, the training she'd receive at a school like Roe Head would at least equip her to find work as a schoolmistress, still one of the few respectable careers open to women.

As she approached her destination, the cart trundled along Roe Head's curving drive before coming to a stop at last. Warily, she stepped from the cart, squinting at the grey stone house set back from rolling green lawns. A frozen Charlotte would have just made out the vague shapes of the school's arched bow windows, but not the little crowd that must have assembled to witness her shuffling dismount. Neither could she know that among the ten or so pupils was one whose forthright personality would go on to challenge her entire way of looking at the world.

Mary Taylor, the future author of the feminist novel *Miss Miles*, was immediately intrigued by Charlotte. The girl looked miserable and antiquated to Mary – a sharp contrast with the fashionable young ladies of the school. Like the newcomer, Mary and her boisterous sister Martha were far from stylish. The blue cloth coats they wore outdoors were too short for them, their black beaver bonnets only plainly trimmed. They even had to take the extra precaution of stitching over new pairs of gloves to try to make them last. But, rather than empathising with Charlotte, Mary scorned the girl's outdated dress and cowed demeanour. Why, she noted to herself, she looks like 'a little old woman'.

At almost 14, and ten months younger than Charlotte, Mary was an attractive young woman with rosy cheeks – 'too pretty to live' according to Margaret Wooler, Roe Head's well-liked headmistress. But the effects of Britain's first major industrial slump had trickled down to Mary's wardrobe when her father, once a prosperous woollen mill owner, accumulated heavy debts. The other students assumed that the popular Taylor sisters cheerfully accepted the consequences of their reduced circumstances, so visibly apparent in their clothing. But Mary's inner feelings of humiliation seem to have cut deeper than her schoolmates could guess.

Later, in the airy schoolroom, she was quick to notice that, though Charlotte had changed into a different frock, this one was just as old. The new girl's timidity and the wildly seeking, side-to-side glances of her poor eyes were another source of amusement. From her chair, Mary observed Charlotte's body hunched over her desk, knowing that this would not do either for the middle-aged Miss Wooler, reminiscent of an abbess in her embroidered white gowns, or for the other Wooler sisters who helped at the school.

Sure enough, when Charlotte's posture was noticed, she was called upon to raise her head. She complied, but in order to keep reading she raised the book in the air too. There it stayed, close to her nose, until the watching roomful of girls couldn't help but laugh. Charlotte's lilting voice, with what Mary took for Irish inflections, also sounded strange to her classmates' ears. Their amusement could only have served to compound Charlotte's feelings of isolation.

It was all so different from the intense, creative atmosphere of Haworth Parsonage, in which she and her remaining siblings – Branwell, Emily and Anne – had flourished. Along with her brother and sisters, Charlotte had previously enjoyed a rigorous and free-ranging home curriculum guided by their intellectual father, with their practical aunt, who also lived with them, instructing the girls in household matters. In addition to these lessons, the children were used to regularly producing poems and short stories for their own entertainment, including a series of manuscripts in miniscule writing that could barely be deciphered without the aid of a magnifying glass, rendering them out of bounds to the prying eyes of adults. Many of these works were set in the confederation of Glass Town, an imaginary world inspired first by the four's childhood games and later their precocious literary tastes. Charlotte had come away to school in the knowledge that, in her absence, her siblings would continue their joint writings without her – that by the time she returned to Haworth, the fantasy landscapes they had built together might have utterly changed.

While the unfettered style of Charlotte's home schooling had made her well-versed in areas out of the range of Miss Wooler's lessons, it had left her largely ignorant in other vital subjects, such as geography or the theory of grammar. At playground games, too, she was considered inept, possessing a physical feebleness that an incredulous Mary put down to Charlotte's self-denying refusal to eat meat – an unusual stance for anyone of her time.

In those early days at the school, Charlotte felt compelled to put in many extra hours of private study, warned by Miss Wooler that, unless she caught up with those of her own age, she would be forced to sit with the younger ones. Although the other students believed Charlotte to be very ignorant, Mary was beginning to understand that there might be more to the new girl than that initial impression of oddness. Her talents were emerging from beneath her air of reserve. Soon, she would impress her classmates with her drawing abilities and her much-envied skill at writing in italics, a technique honed for the Brontës' household magazines made up of the children's stories and poems. Eventually, she'd overcome her shyness, gaining the confidence to weave ghostly tales in the dormitory at night, holding her nightdress-clad audience in the throes of terror.

Charlotte's expectations were surely raised when, one day at the school, the attractive Mary approached her to talk. Even in her short time at Roe Head, Charlotte would have gleaned an understanding of Mary's keen intelligence. Now she may have dared to dream that her schoolmate had sensed similar qualities in her.

But while Mary would eventually warm to the new girl, those initial feelings of condescension hadn't yet disappeared. Any fanciful hopes on Charlotte's part were dashed when Mary pronounced in typically blunt manner, 'You are very ugly.'

With her pale, dried-out skin and untamed frizz of hair, Charlotte had never been considered conventionally beautiful, but, having been brought up in a deeply religious home, she would not have been encouraged to dwell on such vanities. Nonetheless, Mary's words imparted a bruise that would leave Charlotte forever aware of her unlovely looks, the gauntness of her bony frame. And though Mary would never lose her outspoken ways, she would grow to regret her youthful cruelty.

Years later, when Mary eventually apologised, Charlotte's reply was painfully repressed. Describing this adult conversation to her friend's first biographer, Elizabeth Gaskell, Mary would recall Charlotte telling her that she shouldn't repent of her words, that Mary had done her 'a great deal of good'.

Still, the insult had burned itself into Charlotte's consciousness. In 1843, twelve years after this crushing incident, Charlotte, who'd allowed a cousin of Mary to make a portrait of her, was to warn the young woman that the picture would not 'yield pleasure to Mary Taylor – do not give it to her, or if you do – do not expect thanks in return – she likes me well enough – but my face she can dispense with'. Charlotte knew full well that Mary would flatly tell her cousin this if asked, although the opinion would be given in the 'sincere and truthful language' that Charlotte had by then grown to admire.

Back in her earliest days at Roe Head, during that period when the two were still circling each other with wariness, another new girl showed up. Ellen Nussey arrived a week after the official start of term. Like Mary, she was about a year younger than Charlotte and considered attractive. A portrait made at around this time shows a fair-complexioned girl with ringlets and an atmosphere of gentle serenity.

Decades later, Ellen would remember stepping down outside the schoolhouse while the other students were at play in the gardens – all except Charlotte, who, too short-sighted to join in with the games, had been left to her own devices. Ellen was shown into the silent classroom. Believing she was all alone, she took in her surroundings, noting that they seemed pleasant enough. A length of crimson cloth covered the long table in the room's centre and there were a series of shelves weighed down with serious books. Beyond the walls, she could hear the lively voices of the girls. Looking at the volumes on the shelves, Ellen allowed herself, fleetingly, to admit to feeling overawed.

Only then did she notice the small, dark shape by the bow window, weeping without a sound. Feeling both touched and troubled, Ellen took a few steps forwards. The figure shrank back as she approached. When Ellen asked after the source of her distress, the girl managed to explain that she was missing home. And Ellen answered kindly that, 'by and by', she would perhaps be homesick too. Then a quiver of a smile came over the face of the crying girl. Wordlessly they took each other's hands. They would remain there, still and silent, until they heard the approaching footsteps of the other pupils coming in from outside.

Much as Charlotte needed such warm acceptance, as her time at school went by, she couldn't help but find Ellen dull in comparison to Mary. In fact, she considered the well-bred newcomer quite devoid of imagination. Far into later life, she would deride Ellen's eager but unmelodic recitations of poetry and her faltering attempts to talk with Charlotte about books. And yet, it didn't take long for the pair to become inseparable.

Epistolary evidence suggests that they shared a bed at school – still a common practice among young female friends and siblings in this era. In Ellen and Charlotte's case, too, there would have been something almost inevitable about it, since, unlike Mary and her sister Martha, they had turned up at Roe Head without a sleeping partner.

Bit by bit, Charlotte's relations with Mary improved, their shared intelligence and common interests quelling any initial antagonism. Mary and Charlotte – who had allegedly taken an interest in the goings on of Parliament since the age of five – were avid followers of the political manoeuvring of the 1831 Reform Bill, which sought to clean up an irregular franchise system and extend voting rights for men, although not for women. They also discovered that they had similar literary leanings. Charlotte's early promise to show Mary one of the magazines she'd created with her siblings at the parsonage gave her schoolfellow the hope that she would be allowed to enter into this secret fantasy world. In time, she and Charlotte would become good friends, forming a tight-knit threesome with Ellen. Overshadowed today by the more famous trio of the Brontë sisters, often thought to be so devoted to each other that they had no need for anyone else, Charlotte's triangular relationship with Ellen and Mary was also of profound importance to her.

Thanks to the diligent private study Miss Wooler demanded of her, Charlotte's efforts would end up carrying her to the top of the school, where she vied for first place with her two friends. For all Charlotte's dismissiveness of her intellect, Ellen was a clever young woman, and, during her time at Roe Head at least, more than able to hold her own with Mary and Charlotte. Ellen even carried off one of the school's most coveted prizes – admittedly for neatness – but her mild, accepting ways meant that, in Charlotte's estimation, she was no match for the politically engaged Mary.

On some deep level, Mary and Charlotte understood that they could challenge each other's thinking. Charlotte's passionate creativity helped the more down-to-earth Mary to see the world afresh. Similarly, the conservative Charlotte came to value the thorny questions of the day raised by Mary, who hailed from a radical family of nonconformists.

The Taylors and Nusseys were distantly related, but when Charlotte visited the home of each friend the experiences could not have been more different. Although, like the Taylors, Ellen's family had suffered financially through the recent economic decline, they had been prosperous landowners in the district for generations. At this stage, they were still managing to cling on to their home, Rydings, not far from Roe Head. When Charlotte visited, she was met with the grandeur of a castellated building surrounded by towering chestnut trees, one of which had been savagely split apart in a storm. These surroundings, magnificent in comparison to the parsonage at Haworth, would make a lasting impact on Charlotte. Like her first school, Ellen's home became a source on which she drew for *Jane Eyre*. Thornfield Hall, the country seat of her Byronic hero Mr Rochester, was inspired in part by Rydings – a place that, on the surface, seemed the embodiment of wealthy respectability.

The Red House in neighbouring Gomersal, where Mary lived, was less overawing, though Charlotte found it just as captivating. The back parlour, with its framed picture of an erupting Mount Vesuvius on the wall, bore the influence of Taylor ancestors who had travelled in Italy. Two stained glass windows, through which the sunlight glittered, cast hues of purple and amber on the comfortable room. It's hardly surprising that Charlotte should have fallen under the spell of this house as well. Other than the strained relations between the emotionally-stifled Mrs Taylor and her two daughters, interactions between other family members were as vibrant as the furnishings.

Within the Taylors' welcoming home, the then relatively conventional clergyman's daughter found herself outnumbered by Mary and her outspoken siblings. Outwardly reserved by nature, Charlotte usually kept quiet in the face of their arguments but, while others might have taken her silence as agreement, Mary was not fooled. She knew that when conditions were right, Charlotte could show the same fire as any of them. Mary would always hold fast to the memory of a time during their schooldays when Charlotte was drawn into a spirited defence of her hero, the Duke of Wellington, who'd defeated Napoleon Bonaparte's French forces at the Battle of Waterloo about fifteen years before. Charlotte, who considered herself a Tory, had long followed the Duke's warring escapades in the popular press, incorporating him as a dashing household character into the games and writings she enjoyed with her brother and sisters. She, then, had many facts on which to draw to win the argument. Mary, on the other hand, though vehemently sure she ought to oppose the Duke, had found herself rendered unusually speechless since she knew so little about him.

Arguments such as these remained good-natured, but the quarrels of the two young women could sometimes turn deeply personal. Though the reasons behind it have long been obscured by the passage of time, at one point during their schooldays the pair fell out so bitterly that for weeks they didn't speak to each other. Ellen, who remained friends with both throughout the standoff, was puzzled by its cause. Charlotte, too, claimed to be none the wiser, though there are clues of a hidden reason that could not be voiced.

Although Charlotte admired the bold, independent Mary, her feelings for Ellen were more tender. While she debated the pressing issues of the era with Mary and shared her literary leanings, in the evenings, when the lamps were low, she retreated to the bed she must have shared with her other close friend. She and Ellen would slide under the covers in their nightdresses, into a space where they could trade in secrets undisturbed.

Mary treasured the friendship of both her classmates, and had done her best to make amends for her early cruelty to Charlotte. But, as 1831 progressed, this strangely brilliant young woman still remained infuriatingly reticent. Despite Mary's interest in the stories and games Charlotte played at home with the Brontë siblings, her friend had now gone back on the promise to let her see one of the household magazines. Worse still than that rejection, Charlotte had become so inseparable from Ellen that Mary surely felt excluded. This impasse may have been the reason for the lengthy silence that grew between them, a mystery to all others at the school.

Charlotte could certainly be possessive of Ellen, and perhaps it was inevitable that the ardour of her feelings for the girl would lead to friction with Mary. Though the two eventually made up, with Charlotte presumably realising that she needed Mary's abrasive energy just as much as Ellen's soothing charms, the complex emotions that bound the girls together became both stronger and knottier as they matured into women.

Charlotte and Ellen would continue their habit of sharing a bed during overnight visits well into adulthood. Referring to

Ellen as her 'bed-fellow', Charlotte would later enthuse about the 'calm sleep' that only nights with her friend could bring.

By the mid-nineteenth century, romantic friendships between young women had become idealised. But even given the commonplace effusiveness of correspondence of the era, a stronger charge perhaps lights up Charlotte's letters to Ellen. By 1836, when she had reached the age of 20, her writing, for a while, took on the passionate tone of a lover driven to distraction by her sweetheart. 'My darling,' she confided in one such letter, 'I have lavished the warmest affections of a very hot, tenacious heart "upon you" – if you grow cold – its over'.

By this stage in her life, with her father's finances dwindling, Charlotte had been forced to return to her old school to take up a teaching position. Once more uprooted from her parsonage home, her feelings of longing had begun to combine with a yearning for a future with Ellen. Recently, she'd even related to her friend a fantasy about them setting up home together: 'I wish I could live with you always,' she'd confided. 'If we had a cottage and a competency of our own I do think we might live and love on till *Death* without being dependent on any third person for happiness.'

If Mary picked up on the mood between her two friends, she must have felt once again like the third wheel. And yet, while Charlotte's desire for Ellen intensified, she simultaneously grew evermore inspired by the candid conversations she enjoyed with Mary. From daring discussions about women's rights to Mary's frustration at what she saw as Charlotte's personal lethargy, theirs was a far more intellectually stimulating and politicised friendship than the one she enjoyed with Ellen, or even in some ways with her siblings. In the same letter in which Charlotte told Ellen of her dream that they might live together, she went on to make a second confession. Claiming to have been in one of her 'sentimental humours' the previous Sunday, she admitted to Ellen that she had penned her a note, which she had later discarded. Without divulging its contents, she said that she had realised that she ought not to have written it to anyone but Mary 'who is nearly as mad as myself'.

Charlotte would come to rely on Mary's 'madness' – presumably referring to her unconventionally outspoken nature – and never more so than during her stint as an impatient, resentful teacher. In a sense, a return to Roe Head had seemed the ideal job for Charlotte. The familiarity of the place made it more appealing than work as a private governess: she liked and respected Miss Wooler, and would even be replacing one of the other Wooler sister schoolmistresses who'd left to be wed – proof that such a position could indeed lead to the chief prize of marriage. This time round, Charlotte wouldn't even have to cope without her family. Emily would be accompanying her, Charlotte's wages contributing towards her younger sister's tuition.

But the arrangement did not work out as planned. Sensitive Emily, always chronically reserved, suffered even more with her nerves than Charlotte had done during her early days at Roe Head. Physically, she began to ail. Still haunted by the school deaths of her two elder sisters, Charlotte begged her father to take Emily back to the parsonage at Haworth. The more stoic Anne replaced her, and these two sisters would stick it out together. But Charlotte's professional role would soon cause her deep anguish.

Able though she was at her studies, she proved far from a natural educator. Unlike Miss Wooler, Charlotte often felt enraged by what she saw as the stupidity of her charges – largely middle-class daughters of professionals and merchants, girls who would never have the need to earn a living. On the surface, Charlotte played the role of dutiful schoolmistress, but, starved almost to breaking point by her job's restrictions on her writing and thinking time, she gave voice to her frustrations both in conversations with her two friends and in private notes. She asked herself: 'am I to spend all the best part of my life in this wretched bondage, forcibly suppressing my rage at the idleness, the apathy and the hyperbolical & most asinine stupidity of those fatheaded oafs, and on compulsion assuming an air of kindness, patience and assiduity?'

Patient Ellen comforted her by post, sending her words of encouragement, on which Charlotte would often dwell in those rare moments snatched for herself after nightfall.

At one such private hour, she sat alone in the school's dining room as a storm vented its wrath outside. Unable to resist, she fell into a trance-like state, her mind swooping her back to the war-ravaged kingdom of Angria – a more recent addition to the Glass Town saga created with her siblings in childhood. These stories still had a powerful hold on her, and now her mind took her over the crushed groves of a trampled garden, a vast marble terrace shining wet with the rain, and into a room richly decorated with standing lamps and floor-to-ceiling mirrors.

She looked for someone reclining on the chaise longue – a young woman she had seen here before in her imaginings. This figure, conjured from the depths of Charlotte's consciousness, had a book in her hand and an arrogant, self-possessed look. Recording the scene on paper the following night in tiny writing reminiscent of that of her childhood manuscripts, Charlotte luxuriated over the woman's 'exquisite' appearance: her 'heart softly heaving under her dark satin bodice'; 'her small & rosy mouth'; her proud brow 'wreathed with ringlets, & her neck, which though so slender had the superb curve of a queen's about the snowy throat'.

So enthralled was Charlotte that she failed to hear the footsteps outside on the corridor. She reacted with a start when the door to the dining room opened and she found herself face to face with the more humdrum sight of Miss Wooler – apparently in the middle of some household task – carrying a plate of butter.

'A very stormy night my dear!' Miss Wooler said.

And 'it is ma'am,' a resigned Charlotte replied, the evening's fantasy curtailed.

Charlotte's private writings and her similarly charged letters to Ellen could provide only temporary reprieve. But, during the same period, the assertive Mary was planting ideas in Charlotte's mind about permanent alternatives to what they both saw as the drudgery of the schoolmistress's lot.

Since she was still living close by, Mary visited Charlotte frequently, and the pair's shared intellectual interests meant she was far better placed than Ellen to understand the full extent of Charlotte's suffering. Knowing how stifling conditions at Roe Head must be, Mary had been known to arrange for her family to send their carriage to collect Charlotte and bring her to the Red House in Gomersal. But, on one occasion, Mary instead made it her business to come and see her friend at the school.

It must have been strange for Mary to return to Roe Head and cast a grown-up gaze across its familiar sloping lawns, down towards the surrounding fields in which she once played, and the shadowy, wooded lanes beyond.

Perhaps it was to one of these secluded places that Mary led Charlotte for a private conversation about why her friend had taken this job. Or it could be that they were lucky enough to find a corner within the house – in the sleeping quarters upstairs perchance, or one of the rooms leading off from the entrance hallway with its sweeping oak-panelled staircase.

Their conversation would embed itself in Mary's mind. She would always remember Charlotte telling her that, by working hard, she had hoped to put aside some money for herself. But when pressed, Charlotte admitted that after clothing herself and Anne, there was nothing left.

'How can you give so much of yourself for so little money?' Mary demanded.

'It is not brilliant,' Charlotte conceded. 'But what can I do?'

Burning with indignation, Mary found this another of those rare occasions when she was struck dumb by Charlotte's words.

Though the letters the pair exchanged at this time have not survived, hints gleaned from Charlotte's milder correspondence to others suggest that, over the following weeks and months, Mary would become privy to the full extent of her friend's misery – confessions Charlotte could not bring herself to make even to Ellen or her beloved siblings.

Mary, who could never tolerate moping, had long argued that Charlotte ought to make more of her literary abilities, and that she should explore other possible paths in life than those of a schoolmistress or wife. Her hectoring, though less comforting than the balm of Ellen's commiserations, ultimately encouraged Charlotte to reconsider her own potential.

Since Mary's influence was crucial in firing Charlotte's ambitions, it seems strange that so little is known of her today – especially when Mary's provocations, though not always immediately welcome, were instrumental in propelling her friend to take those tentative first steps towards a career as an author. But the well-worn image of Charlotte as one of three isolated sisters has thrown a cloak over the other important female relationships that she sought outside the home.

When Charlotte was back at Haworth for the holidays of Christmas 1836, those arguments from an exasperated Mary seem to have drowned out even her feelings of pity for herself. Taking her friend's advice to heart, along with the encouragement of her literary brother, Branwell, Charlotte gathered up the courage to send samples of her verse to none other than Robert Southey, the Poet Laureate.

Close to three months would pass before she received a reply from the great man. It would transpire that he'd been away travelling around the south of England when Charlotte sent her letter.

Surely in a state of anticipation, she broke the red sealing wax and bowed her head over the first page to make out the Lake

Poet's lines penned in a precise, black-ink script. Her message caught up with him in Hampshire, Southey told her, but, being so busy at the time, he had been unable to reply. Now that he had returned to his home, far north in Keswick, he informed her that he had allowed her letter to slip to the bottom of a hefty pile of post accumulated in his absence, 'not from disrespect, or indifference to its contents, but in truth, because it is not an easy task to answer it, nor a pleasant one to cast a damp over the high spirits, & the generous desires of youth'.

Fearfully, Charlotte read on. It must have been a further blow when, halfway through, she reached Southey's judgement. She did have talent, he acknowledged, but she must abandon any plans in this direction. 'Literature cannot be the business of a woman's life', he admonished, '& it ought not to be.'

Charlotte must have wondered how best to respond to his sterner words. But it did not take her long to work out a strategy. 'I must thank you for the kind & wise advice you have condescended to give me', she wrote – in a tone of which Southey, on receipt of her letter, would heartily approve. While he would feel assured of her ample contrition, there was also an inner strength to Charlotte that could not be subdued. Having assured the poet that she was careful to concentrate on her proper duties all day, she mischievously added that, in the evenings only, 'I confess, I do think'. And she signed off with the arch promise that, should the wish ever arise again to see her name in print, she would 'look at Southey's letter, and suppress it'.

Mary might have worried about her friend's passivity, but these words have a different story to tell. They whisper that there was already a hunger for change in the young woman and a creativity that, despite Mary's fears, raged within that meek exterior. The same inner tenacity would hold out several years more until Mary hatched a bold plan of escape for the two – but one that would force Charlotte to choose between responsibilities owing to her family and the sweet-natured Ellen, and branching out into the world with Mary, for real and literary adventures anew.

CHAPTER 5

TWO ADVENTUROUS SPIRITS

The year of 1841 would see its share of frustrations and sadness for all three old Roe Head schoolmates, making plans for escape both more difficult and more urgent. Ellen Nussey, who back in the mid-1830s had enjoyed a modicum of independence, including a spell living with her brother in London, was back entrenched in her Yorkshire parish – this time at the family's new and more modest home, Brookroyd, a short walk from Rydings, their former, grander residence. The Nusseys, who had become reliant on Ellen's caregiving, regularly prevented her from travelling to Haworth.

For Mary Taylor, the death of her bankrupt father at the end of 1840 still cast a long shadow, exacerbating existing tensions between her three brothers and mother over Mr Taylor's remaining property and business interests. All the children would eventually disperse from Gomersal, with the youngest two going abroad that year – Waring setting sail for the far-off British colony of New Zealand and their fun-loving sister, Martha, heading for a finishing school in Brussels, where an uncle and cousin lived close by.

As for Charlotte, now that she'd left two consecutive teaching posts, each with Miss Wooler, she had found work as a private governess. The 25-year-old had entertained hopes of gaining some greater freedoms by establishing a school of her own with her two sisters. But a package she would receive from Belgium – where Mary and one of her brothers had accompanied Martha for a month's tour – would divert the course of these ambitions.

It must have been with delight that Charlotte pulled away the string, to reveal the elegant black silk scarf and kid gloves sent by Mary. These fine Belgian garments were exotic indeed, a far cry from her usual plain wardrobe. But knowing of the late Mr Taylor's debts, still yet to be fully repaid, the thought of her friends squandering their precious pocket money dampened Charlotte's enjoyment. Nonetheless, ensconced within the village home of her current employers, she allowed Mary's accompanying letter to transport her. Gone now was the dreariness of her governess's existence with the family of a Bradford merchant: Charlotte's painful timidity in the company of the lady of the house, the hours of sewing that supplemented her teaching duties, the unruliness of the children. These irritations all faded from Charlotte's mind as the beauty of famous works of art and towering cathedral spires emerged in their place – sights borne forth from Mary's words. Before long, Charlotte felt overcome with emotion, a lump forming in her throat as her whole being ached with a 'wish for wings'.

For a minute or two, the desire 'to see – to know – to learn' expanded, unchecked. But then reality intruded once more and everything evaporated. Charlotte determined to refocus her attention on the more manageable ambition of opening a school with Anne and Emily, never to think again of thoughts as foolish as these.

At least, this was what she would tell Ellen initially. But she would go on to confess in a later letter that Mary had 'cast oil on the flames'. And so, only seven weeks later, as summer shaded into autumn, Charlotte took up her pen again to write something of a very different nature, this time to her aunt.

Back in 1821 when Charlotte was only five years old, Elizabeth Branwell had arrived at Haworth to help care for her dying sister. After Mrs Brontë's passing, Aunt Branwell had felt called to remain at the parsonage, to keep house for her clergyman brother-in-law and provide a steady influence in the lives of his young son and daughters. Though never given to displays of warm affection, she liked to indulge in a bit of merrymaking when the mood took her. On Ellen's first visit to the parsonage, she'd shocked the sheltered young woman by jokingly offering her a pinch of snuff from the little gold box she always kept close by. A proud unmarried woman, she was more than ready to argue her case with Patrick Brontë when they came to occasional disagreements, and she insisted on paying him for her keep. Through careful management of her £40 annuity – particularly an astute investment in the York and North Midland Railway Company in the 1830s – Aunt Branwell had accumulated well over £1,000 in savings by the time Charlotte wrote to ask if she would be willing to grant her a loan.

Charlotte told her aunt that friends – presumably Mary and Martha – advised that, to ensure the success of her future career as a schoolmistress, she ought first to spend six months in Europe, improving her command of languages. Seated at her writing desk, Charlotte methodically laid out her case, arguing that: 'In half a year, I could acquire a thorough familiarity with French. I could improve greatly in Italian, and even get a dash of German.' These advantages, she pointed out, could be turned 'to vast account' when she and her sisters set up their school. With this end goal thus firmly outlined, Charlotte suggested that Emily, who'd been back at home since

1839 and remained the most reserved and yet most untameable of the sisters, should accompany her to the continent. The more adaptable Anne, who, like Charlotte, was living away as a governess, could take Emily's place at some point in the future, she said.

Charlotte was careful to let Aunt Branwell know that she had 'no other friend in the world to whom I could apply on this subject except yourself'. Appealing to the independent nature of this aunt in her mid-sixties, she continued in a voice that could almost have come from the bold Mary: 'Papa will perhaps think it a wild and ambitious scheme; but who ever rose in the world without ambition? When he left Ireland to go to Cambridge University, he was as ambitious as I am now. I want us *all* to go on.'

Charlotte's approach must have been convincing for, a fortnight later, she wrote to Ellen again, this time with the announcement that there could be a chance of her going away after all. Charlotte requested that her confidante keep the information to herself, explaining that Mary had advised her to take this precaution – something that would have rubbed salt in the wounds of the bewildered Ellen, shut away at home in Birstall. How far arrangements had progressed since Charlotte last wrote to declare that she had quelled all such fanciful thoughts!

Charlotte must have known that Aunt Branwell would only part with £150 of her savings if she believed it would be a sound investment. And so, desperate to satisfy her 'wish for wings', Charlotte felt bound to present her plans as a way to further her job prospects. Somewhere inside, though, she must have feared that adopting this stance would commit her to the schoolmistress's path that had already caused her such misery. Letters written from the home of her employers, while less rage-filled than the private jottings she'd penned as a teacher at Roe Head, continued to paint a picture of a deeply unsatisfied young woman who hungered for creative liberty. Still, any worries about where this future would take her were pushed into the background by the excitement of making travel arrangements.

Despite Charlotte's heartfelt entreaties, Ellen, no doubt still smarting from the shock that her friend was really leaving, declined to visit her to say goodbye. Over the past months, she had observed the plans only through Charlotte's letters, thus failing to realise how seriously the 25-year-old was contemplating a move abroad until it was too late to stop her. The pair had quarrelled over the matter. While Ellen insisted that it was her family who prevented her from bidding farewell in person, a comment by Charlotte that she could not 'quite enter' into the mindset of the Nusseys suggests that she thought that Ellen was using this as a convenient excuse.

The task of finding a Belgian school that was both suitable and inexpensive offered Charlotte a distraction from her troubles with Ellen. Though still debt-ridden, the Taylor family fortunes remained less immediately precarious than those of the Brontës, and the Château de Koekelberg – where Mary was about to enrol as a pupil along with Martha – was deemed too dear for Charlotte and Emily. Back in Yorkshire after her summer tour, Mary invested a good deal of her own time and money in sending her friend information. As ever, her supportive words did much to rally Charlotte's spirits. After the intercession of various others, including the wife of the British chaplain in Brussels who helped to put Patrick's mind at rest, they eventually settled on the Pensionnat de Demoiselles Heger-Parent, situated close to the heart of Brussels and run by the respectable Monsieur and Madame Heger.

What must the townspeople of Haworth have thought when three of the most eccentric of their community set off that day in February 1842? The melancholic reverend with his soldierly posture, and his two daughters – willowy Emily, whose shifting blue-grey eyes refused to meet the gaze of onlookers, and the smaller, bespectacled Charlotte – would have made a sight indeed, laden down with their locked trunks.

Their first major stop would be Leeds railway station, where they'd arranged to meet with Mary and her clever older brother Joe, an experienced traveller, much admired by Charlotte. Following the eleven-hour journey to London, the next three days before their departure by steamship would be a whirl of activity. But Charlotte's and Mary's recollections of this time could not have been more different.

For Charlotte, who'd long dreamed of visiting London, the prospect of even a short stay here filled her with awe. This was, for her, the start of the adventure and a chance to steep herself in the capital's great works of art. The group's lodgings at the Chapter Coffee House on Paternoster Row lay within the shade of St Paul's. Like Lucy Snowe, the heroine of her future novel, *Villette*, when Charlotte woke in the morning and looked out on the blue cathedral dome, she felt the once-constrained wings of her spirit beginning to shake themselves loose.

St Paul's was the one landmark that would leave a lasting impression on Mary, too. Despite her similar enthusiasm for sightseeing, expressed only months earlier, she now cast a jaded eye over Charlotte's excitement. The urbane Joe gamely volunteered himself as the group's guide, but Mary merely tagged along with the Brontë sisters and their father. While Charlotte, and even the often taciturn Emily, had much to say about what they saw, the more worldly Mary could only look forward to the months ahead when, along with Martha, the young women would all be unchaperoned in Brussels.

Following the sea crossing and arduous journey by stagecoach, the party arrived in the Belgian city after dark. As Mary would remember it at least, all three young women were much preoccupied and gloomy by the time they set off the next morning for their different schools: Mary heading with Joe for the Château de Koekelberg to the north-west of the city, and Charlotte, Emily and their father making their way to the Pensionnat Heger.

The arrival of the Brontë sisters was the first link in a chain of events that would judder on for decades to come, ultimately drowning out other aspects of Charlotte's time in Brussels, including Mary's important role in bringing it about. But on that dull February morning, Charlotte and Emily must have seemed a most unassuming pair, hardly the types that could bring notoriety to the pensionnat. All that distinguished them from the other schoolgirls was the relative ripeness of their years – at 25 and 23 – and their unfashionable garb. The large collars and huge sleeves of Charlotte's frock did nothing for her diminutive frame, while the lack of fullness to Emily's skirts only served to accentuate her straight-up-and-down figure. The sisters and their father had been accompanied for this last part of the journey by the British chaplain of Brussels, who had family connections in Yorkshire. It's likely he did most of the talking, introducing his charges first to the female porter at the door, and then to Monsieur and Madame Heger. This would have given Charlotte and the still shyer Emily the chance to quietly appraise the couple, their three children and the strange surroundings that would become their new home.

The two-floor building on the Rue d'Isabelle included rooms for the school's three classes and a dining hall with a pair of long tables, an oil lamp hanging over each. On the level above, a communal dormitory was lined with small beds shrouded in individual white curtains. The school's walled garden was hidden from the street. Amid this peaceful oasis filled with historic fruit trees, a wilderness took up one side – a dark, brooding mass of foliage, which carried an air of the illicit. A decade later, this spot that had lingered in Charlotte's mind ever since would appear in *Villette*, in an only lightly fictionalised form.

Claire Zoë Heger, the director, had set up the school prior to her marriage. She was an attractive, hugely capable woman in her late thirties, but it was her husband, the younger Constantin Heger, who made the stronger impression on Charlotte. Short of stature and with a dark complexion, this teacher of rhetoric struck her as ugly and with something of a wild animal about him. At least, this was how she would attempt to rationalise her early reactions to a man who awakened the kind of strong emotions that she'd previously poured into her fevered writings set in the fantasy kingdom of Angria.

While, across town, Mary was finding her bearings at the Château de Koekelberg, Charlotte and Emily struggled to adjust to life at the Pensionnat Heger. They shied away from socialising with their younger schoolmates, who soon came to regard them as excessively earnest. With the permission of Madame and Monsieur Heger, the sisters completely curtained off their corner of the twenty-person dormitory so that they could attain a greater degree of privacy for themselves.

In April 1842, once the Easter holidays arrived, it must have been a relief to finally have time to pay a visit to the Taylors' school in leafy Koekelberg, on the city's outskirts. Ahead of this much-anticipated reunion, Mary had written a newsy letter to Ellen, which was waiting to be posted. In her neat, flowing script, she talked of the activity of her days and how, in the evenings, she went to bed 'sometimes at nine o'clock heartily tired & without a word to throw at any one'. In her usual outspoken manner, Mary laughed at the lack of language skills of her fellow pupils, mimicking a French girl speaking English and declaring that 'the Germans make a mess of both languages the german teacher worst of all'. These sweeping statements betray the casual national stereotyping that would also be a feature of several of Charlotte's Belgian letters. But Mary's vivid depictions of the finishing school atmosphere – so alien to the independent life path she was determined to forge for herself – also give a taste of the burgeoning creativity that would come to bear years later in *Miss Miles*, her feminist novel that celebrates the importance of female friendship.

Mary's letter painted quite a picture of the Château's community. Monsieur Huard, the drawing master, was 'a man of some talent, a good judgement, & an intelligible manner of teaching', who she said would have been her favourite 'if he did not smell so of bad tobacco'. Having mocked her own lack of grace in dancing class, and praised Martha's improvement, she continued, 'All our awkwardnesses however are thrown into the shade by those of a belgian girl who does not know right foot from left & obstinately dances with her mouth open.'

Mary had folded the large sheet of paper in half. Having written on either side of that first page, she showed Charlotte the space left for her and Martha. When Charlotte sat down to write, her words, however, did not flow. No doubt still hurt by the lack of a proper goodbye between them, Charlotte's language, in this communal letter, is unusually stilted. Gone is the reconciliatory tone of early communications in which she tried to make Ellen understand her reasons for leaving. In just half a page, in comparison to Mary's two, she wrote that she and Emily were comfortable, that Mary and Martha were unchanged and, most tellingly, that Ellen had not been forgotten 'as you feared you would be'.

Several days later, while Mary sat staring fiercely at a German dictionary, the far less diligent Martha would finish her portion of the letter. Her note, also brief, though less so than Charlotte's, remarked that 'There is a very sweet, ladylike, elegant girl here, who has undertaken to civilise our *dragon*', meaning Mary. Martha joked that her sister was 'actually improving a little under her hands'.

In reality, as Ellen probably guessed, nothing could have been further from the truth. Over the next months, while Charlotte knuckled down to the regime of lessons in French and the rigours of the Pensionnat Heger's curriculum, Mary, true to her restless nature, tired of what she regarded as the hypocrisy of the refined Château. When Martha returned home for an extended visit to Yorkshire in late spring 1842, Mary declined to accompany her. By September, she was preparing to move on to Germany, to continue studying German and music, and to earn her keep teaching English.

Despite having done so much to bring Charlotte out to Brussels, Mary, ever eager for new experiences, seems to have given little thought to how her friend would fare without her. Under different circumstances, Charlotte might have felt let down, but by then she was positively thriving at the Pensionnat Heger. Although she and Emily had failed to build a rapport with the other students, their intelligence had drawn the attention of the temperamental Monsieur Heger, who singled them out for private lessons – an act that increased the animosity with which the two were viewed, but filled Charlotte with pride and pleasure. She and Emily made such good progress that, with their half year at the school almost up, Madame Heger said she would let them stay on as pupils on the condition that Charlotte take over the English lessons, allowing the director to save money by dismissing the English master. The frequently homesick Emily would be employed to teach music, and, although neither young woman would receive a salary, their own lessons in French and German, and board at the pensionnat, would be free.

On balance, Charlotte considered it a good offer. Both sisters had supposedly begun this European escapade in order to increase their future standing as heads of their own school, but neither had been missing their past existences as classroom teachers and governesses. Charlotte, in particular, thanks to her love of studying, and her growing admiration for Monsieur Heger, felt a strong pull to remain in Brussels. Missing home at times, she occasionally wavered – writing to the unenthusiastic Ellen back in Britain for her views. Overall, though, like her friend across town at the Château de Koekelberg, this was a time of great hope for Charlotte.

But then Mary's sister, Martha, suddenly fell ill. When she'd come back to Belgium from Yorkshire, the 23-year-old had appeared as healthy as ever. By late September, however, she was showing signs of what was subsequently identified as cholera, that ghastly waterborne disease. Its grip tightened so quickly that Mary, preoccupied by this nightmare, did not at first send word to the Brontë sisters. But, as soon as Charlotte heard the news, she set off for the Taylors' school. Armed with only scant information about Martha's condition, she arrived at the Château expecting to see both her friends but found only Mary, waiting with the terrible news that Martha had died the previous evening.

The revelation came as a great shock to Charlotte, who wondered how a young woman as vibrant and full of life as Martha could suddenly be gone. Despite her own early experience of losing Maria and Elizabeth, the thought that death could be on the horizon for Mary's sister had not occurred to Charlotte. To someone raised in nineteenth-century England, cholera was no unfamiliar spectre. Charlotte knew of the agonies borne by its sufferers: the extreme sickness, dehydration and muscle cramping, the terrible awareness that there remained no cure. And yet, it was still utterly bewildering to be out here, all these hundreds of miles away from Yorkshire, and now without the vivacious Martha.

In the sombre atmosphere of the Château, Charlotte gleaned something of the extraordinary level of care Mary had given to her sister. Practical and determined, in the weeks to come, she'd show no hint of letting go of her emotions, striking Charlotte as the very epitome of self-control.

Charlotte, of course, would have been aware that to simply get on with things, on the surface at least, was very much her friend's way. Shortly afterwards, Mary's relatives, the Dixons, who lived close by, took her into their home and would have gladly allowed her to remain there for a while. But she still had her sights set on going to Germany and, tempting though the Dixons' offer must have been, she continued to make the necessary arrangements.

With a visit to Martha's grave at the city's Protestant cemetery still fresh in her mind, a grieving Charlotte once again received distressing news, this time from the home she'd left behind. Aunt Branwell had fallen dangerously ill. Emily and Charlotte decided to depart for Britain at once, but a second letter arrived the next morning bringing the further blow that the woman who'd financed this life-changing trip had passed away. Like Martha, who'd seemed a picture of health, Aunt Branwell had always had a strong constitution. It appeared simply unbelievable to Charlotte that she would never again see either of these two women who'd played such important roles in bringing about her foreign adventure.

While Mary never seriously entertained the possibility of returning to Gomersal after her sister's death, both Charlotte and Emily felt compelled to go back to Haworth as planned to pay their respects to their aunt. They arrived, too late for the funeral, to find their father much subdued and their brother Branwell, who'd been at his aunt's side in her last days, in a severe state of grief. As Anne had also returned temporarily from her governess's post to take over the running of the household, the four siblings were at least able to draw strength from each other, even under these saddest of circumstances.

Still in Brussels for now, Mary must have worried about Charlotte, wondering perhaps if, having settled back in with her family, she would throw away her current freedoms for a return to the limitations of her former existence. Mary perhaps envisioned her friend within the grey stone walls of the parsonage, a place she had visited in happier times with Martha. Or, like Elizabeth Gaskell in her biography some years later, she may have pictured the Brontë sisters walking the rough tracks of the snow-crusted moors, and asked if the life Charlotte had left behind in Brussels felt now no more than an incredible dream.

Charlotte's tutor, Monsieur Heger, who'd been so entranced by the abilities of his British students, apparently had similar fears. He'd given them a letter, written in French, to pass on to their father expressing sympathies for the family's loss and praising Emily's and Charlotte's talents. The good character traits the young women had learnt at the parsonage, he wrote, were largely responsible for their progress at the pensionnat. Yet Monsieur Heger also stressed the necessity of the sisters returning to Brussels to complete their education. Just one more year was needed, he said, for Charlotte to gain the confidence and poise to succeed in teaching French. He couldn't bring himself to be quite this effusive in his praise for Emily, but she, too, he claimed, was losing some of her natural shyness.

It probably came as no surprise to her father that Emily showed little eagerness to return to Belgium. Unlike her sister, she'd never embraced Monsieur Heger's exacting teaching methods. While Charlotte seemed happy to exercise her literary artistry by throwing herself into the writing of French essays, Emily had yearned for the familiar landscapes of home and for more time to work on the Gondal saga that she and Anne had developed from the Brontës' original Glass Town writings, and which she had continued into adulthood. Charlotte, on the other hand, decided to do as her tutor suggested and go back to Brussels, guided by that 'wish for wings' encouraged by Mary, and also, perhaps, by the enthusiasm of Monsieur Heger and her deepening attraction to him. But, if she set off from Haworth with high hopes for the next year, the arduous journey to Belgium now reads like a bad omen for what was soon to come.

This time, there would not be the security of travelling as part of a group. Charlotte, a still outwardly timid 26-year-old, gathered her nerves to take the train to London alone. Due to severe delays, she did not arrive until ten at night and, fearing the possible censure of turning up at the Chapter Coffee House at that improper hour, the inexperienced traveller decided it would be safer to take a horse-drawn cab to London Bridge Wharf. Here, the steamship for Ostend waited, ready to set sail in the morning.

It must have been a shock for those crew members on deck when a female voice called out from a small boat that had appeared in the dark by their vessel. Having persuaded a waterman to row her out from the dock, the tiny Charlotte shivered in the January air: cold, crisp and damp all around. Wary though she was of making demands, it was a thrill to be out at this time on the river with the lamps and hushed noise of London distant in the background.

From the deck of the ship, a sneering male voice called out, 'No passengers might sleep on board.'

But with the boldness that she had learnt from Mary and the determination of mind that was very much her own, Charlotte rose precariously to her feet as choppy waves lapped the sides of the waterman's boat. Standing as tall as her short height allowed, she called back that she wished to speak to someone in authority. Much consternation ensued, but when, eventually, such a person was brought on deck, Charlotte's quiet resolution so impressed the man that he allowed her to come aboard and take up residence in a berth.

On her arrival back at the pensionnat, Madame Heger greeted the sole returning sister with kindness, but it wasn't long before Charlotte's gratitude towards the director began to ebb. In a letter to Ellen, five months later, she would tell of her extreme isolation, especially during the holidays when other teachers and pupils spent time away from the school. Had Mary still been in Brussels, Charlotte could have made plans to see her. Instead, it sometimes happened, she said, that she was left for hours alone – 'with 4 great desolate classrooms at my disposition – I try to read, I try to write but in vain I then wander about from room to room – but the silence and loneliness of all the house weighs down one's spirits like lead.' In her days as a teacher at Roe Head, she'd craved solitude, but now the quiet she'd once so desired brought on a level of depression that blocked her creativity.

There were, though, important differences between now and then. At Roe Head, Charlotte had been accompanied much of the time by either Anne or Emily, and her two closest friends lived within an easy distance. Here in Brussels, Ellen was 500 miles away, and Mary across the German border. Despite Charlotte's many frustrations with life under Miss Wooler's rules, her former headmistress had been a steadying presence. The same could not be said of Madame Heger or her volatile husband, whom Charlotte nicknamed the Black Swan and whose influence can be felt in the dark-complexioned appearance and explosive moods of the character Monsieur Paul Emanuel in *Villette*. Monsieur Heger's gifts of books and the rigorous demands of his teaching would leave a lasting impact on his student, helping to refine her writing style. The effect he had on her secret erotic self was more immediate still, for in the months when Charlotte was alone in Brussels her feelings for her tutor deepened. What had once been an excited revulsion, then a strong admiration, would eventually become an all-consuming passion.

Perhaps unsurprisingly, given the past sensually charged relations between them, she said nothing of these emotions to the more conventional Ellen, who had never been in favour of Charlotte's European adventure. Whether she spoke of them to her other, worldlier friend we cannot know because Mary – apparently fearful of their falling into the wrong hands – would later destroy almost all of Charlotte's letters. We can discern, however, that Mary had become concerned enough to ask her cousin, Mary Dixon, to keep up a relationship with Charlotte. Not long afterwards, the two Brussels expatriates would pose as portrait models for each other – leading to that request by Charlotte that her finished picture not be shown to Mary Taylor, who would find no pleasure in it.

While Mary worried about Charlotte during this period, Charlotte also worried about Mary. She had sensed from the letters she'd received from Germany – which have not survived – that, though her valiant friend never complained, neither was she enjoying herself as much as she pretended. Since an extant letter from Mary to Ellen in early 1843 was full of enthusiastic declarations about her new life, this leaves the niggling question of what details Charlotte and Mary shared in their private communications. Charlotte knew, from the haunting early experience of losing her own sisters, that, despite Mary's resolution to put the trauma of Martha's death out of her mind, the wounds of bereavement take a long time to heal. Likewise, Mary may have had at least an inkling of the true reason for Charlotte's distress.

By the summer, Mary Dixon had departed from Brussels for health reasons, to undergo bracing cold-water treatments first in Germany and then back in Yorkshire. In August, more isolated than ever, Charlotte begged Ellen to write to her, calling on her friend's sense of Christian charity to send a 'long, long letter – fill it with the minutest details'. Homesickness kept creeping over her, she said: 'I cannot shake it off'.

Another missive, penned a month later, this time to Emily, painted a desolate image of the life of which Charlotte had once dreamed. She would 'fall into the gulf of low spirits', she told her sister if she stayed on her own at the pensionnat, 'so I go out and traverse the Boulevards and streets of Bruxelles sometimes for hours together.'

Coming back after one such walk, she felt so overcome by feelings of revulsion that she set off again, winding her aimless way through the streets surrounding the Rue d'Isabelle, ending up outside the Catholic church of St Gudule's, at the tolling of the evening bell. For some reason, unfathomable to her – the nineteenth-century daughter of a Protestant preacher with the era's commonplace prejudice against Catholicism – she found herself drawn inside its great doors.

Here she wandered alone along the aisles, past circular columns on either side, the stained glass of the windows casting coloured shadows on the grey stone walls. A few elderly women were bent in prayer, waiting for Vespers to begin. Charlotte stayed to watch and listen. When the priest's final words had been said, she still could not bring herself to go home. To either side of the church were ornately carved confessionals. She noticed a few people crouching down in the available spots on the dark wood steps outside each one. Suddenly, she was seized by a 'freak' desire to do something – anything – to 'vary my life and yield a moment's interest'. Having watched a couple of penitents go through the process, and now feeling ready herself to whisper through the bars to the priest within, she approached one of the confessionals.

In another scene that would make it into the pages of *Villette*, Charlotte knelt down. After a short wait, the small door covering the grating was opened and she understood that this was the sign for her to begin. But Charlotte had no idea what to say. As she would later relate to Emily, she saw herself back alone on the Thames in the waterman's boat, in the dark by the steamship.

At last, she managed to find her tongue, telling the priest, in French, that she was a foreigner, and that she had been brought up a Protestant.

'Are you still a Protestant?' came his unseen reply.

She could not bring herself to lie. 'Yes,' she said.

He told her that she could not then enjoy the privilege of confession.

But, just as she had that chill night on the river, Charlotte mustered the strength to stay her course. And, in the end, the priest relented. It was his hope, he said, that this might be the first step in her return to the true church. So Charlotte leant close to the grate and, in a voice no doubt tightened by nerves, began to confess.

What she told the priest remains unknown, but it is tempting to speculate that, within the secrecy of the confessional, her growing feelings for Monsieur Heger at least informed her words. As Mary seemed to have sensed, even from Germany, her friend's life at the pensionnat had become increasingly untenable, Charlotte having become greatly distrustful of Madame Heger. This resentment was no doubt magnified by her growing attachment to Madame's husband – something an astute woman like the head of the school could have hardly failed to notice.

Charlotte's duties, when she'd first returned to Brussels, had included teaching English to Monsieur Heger and his brother-in-law. These sessions, though, had been discontinued, and the French tutorials Monsieur Heger gave to Charlotte significantly limited. But when, not long after this extraordinary evening at the Catholic church, the desolate young schoolmistress attempted to hand in her notice, she was stopped by the force of the man's determination that she remain. He might have been willing to bend, presumably, to his wife's demands that he curtail the time he spent with his protégée, but the thought that he might lose her altogether seems to have come as a wrench he could not bear to endure.

There were so few joys in Charlotte's life at this time – the sight of the young Queen Victoria's carriage passing through the Rue Royale while on an official visit in September 1843 providing a rare moment of excitement. Mary, ever mindful of her friend's suffering, sent a letter from Hagen in Germany, urging Charlotte to join her in her new life across the border. Mary, too, had found a job teaching English to men – controversially, in her case, to young and unmarried ones. She had begun studying piano with the well-known Friedrich Halle – father of the conductor Charles Hallé, who later added an acute accent to the family name. Mary admired her teacher's expertise, but tried his patience by arguing persistently over what she believed was his over-enthusiasm for Beethoven. She had also begun studying algebra, which she liked because 'it is odd in a woman to learn it, and I like to establish my right to be doing odd things'.

When Mary wrote to Charlotte, she must have hoped that the strength of her words would prove enough to shake her friend. But while they seem to have given Charlotte the final push she needed to insist Monsieur Heger accept her notice, Mary must have been disappointed to learn that Charlotte's next destination was not to be Germany. Instead, she would be returning to her old moorland home.

Before Charlotte left Brussels for good, Monsieur Heger gave her a sealed diploma, certifying her competencies as a teacher. He had even suggested she take one of his small daughters with her as a first pupil for her planned school. Despite the fact that it would have allowed them to maintain contact, Charlotte had turned down this proposal, citing Madame Heger's likely disapproval.

Back at the parsonage once more, Charlotte wrote a mournful letter to Ellen, in which she mused that 'there are times now when it appears to me as if all my ideas and feelings except a few friendships and affections are changed from what they used to be'. It was good to have Emily's company again, but her father's noticeable age and his failing eyesight, which had worsened significantly in her absence, were matters of great concern. What she wished for now, she confided in Ellen, was 'active exertion – a stake in life'. Haworth seemed to her 'such a lonely, quiet spot, buried away from the world', but she couldn't bear the thought of leaving her father again.

With Anne returned to her employment as a governess, any plans for Charlotte and her sisters to set up a school were also left on hold. Mary, who understood better than anyone else how ill-suited Charlotte was to the life of a teacher, could at least be pleased at that. But it would have distressed her to learn that, back at Haworth, Charlotte had once again fallen into the habit of restraining her own desires and bending to the needs of others.

Still, the spring brought with it the welcome relief of a reunion between their schooldays trio. When Mary returned for a month from Germany, Charlotte hastened to Gomersal to meet her, as did Ellen, who arrived there in the evening. Later, Ellen would recall her feelings as she went into the gardens of the Red House, where, thanks to the fading light, she could make out only the silhouettes of two female figures.

Walking among the shadowed shrubs and flowers and talking 'with all their might', they certainly looked like Mary and Charlotte. But from this distance Ellen could not recognise the pair's voices and so could not identify them for certain. She may have been made hesitant by, what even through the dusk, was the evident force of their conversation.

When Charlotte and Mary noticed Ellen's cautious silhouette approaching, they were thrown similarly off guard. Into the blackness they squinted until finally they realised who it was and called out glad greetings of welcome, suddenly full to the brim with warmth.

Ellen would never learn of the words passed between her two friends that night, and, as in the case of Charlotte's church confession, we too must remain out of earshot. But we know that this was an impassioned conversation. And we know that Charlotte, who would soon begin an astonishingly frank and yearning sequence of letters to Monsieur Heger, was deeply dissatisfied with her current situation. We know, too, that both these unusual and ambitious young women still hungered for genuine adventure. Perhaps that evening Charlotte spoke of some of her unfulfilled dreams, and Mary, in her brusque but kindly way, tried once again to persuade Charlotte to join her in Germany.

Whatever the truth, *this* we know for sure: just months later, in the autumn of 1844, Mary sent Charlotte a letter that would shock her to the core. She was writing with the news that she planned to go through with something she'd fantasised about before, but that her friend had never believed would happen. Mary would now be leaving the Northern Hemisphere behind and emigrating to New Zealand. It was, as a stunned Charlotte would relate to Ellen, as if 'a great planet' had fallen from the sky.

CHAPTER 6

ONE GREAT MYTH

On a mild winter's day in June 1848, Mary Taylor set off from her lodgings in the small settlement of Wellington with a single clear purpose. She had in mind an important letter – as yet unwritten – containing a stern message for her friend Charlotte Brontë. Heading away from the town's few streets of timber houses, Mary followed the curve of the eastern shore, walking in typically determined fashion in the direction of Mount Victoria. From its top, she hoped to spy a ship that could carry her words all the way back to Britain.

Mary's route would take her along rougher roads and over swampland before she reached the base of the hill. Six hundred and forty-eight feet up stood the shipping signal station, and it was towards this destination that Mary began her ascent. Four years had passed since that evening in the garden with Ellen Nussey and Charlotte. Like her two friends, at 31 years old, Mary remained unmarried. Unlike them, here in New Zealand, she had carved out the kind of independent living that she could never have hoped to enjoy back in Yorkshire, or even in Belgium or Germany.

Since her arrival in July 1845, Mary had built a five-roomed house on newly established Cuba Street, which she let out for profit while living elsewhere, supplementing her income by giving piano lessons. And, when her brother Waring went away, she took care of the day-to-day running of his import and trading company, honing her innate business skills.

What adventures she'd had since she last saw poor Charlotte! For Mary, today's climb must have felt every one of the 11,500 miles from her old friend cooped up in the parsonage at Haworth. The last time they'd met, not long before Mary's four-month crossing, she'd been dismayed when Charlotte announced that, though richness and variety of life might be possible for other people, she had given up on such things for herself. Mary had argued otherwise, but, what with Charlotte's unerring sense of filial duty, it had been no use. And so it was with a heavy heart for Charlotte's prospects that Mary sailed away for New Zealand.

The two had continued to keep in touch, but owing to the unreliability of seaborne communications, with some letters taking months to arrive and others seemingly disappearing en route, this pitiful image of her friend had embedded itself in Mary's mind.

Charlotte's return to the parsonage, however, had allowed her to focus on her literary plans. In 1846, in a project she spearheaded, she and her sisters had self-funded the printing of a collection of their poems. But despite good reviews in the *Critic* and *Athenaeum*, they had only managed to sell two copies. Even before they learnt of this sorry outcome, Charlotte had begun seeking a publisher for the trio's novels. Anne's *Agnes Grey* and Emily's *Wuthering Heights* eventually found a firm willing to take them on, but Charlotte's novel, *The Professor* – her first attempt at writing of her experiences in the Brussels home of the Hegers – was turned down multiple times, and would remain unpublished until after her death. It must have been galling on so many levels. When she was rebuffed by her former tutor – who, no doubt alarmed by her increasing obsession, had begun to ignore her letters – she'd been afflicted by fevered sleeplessness and an inability to eat. And now her book that memorialised him had also been rejected. It is testament to her determination that she pressed on undeterred, and began a new book, *Jane Eyre*, which she would complete within the space of a year.

Until recently, Mary's three-year absence from Britain had given her little chance for reassessment of Charlotte's lot. Even today, as she looked down on the waves – with all she knew now – Mary could not shake her belief in her friend's sadly wasted existence. Strange perhaps, since Mary had just discovered that Charlotte had recently achieved one of her chief ambitions: in the guise of 'Currer Bell', she had become a published novelist.

After all her considerable disappointments, the immediate success of *Jane Eyre* had taken Charlotte by enormous surprise. Her tale of an impoverished and determined young governess who triumphs over adversity had excited critics and public alike. Charlotte's weeks were now cheered by heartening news from her London publisher. A third print run had been commissioned within months, offering Charlotte the sweet prospect, for the foreseeable future, of no longer needing to contemplate a return to her former life as a governess. While controversy raged over the true identity of the book's author – with even Ellen kept in the dark for months – soon after its publication in October 1847, Charlotte had parcelled up the three volumes of the first edition and sent them on their long voyage to New Zealand.

Now that she had finished reading the novel, Mary stood on the hill, looking down for a suitable vessel. But in this distant outpost of the British Empire there was only a small boat with a single mast, and the HMS *Fly*, an eighteen-gun sloop. A pity, thought Mary, since normally a passing cattle carrier might have been called upon to take her mail. Still, it stood to reason that the strong easterly winds of late had prevented much of the usual sea traffic from coming into the bay.

It would, in fact, be several weeks before a suitable ship arrived – and only after the winds changed again that it could depart once more on its journey. Almost five further months would go by before Mary's words reached Haworth. By then, although Charlotte read the letter through, it would be more time still before she could muster the enthusiasm to reply.

Mary's July missive arrived at Haworth at the most difficult of times for Charlotte. From Mary's distant vantage point in Wellington, when she thought of her friend's unhappiness, she tended to focus on the overbearing demands, as she saw them, of Charlotte's ageing father. But, in reality, the 71-year-old's worsening health was not even close to Charlotte's main concern. Recent events at the parsonage had been considerably more traumatic.

Throughout what ought to have been a joyous period for this newly successful author, Charlotte's brother's problems, exacerbated by his dependence on alcohol and opium, had become a constant worry. Branwell had been living largely at home since the disgrace of his dismissal from his last job as a tutor, probably following an affair between him and the mother of his pupil. By the date when Mary made that climb up Mount Victoria, Charlotte was confiding in the geographically closer Ellen that the brother she'd once so admired was 'much shattered'. He had most likely developed tuberculosis. When he died in September 1848, almost a year after the publication of *Jane Eyre*, his sisters had still not let Branwell in on the secret of their literary success. Emily, under the pseudonym Ellis Bell, had published *Wuthering Heights*. Anne, as Acton Bell, had seen both *Agnes Grey* and *The Tenant of Wildfell Hall* make it into print. But, as a bereft Charlotte related to Ellen, 'we could not tell him of our efforts for fear of causing him too deep a pang of remorse for his own time misspent, and talents misapplied'.

Following Branwell's death, all his grief-stricken sisters fell ill. Charlotte recovered fairly quickly, and Anne, whose health had worried Charlotte since their days at Roe Head, also rallied. But Emily, suffering from what they tried to persuade themselves was merely a cold, continued to decline. By mid-December, when Mary's letter at last reached Charlotte's hands, the family could no longer deny that Emily's condition was serious.

It is no wonder that, in the midst of such emotional turmoil, Charlotte could not summon the strength to respond to Mary straight away. Within the dim-lit interior of a home shrouded in sadness, Mary's lively descriptions of life in New Zealand must have felt so at odds with Charlotte's present circumstances. Here in the quiet parsonage, reminders of Emily were everywhere: the kitchen where, in better health, she used to knead the bread dough while reading from a book propped up beside her; the dining room, where – in a habit learnt from their former headmistress Miss Wooler – the three sisters once walked round and round the table until late in the evenings, discussing their writing; the children's study, now Emily's bedroom, the place where they created their miniature manuscripts. Though she was no stranger to sorrow, Charlotte had never before known agony like this. With Emily now on the verge of death, even the most uplifting parts of Mary's letter could have brought her little delight.

The biggest disappointments came in the opening paragraphs, in which Mary gave her opinion of Charlotte's novel. While she praised *Jane Eyre* for being 'so perfect as a work of art' she criticised it for not having a greater political purpose.

'You are very different from me', Charlotte read, 'in having no doctrine to preach'. It was, according to Mary, 'impossible to squeeze a moral' out of the book. 'Has the world gone so well with you that you have no protest to make against its absurdities?'

Across continents and a time lapse of several months, Mary's voice seeped from the blue-tinged paper. Even from half a world away, it still had the power to pierce the hush of the parsonage – a space previously punctuated only by the muffled voices of the servants and the ticking grandfather clock in an alcove of the staircase.

Given that among the many positive reviews of *Jane Eyre* others had criticised its apparently dangerous challenge to the status quo, Mary's rebuke must have come as a surprise. In the same month that Charlotte received the letter, the *Quarterly Review* attacked the mysterious Currer Bell's book for being decidedly 'anti-Christian'. Comparing it to Samuel Richardson's scandalous tale *Pamela*, published over a century earlier, the female reviewer remarked that she would have thought a hero such as Rochester would have 'no chance, in the purer taste of the present day'. As for Jane, her 'pedantry', her 'stupidity', her 'gross vulgarity' came in for criticism. Throughout the book, which the article doubted could be written by a woman, there was, it said, 'a murmuring against the comforts of the rich and against the privations of the poor, which … is a murmuring against God's appointment … there is that pervading tone of Godly discontent which is at once the most prominent and the most subtle evil which the law and the pulpit, which all civilized society in fact has at the present day to contend with'.

It is hard to imagine the Tory schoolgirl Mary had known in the 1830s being accused of holding such supposedly outrageous opinions. And so the *Quarterly Review*'s condemnation suggests that, in the sixteen years since, elements of Mary's radicalism had rubbed off on Charlotte – shaping her thinking and writing, even now they were separated by such a great distance. But Mary, clearly, didn't see this. Instead, her letter complained that, unlike the novels of Charlotte's sisters, Emily and Anne, *Jane Eyre* would do nothing to challenge readers' lazy assumptions about the established social order. How could Charlotte have written three volumes, Mary wanted to know, 'without declaring war to the knife against a few dozen absurd do[ct]rines each of which is supported by "a large & respectable class of readers"?' Emily, Mary opined, 'seems to have had such a class in her eye when she wrote that strange thing Wuthering Heights'.

The unjustness of Mary's allegations not withstanding, her letter surely instilled more complicated emotions in Charlotte – momentary envy perhaps at this praise of her sister's work mixed with guilt over such feelings at a time when Emily was sinking irrecoverably into the final all-consuming stages of tuberculosis. Within days, on 19 December, she would become the fourth of the Brontë siblings to die, and the second in the space of three months.

Back in July 1848 when Mary sealed up her letter, unaware of these coming ordeals, she'd presumably hoped that by taking Charlotte to task she would encourage her friend to make her next novel more openly political. As to Mary's own literary ambitions, she had written 150 or so pages of a novel, but had to admit that she was struggling to get past this point. She'd also sent a few articles to the editor of the radical *Tait's Edinburgh Magazine* but had never heard back from him. Another piece had gone off to *Chambers Edinburgh Journal*, to be met with the reply that they felt it was unsuitable for them.

All this must have been disheartening, but Charlotte had experienced far more severe knockbacks. And, unlike Mary, so distracted by her brave new life in Wellington, she had ploughed her creative and personal frustrations into her writing.

As 1849 dawned, though, Charlotte was also finding it hard to concentrate. With she and Anne the only remaining siblings, and their bereaved father increasingly leaning on his eldest daughter as a matter of survival – telling her he should sink if she failed him – Charlotte's worries for the well-being of what was left of her family only increased. From a letter passed on by Mary's brothers, she'd learnt about an earthquake in Wellington that had occurred three weeks after the death of Branwell. Having received no word from her friend since that date, Charlotte fretted about Mary too.

By the time Charlotte confided these fears to Ellen, Mary had, in fact, sealed up another letter and sent it off on its long voyage to Haworth. Written in April 1849, it told that she was expecting the arrival of a younger cousin, also called Ellen. Mary had already thought up 'dozens of schemes' of occupation, the most ambitious of which was establishing a shop. Mary said that she had written an article about the earthquake and its aftershocks and submitted it to *Chamber's Edinburgh Journal*. This, like the pieces she'd mentioned in her letter posted in July 1848, would remain unpublished. While Mary said that she intended to write more, she seemed to doubt herself. She asked Charlotte not to remind her of this statement in a year's time. 'I write at my novel a little,' she continued, and talked of another book that she referred to as her baby – a text that she hoped would one day 'revolutionise society and faire époque in history'. Claiming that, in her case, it was '*active* work' that encouraged her writing, she admitted that she was more currently engaged in 'doing a collar in crochet work'.

At the best of times, Charlotte would surely have raised an eyebrow at Mary's convenient excuses. Since Branwell's death, Charlotte had experienced obstacles of such magnitude that she had put her new novel aside. But, in the end, finishing *Shirley* would turn into a form of salvation. In the immediate aftermath of Emily's death, Anne's health became a matter of grave concern once more. Like Emily and Branwell before her, she was probably suffering from tuberculosis. Hoping that a change of air would do her good, Anne persuaded her reluctant sister to accompany her to the seaside town of Scarborough. However, on their arrival in May 1849, Anne deteriorated rapidly. At lodgings within sight of the waves, death soon stole the last of Charlotte's siblings. After returning to Haworth, Charlotte buried herself in her manuscript. As she said to her editor, William Smith Williams, whatever its eventual level of success with the public, 'writing it has been a boon to me – it took me out of dark and desolate reality to an unreal but happier region.'

With the impossibility for fluid communication between her and Mary, Charlotte surely felt glad that she now had people other than her schooldays friend with whom she could talk about writing. In addition to her editor, she'd begun to establish relationships with some of the best-known literary figures of the day, including William Makepeace Thackeray, whom she'd met during a visit to London, and George Henry Lewes, who would one day become the partner of George Eliot. With the latter, she had established something of a rapport on the page, even arguing with this well-known critic about the talents of Jane Austen. Lewes was a great admirer, his essays – written some decades before James Edward Austen-Leigh's memoir of his aunt – marking him out as one of the era's rare readers to appreciate her genius. Charlotte's appraisal, on the other hand, was decidedly less complimentary. 'Why do you like Miss Austen so very much? I am puzzled on that point,' she asked. Charlotte compared *Pride and Prejudice* to a 'daguerreotyped portrait of a common-place face; a carefully-fenced, highly cultivated garden with neat borders and delicate flowers – but no glance of a bright vivid physiognomy.'

While Thackeray and Lewes would always remain acquaintances of hers rather than close friends, in August 1850, another popular author of the day entered the life of Charlotte Brontë – someone who, like Ellen and Mary, would go on to define her legacy.

In New Zealand it was winter, but in Britain, these were the last weeks of summer. Contrary to Mary's gloomy imaginings, Charlotte had been far from shut away in Haworth in recent months. She was not long back from a month's stay in London, during which she sat for her portrait, followed by a sightseeing tour of Scotland. Tired though she was, she had now reluctantly accepted the invitation of new friends, Sir James and Lady Janet Kay-Shuttleworth, to stay at a house they had rented high above the misty banks of Lake Windermere. On 19 August, after a long and trying northbound journey, it was eight o'clock in the evening by the time Charlotte arrived at the small station. Sir James was waiting for her with his carriage, ready to drive them through the wooded lanes that led to Briery Close. Despite her tiredness, Charlotte – who from her days of writing to the Lake Poet, Robert Southey, had romanticised this part of the world – was struck by the brooding beauty of the Cumbrian fells.

She was not the only guest invited. The next evening, Elizabeth Gaskell, the writer of *Mary Barton*, would arrive at the house. She and Charlotte had never met, but, since the publication of *Jane Eyre*, Elizabeth, like so many others, had been following rumours about the real identity of its author.

After *Shirley* came out in October 1849, 'Currer Bell' had sent Elizabeth a copy of the novel through her publisher, leading to an exchange of one letter each between the pair. Though Charlotte's missive had not divulged her name, it had let Elizabeth in on the tantalising truth that she was a woman. Some months afterwards, during one of her stays in London, Charlotte had come face to face with several well-known figures of the literary world. Though some had respected her wish to remain incognita, others – such as her earlier correspondent Thackeray – were apparently incapable of keeping her secret. After meeting Charlotte at her publisher's house, he had gone straight round to his gentlemen's club and announced to the gathered members, 'Boys! I have been dining with "Jane Eyre".' It seems little wonder then that by the following year, literary London was rife with gossip over the identity of Currer Bell. For the wealthy Kay-Shuttleworths, the prospect of being the ones to introduce Charlotte and Elizabeth to each other must have been simply too enticing to resist.

It was dark when Elizabeth entered the house, but the well-appointed drawing room was all adazzle. Charlotte, perhaps feeling that she and her fellow-guest knew each other through their correspondence and novels, abandoned her customary shyness, coming straight up to shake hands. The two exchanged pleasantries and then Elizabeth, who at close to 40 was six years Charlotte's senior, went upstairs to lay down her things and remove her bonnet. Later, over tea, while Charlotte worked away at her embroidery, Elizabeth would take a good look at this slightly built woman, making a mental inventory of her features – details that she'd record in writing and use to beguile, first her friends, and later a far larger reading public. Elizabeth noted the light brown hair and expressive eyes of more or less the same colour, the 'reddish face; large mouth & many teeth gone'. Less cutting in her judgement than Mary's schoolgirl impressions, she decided, nonetheless, that Charlotte was plain. But she was taken by the sweetness of the novelist's voice and how she 'rather hesitates in choosing her expressions, but when chosen they seem without an effort, *admirable* and *just* befitting the occasion'.

From her hostess, Lady Janet, Elizabeth would soon receive an exaggerated version of Charlotte's life in Haworth with the supposedly crazed Reverend Brontë – a man who allegedly burnt hearth-rugs and sawed chairs into pieces in fits of pique. Elizabeth lapped up suggestions that Charlotte's father's unstable mental state had led his wife to an early grave. In the years to come, Elizabeth's dealings with him would moderate her opinions, but her continued belief that he inflicted hardships on his daughters would prime her to accept the image of Charlotte's sad existence that Mary would later lay before her.

In August 1850, the same month that Charlotte and Elizabeth came face to face for the first time, Mary sent Charlotte her thoughts on *Shirley*. As with *Jane Eyre*, she'd had to wait a long time to receive her copy, and it would be a good while more before Charlotte was able to read her response.

The consignment containing Charlotte's latest novel had arrived with Mary one Monday afternoon. She and her cousin Ellen, with whom she now lived and ran an adjoining shop, were getting ready for a small party, but had abandoned these preparations to open the box and read all the letters. Mary hadn't found the time to start reading *Shirley* that day or on Tuesday either, since – clearly untroubled by the clumsiness she'd exhibited in her Brussels classes – she and Ellen had stayed up dancing until three or four o'clock in the morning. But on the Wednesday, Mary had begun the book. Given her criticisms of the last novel, Charlotte must have looked forward to her friend's verdict with considerable apprehension. But, unlike many critics, including the previously kindly George Henry Lewes, who had written an unenthusiastic assessment for the *Edinburgh Review*, Mary would come to the conclusion that *Shirley* was superior to *Jane Eyre*.

Set against a backdrop of industrial agitation in Yorkshire during the time of the Napoleonic Wars, the new novel dealt more explicitly with social issues. And so it seems that Charlotte had taken Mary's criticisms of *Jane Eyre* to heart. According to Mary, *Shirley* had 'so much more life & stir – that it leaves you far more to remember than the other'.

As she had done with *The Professor* and *Jane Eyre*, and would do again with *Villette*, Charlotte had drawn inspiration from many individuals personally known to her. In the case of *Shirley*, this included the Taylor family whom she reimagined as the Yorkes. Back in Gomersal, Mary's mother remained furious at the cold way in which Charlotte had depicted her. Her daughter's letter made no comment on this, but it took issue with the portrayal of Mr Taylor, whom Mary said Charlotte hadn't made sufficiently honest. This seemed to have been an important point for Mary, whose admiration of her late father remained strong. It was he, she said, who'd taught her 'not to marry for money nor to tolerate any one who did'. As for Rose Yorke, the character based on her, Mary joked that Charlotte had made her 'a little lump of perfection'. But it must have been a relief for Charlotte to learn that her friend felt that she had captured the atmosphere of the Taylor home, and that she thought highly of the book.

Mary's own novel continued to come on only in fits and starts. All she had to say on the subject was that she wrote 'a page now & then'. Typically, though, she retained her optimism, saying that, whenever she found a free moment to read over what she'd produced, it looked 'very interesting'.

Charlotte must have picked up on some of the hidden frustrations beneath such cheerful pronouncements because she was to comment to Ellen Nussey, on receipt of this letter early in 1851, that Mary was not in the best emotional state. As the year wore on, Mary's spirits were to sink lower still when the health of her cousin Ellen began to show signs of deterioration. She, like Emily, and probably Branwell and Anne, had become a victim of tuberculosis. By early January 1852, even those back in Yorkshire could guess that Mary's cousin would not be long for this world. Charlotte predicted that Mary would be devastated if Ellen Taylor were to die. But, parted as they were by such a great distance – the long gaps between the sending and receipt of letters meaning that their conversations often ran at cross purposes – by the time Charlotte voiced these worries to Ellen Nussey, they were out of date. Ellen Taylor had already passed away on 27 December.

This, then, was how Mary began the new year, all alone in her timber house. In the early months of 1852, she sat down to write to Charlotte, telling her how life felt so quiet, so lonely, without Ellen. Now, it seemed that it was her cousin who'd kept her so busy – at first with their work in the shop together and then lately with nursing duties. With Ellen dead, Mary occupied herself with cleaning a home once so chaotic that Charlotte had joked to her old headmistress Miss Wooler that, from what she'd heard, the cousins could never win the Roe Head Neatness

Prize. Now, Mary kept everything scrupulously tidy and pictured herself as an unoccupied old woman, reduced to scrubbing her floors before they got dirty and polishing the outsides of all her pans. As with a previous broken-off attempt to write this letter, her heavy sorrow stifled her words. Tonight she wished that she and her old friend could really speak face to face. 'O for one hour's talk!'

On learning, several months later, that Ellen Taylor had died, Charlotte began to feel that it would be best – not just for herself but for Mary too – if her friend came home. During the same period, Charlotte continued to strengthen her relationship with Elizabeth Gaskell, even persuading her publisher to delay the date on which they brought out her novel, *Villette*, ultimately in January 1853, because it would have clashed with the publication of Elizabeth's book, *Ruth*. Despite enjoying this closeness with a writer of comparable commercial stature, Charlotte continued to place a great importance on her bond with Mary – her first literary friend outside of the Brontë family. And in an unlikely turn of events, at a moment when both Ellen Nussey and Elizabeth shied away, Mary would soon send Charlotte some much-needed support, all the way from the other side of the world.

As a woman in Victorian England in her late thirties, Charlotte, like her unmarried friends Ellen and Mary, assumed that she would now never wed. In her twenties, she had received two proposals but turned them both down. To one suitor, a clergyman brother of Ellen's, she'd said that she was 'not the serious, grave, cool-headed individual' he supposed, and that she would not be able to make him happy. Later that year, she'd refused another man of the cloth. Twelve years later, in 1851, she was also the recipient of, if not a proposal exactly, a promise of sorts by James Taylor, an editor at her publishing house. Following a visit from him to the parsonage, Charlotte had asked herself if the two would make a good match: 'Could I ever feel for him enough love to accept of him as a husband?' As with the previous offers she'd received – and taking a similar line to Mary in matters of the heart – Charlotte, who decided she couldn't imagine loving this man romantically, turned him down.

Unknown to her, someone with whom she'd been living in close proximity for years had been growing increasingly attracted to her. The Reverend Arthur Bell Nicholls, her father's assistant curate since 1845, was not usually given to outbursts of emotion, but in December 1852 Charlotte suddenly came to understand the meaning behind 'his constant looks – and strange, feverish restraint'.

One evening at the parsonage, Arthur, a well-built man with dark features and uncommonly long whiskers, finally unburdened his feelings. Charlotte had withdrawn to the dining room after tea, leaving her father and his curate to their conversation. At around nine o'clock, she heard the parlour door open – a sign that Arthur must be about to leave – but, rather than the expected jolt of the front door, he stopped where he was in the hallway and tapped the dining room door.

In a scene that could come straight out of one of her novels, this man whom Charlotte had once written off as drab and dull, appeared a moment later in the dining room, suddenly much more interesting in her eyes, shaking as he was with emotion. In a low voice, he told of the 'sufferings he had borne for months', that 'he could endure no longer'. Revealing the strength of his affections was clearly a trial, and Charlotte felt moved in response.

'Have you spoken to Papa?' she asked.

'No,' he said; he dared not.

Overwhelmed by his wan appearance, and mindful no doubt of her father's nearby presence, Charlotte urged Arthur to leave the house, promising a reply 'on the morrow'.

Once he was safely away, Charlotte crossed the hall to the parlour. If she hoped that her father would share her sympathy for Arthur, she was quickly put straight on that. As she would later confide in Ellen, 'Papa worked himself into a state not to be trifled with – the veins on his temples started up like a whip-chord – and his eyes became suddenly blood-shot.' Though Charlotte had never been attracted to Arthur, she felt incensed by the injustice of it all. Nonetheless, she quickly promised that she would give her refusal.

This outcome pleased her father, who would waste no time in letting Arthur know that he regarded this as an unthinkable act of subordination. He was angered, not just by the man's failure to ask his permission before approaching his daughter, but also his daring to think he could be worthy of Charlotte, given his lack of financial security. Even months later, Patrick remained so furious that he would communicate with his curate only by letter. Arthur, realising that his position had become untenable, began making arrangements to emigrate to Australia as a missionary. But, in the end, being a far less adventurous character than someone like Mary, he scaled back these lofty dreams and decided simply to go away from Haworth.

In May 1853, not long after Arthur left the village, Charlotte, feeling exhausted and guilty for her part in his misery, developed a cold that deepened into influenza. Her father, too, surely weakened by the stress of the past months, suffered a stroke, which for a time reduced his weak eyes to a state of total blindness. Charlotte, who had obeyed his wishes and rejected Arthur, was now left contemplating the prospect of a life without either of them. Thus, she decided to answer the last of the six sad letters she'd received from Arthur since his departure. Before long the two established a regular correspondence, keeping it a secret from almost all others.

Ellen was one of the few let in on developments. Apparently seeing Charlotte's new closeness with Arthur as an act of betrayal, she wrote to Mary in New Zealand, hoping to garner support. Ellen suggested that, as a spinster like the two of them,

Charlotte should concern herself, not with the possibility of happiness, but 'bearing' her current position and 'enduring to the end'. Mary, though, who approved of partnerships not based on economic gain, and saw marriage to Arthur as a chance for her friend to strike out in life away from the parsonage, leapt to Charlotte's defence.

Writing in early 1854, she told Ellen that she talked 'wonderful nonsense'. 'If its C's lot to be married shd n't she bear that too? or does your strange morality mean that she shd refuse to ameliorate her lot when it lies in her power.' It would be August before the letter reached its disgruntled recipient and by then it would have delighted Mary if she'd known that Charlotte's father had at last recanted his objections to the couple's union.

In June 1854, they were married. Ellen, while still unhappy, travelled to Haworth to attend the wedding. Among the small party of guests was Miss Wooler, now in her sixties, who, on learning of the quarrel between the two friends, had advised them to make up. She also took on the last-minute duty of giving Charlotte away at the altar when her father suddenly refused to attend the ceremony. Although the far-off Mary was apt to over-estimate the level of Patrick's control over his daughter, the saga with Arthur, culminating in his new father-in-law's petty stand on the pair's wedding day, suggests that there was some truth in her claims. It was Mary's hope that, as a married woman, Charlotte would finally be able to acquire the happiness that Mary felt she had been lacking for so long.

Elizabeth Gaskell, by then the author of *Cranford*, had successfully combined a flourishing literary career with the duties of a minister's wife, and yet she was far less optimistic. When she had first learnt about the clandestine love affair, she'd found herself swept up in the romance of it all. But since hearing more about Charlotte's fiancé, whom she had never met, she had reversed her initial optimism. In letters to a friend she confided the fear that the '*very* stern & bigoted' Arthur would seek to keep

Charlotte away from those – such as a Unitarian like Elizabeth – who didn't share his 'narrow' religious beliefs.

In marrying Arthur, Charlotte would not, in the end, be breaking with her past life in anything like the way Mary had hoped. Charlotte had eventually persuaded her father to relent by promising that the couple would remain at the parsonage with him. Sadly, her relationship with Elizabeth did indeed go the way of this friend's predictions, though Arthur seems not to have been the cause. Shortly after her marriage, Charlotte wrote asking her fellow author to come to stay, particularly so Elizabeth and her new husband might get to know each other. But Elizabeth, wrapped up in a new friendship with Florence Nightingale – soon to be made famous by her nursing work in the Crimean War – put off the invitation. Letters, which the two authors had once frequently exchanged, began to dwindle. By the beginning of January 1855, Elizabeth found herself regretting that Charlotte seemed to have stopped writing to her entirely.

A fortnight later, and unbeknown to Elizabeth, Charlotte began to develop the kind of feverish symptoms often associated with tuberculosis. In her case, however, the source would turn out to be her first pregnancy – an unexpected cause for celebration at 38 years of age. This fact may have initially assuaged the fears of her husband, but as the weeks passed and Charlotte's sickness did not abate, Arthur began to send letters to Ellen that hinted at his worst fears. In March 1855, Charlotte rallied a little and, as she told Ellen in a note written in a shaky pencil script, she took 'some beef-tea – spoonfuls of wine & water – a mouthful of light pudding at different times'. But later that same month, she slipped into partial unconsciousness. On the 30th, her father, whose recent conduct had fallen so far short of exemplary, wrote a courageous and dignified letter to Ellen, preparing her for the imminent death of her beloved friend – which ended up occuring early the next morning.

He asked Ellen to inform Miss Wooler, and he contacted Elizabeth himself. Someone must have written to Mary at around this time. But, as ever, it would take several months before she received the news. Mary's sorrow on hearing that Charlotte had died can only be imagined. By then, she'd learnt that Charlotte and Arthur had been living at the parsonage for the duration of their marriage and it surely pained her further to realise that her friend had never gained a freer life. This seems to have made Mary particularly amenable to the advances of Elizabeth, who tracked her down by letter with the news that she would be writing Charlotte's biography.

Here, at last, or so it appeared to Mary, was a chance to give the public an accurate picture of the creative and cruelly stifled friend she'd known. Elizabeth, from what Mary could tell from her letter, seemed to be a competent woman, although Mary wondered how on earth she would cope with all the differing stories about Charlotte. Still, here in Wellington, feeling that she must do something to help, Mary put together pages of recollections – a letter that would be delayed on its long journey to Britain, due to the lack of sufficient postage, but would eventually reach a grateful Elizabeth.

The past year or so had been far from Mary's most successful. Not so very long ago, she had thought that, thanks to her various business ventures, it wouldn't be long before she'd make enough money to leave Wellington behind and return to Yorkshire with the means to live with the same independence that she enjoyed overseas. Now, though, stuck in her timber house without her cousin, despite the presence of her brother nearby, Mary felt increasingly alone. So it must have been a comfort to know that, even from this distance away, the words she had written for Elizabeth would have the power to shape the public's view of the oppression exerted on her selfless friend.

It would be another decade more before Mary finally began to publish her own work, but in a sense her first foray into print came in *The Life of Charlotte Brontë*, in which Elizabeth would quote large parts of the letters she'd received from Mary verbatim. Mary, who'd told Ellen Nussey that she could 'never think without gloomy anger of Charlotte's sacrifices to the selfish old man', hoped that Elizabeth's book would stoke the sort of anger felt by her among its many readers. The initial print run created similar levels of excitement to that of Charlotte's first published novel, *Jane Eyre*. But the easy acceptance with which the world looked upon the events of Charlotte's life left Mary indignant. Elizabeth, mindful of the Victorian mood, had expunged any hint of scandal from the *Life*: presenting Monsieur Heger, once the focus of Charlotte's affections, only as a tutor whose scholarly nature she admired; and the wild writings of Charlotte's youth as curiosities, comprehensible to the 'bright little minds' of the Brontë children alone.

Overall, Charlotte came across as long-suffering and impossibly forbearing. But the portrayal of her many hardships did not result in the public fury anticipated by Mary, or any genuine appetite for change. Elizabeth's portrait would simply make the image of the controversial author of *Jane Eyre* more palatable to her friends and critics. George Henry Lewes felt that the biography presented 'a vivid picture of a life noble and sad … a lesson in duty and selfreliance'. Sir James Kay-Shuttleworth, who'd introduced Elizabeth to Charlotte, wrote that he hoped the widowed Arthur, who did not share his enthusiasm for the book, would 'learn to rejoice that his wife will be known a Christian heroine, who could bear her cross with the firmness of a martyr saint'. When Mary heard of these kinds of responses, no wonder she felt dismayed.

In July 1857, still living in Wellington, she penned a letter to Elizabeth, thanking her for sending the copy of the *Life* – the first, Mary believed, to arrive in New Zealand. Of the two reviews she'd read, Mary complained that 'Neither of them seems to think it a strange or wrong state of things that a woman of first-rate talents, industry, and integrity should live all her life in a walking nightmare of "poverty and self-suppression." I doubt whether any of them will.'

She would be further demoralised when, following a slew of complaints to the publishers from, among others, the friends and family of Reverend William Carus Wilson – the headmaster of Charlotte's hated first boarding school – Elizabeth was forced to retract and rewrite several sections, and issue a public apology. Mary wrote to Ellen in January 1858, that she thought Elizabeth seemed to be a 'hasty, impulsive person'. 'Libellous or not,' she maintained, 'the first edition was all true.'

Mary would return to Yorkshire in 1860, when she was in her forties. Having shored up her own finances through her business ventures in New Zealand, she built herself a house, High Royd, near to her childhood home in Gomersal. Here, she lived what neighbours regarded as an eccentric and certainly independent life. Ellen, too, came to regard Mary as decidedly odd, and, although the pair lived close to each other, they grew increasingly distant.

Mary continued to travel into old age and finally committed herself to the act of writing from which she'd been so distracted in her thirties. Her first published work was a series of articles for *Victoria*, a progressive magazine edited and printed by women. Later came her chapters of the travelogue *Swiss Notes by Five Ladies*, following a mountaineering expedition to the Alps when Mary was 57.

Unlike Anne Sharp, who never saw an official account of Jane Austen's life, the first being sanctioned some five decades after the author's death, Mary would witness the appearance of various works of biography over the coming years. Ellen Nussey published her 'Reminiscences of Charlotte Brontë' in *Scribner's* magazine in 1871. Casting herself as the custodian of Charlotte's memory, she would go on to cooperate with several future Brontë biographers. Mary, on the other hand, obliging though she could be on occasion, became increasingly unwilling to talk to researchers as time went by. Sadly, her reticence allowed a more socially acceptable mythology to build up around Charlotte's female relationships, which excluded the kind of politicised friendship that she had enjoyed with Mary.

Miss Miles, the novel – that, owing to Mary's long period of adventuring, took four decades to complete – was published in 1890, three years before Mary's death at the age of 76. Though largely ignored by the reading public, its exploration of the lives of working women was ahead of its time. The book stands as a testament to all that she held most true, its plot celebrating the enduring power of female friendship – with the personal relationship between Mary and Charlotte refracted and reflected many times over in its interlocking stories. Its characters include the outwardly placid Maria Bell, a schoolteacher who grows up in a moorland parsonage, and the Sarah Miles of the title, someone who believes passionately in the power of education as a means to independence. Mary's message in *Miss Miles* is reminiscent of her youthful debates with Charlotte. There exists an alternative path in life for women, she insists, at least for those willing to reject the expectations of society and fight instead for their own happiness.

PART 3

GEORGE ELIOT
AND
HARRIET BEECHER
STOWE

~ a hand stretched forth in the dark passage of life
to see if there is another hand to meet it

Harriet Beecher Stowe to George Eliot
25 May 1869

~

CHAPTER 7

THE STUFF OF LEGEND

A wonderful surprise lay in wait for George Eliot as she drew up outside her north London villa in May 1869. The weary 49-year-old, who'd been writing for over a decade under this masculine nom de plume, had spent an exhausting spring in continental Europe. She'd been travelling with the philosopher and critic George Henry Lewes. Controversially, the couple lived together as husband and wife, though they were not legally wed. Marian – or Mrs Lewes, as she was known off the page – had gone in search of new sights, the rekindling of memories from previous trips abroad, and the much longed-for warmer weather that always did wonders for her health. But unusually cold winds and rain had plagued the couple's travels. Added to this were worries about her sick stepson, currently making his way back from his South African home, and Lewes's mother, now in her eighties, also in poor health.

It was in a relieved frame of mind that Marian returned to her house, the Priory, in the elegant neighbourhood of Regent's Park. As the carriage reached the end of the drive, she glimpsed the tiled roof and large chimney stacks emerging above its high surrounding wall. It had been fifteen years since she and Lewes began 'living in sin' – an act that had led to Marian being shunned by London's polite society, concerned female writers who might otherwise have befriended her, and even her own siblings. But such strains were surely far from her mind as she and Lewes stepped down from the carriage footplate. Inside the property's neatly kept garden, a path surrounded by plentiful rose bushes led into the inner sanctuary of home.

Though situated close to the park's zoological gardens, the newly opened Underground and busy local canal, the Priory's grounds and walled fortifications shielded it from the capital's hustle and bustle. After all the journeying of the past two months, Marian could note the quiet with pleasure. Their temperamental maidservants, sisters Amelia and Grace Lee, were waiting inside with the customary greetings, ready to unburden their master and mistress of the cloaks, hats and gloves that they'd worn for the carriage ride.

There was much to cheer Marian after nine weeks spent in the homes of friends and foreign hotel rooms: familiar leather spines of books on shelves, the grand piano – even given its somewhat plodding sound – and her favourites among the many framed pictures all fitted onto backdrops of custom-made wallpaper created especially for her and Lewes. The handsome returns from Marian's writing had allowed them to buy the Priory for a costly sum, and to engage the services of a fashionable designer to redecorate. But though she was the main breadwinner, Marian, who wished the world to regard her as conventionally married, seemed content for Lewes to remain ostensibly in charge of the household finances – an arrangement that freed up more time for writing and reading.

Needless to say, now that she had returned to Britain, she had many tasks to fulfil: appointments to keep, domestic orders to deal with, her journal – abandoned for the entirety of her

A watercolour by Cassandra Austen of her 12-year-old niece, Fanny, painted during Anne Sharp's two-year tenure as the girl's governess *(Jane Austen's House Museum)*

Godmersham Park in Kent, the home of Jane Austen's brother, where Anne was a member of the household staff *(https://commons.wikimedia.org/wiki/File:Godmersham_(1779).jpg)*

A portrait included in the Friendship Book of court librarian James Stanier Clarke, which some claim he painted of Jane following her visit to the royal library at Carlton House in 1815 *(Reproduced with permission of Simon Wheeler)*

Above: Jane in her mid-thirties, drawn by her sister Cassandra in about 1810 *(World History Archive / Alamy Stock Photo)*

Left: The posthumous and romanticised portrait, based on Cassandra's sketch, commissioned to create the frontispiece to *A Memoir of Jane Austen (Heritage Image Partnership Ltd / Alamy Stock Photo)*

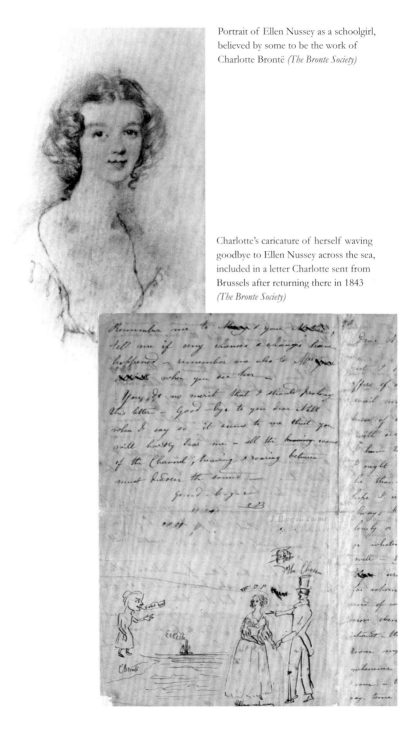

Portrait of Ellen Nussey as a schoolgirl, believed by some to be the work of Charlotte Brontë *(The Bronte Society)*

Charlotte's caricature of herself waving goodbye to Ellen Nussey across the sea, included in a letter Charlotte sent from Brussels after returning there in 1843 *(The Bronte Society)*

Mary Taylor regarded George Richmond's 1850 portrait of Charlotte as overly flattering, and questioned the decision to include a copy in Elizabeth Gaskell's *Life of Charlotte Brontë (World History Archive / Alamy Stock Photo)*

Mary Taylor (far left) on a mountaineering expedition in Switzerland in 1874, when she was aged 57 *(Kirklees Museums and Galleries)*

Earliest known photograph of Mary Ann Evans, as George Eliot was then known, taken in the 1840s *(Coventry Archives)*

The drawing room at the Priory – the scene of the regular Sunday gatherings Marian hosted with her partner George Henry Lewes *(Chronicle / Alamy* Stock Photo)

Harriet Beecher Stowe in the late 1870s, during the period of her friendship with Marian *(Alpha Historica / Alamy* Stock Photo)

Harriet with her husband Calvin Ellis Stowe (both far right) on the porch of their idyllic Florida home *(Hulton Archive / Staff)*

Katherine Mansfield at
Garsington Manor in
Oxfordshire, around 1916, the
year when she became friends
with Virginia Woolf *(National
Portrait Gallery, London)*

Society hostess Ottoline Morrell (far left) in the gardens at Garsington, 1915, with Virginia's sister
Vanessa Bell (far right) and Virginia's friend Lytton Strachey (seated on chair), who introduced her to
Katherine *(National Portrait Gallery, London)*

Virginia in her mid-thirties, at Garsington Manor, where she first met Katherine *(National Portrait Gallery, London)*

trip – to bring up to date. But in the drawing room, there was
the sweetness from the customary vases of flowers to uplift
her, and the happy memories of their regular Sunday gatherings
in the company of fellow intellectuals. Little did Marian know
that among the stacked correspondence accumulated during her
travels was an item that, when she slit open its seal, would do
even more to raise her tired mood.

The letter, which she must have all but given up hope of
ever receiving, had begun its long voyage across the Atlantic
three weeks before. It had been sent by another novelist whom
she'd never met, but whose bestselling fame surpassed even
her own.

Harriet Beecher Stowe, eight years her senior and close
to 60, was an international celebrity and someone Marian
had long admired from afar. Harriet's anti-slavery novel *Uncle
Tom's Cabin* remained the publishing sensation of the age, its
fictional characters having become so well known that their
images appeared on everything from handkerchiefs to ceramics,
while unauthorised Uncle Tom shows flooded the vaudeville
stage. The book was even regarded by some as a cause of the
American Civil War, ended just four years previously. Legend has
it that during a visit Harriet made to the White House, President
Abraham Lincoln greeted the author, who was short of stature,
with the words: 'Is this the little woman who made this great
war?' Her critics were vocal and numerous, but Harriet had fans
aplenty, too. In 1852, on the publication of *Uncle Tom's Cabin* in
its original newspaper serialisation form, readers bombarded the
editor with enthusiastic letters. When Harriet went on to tour
the land of Marian's birth, twelve months later, crowds turned
up in their droves, and she was wined and dined by London's
high society. At one such dinner, hosted by the Lord Mayor,
Harriet was seated opposite Charles Dickens, who had mixed
feelings about her work. Queen Victoria, on the other hand,
was an all-out fan of the novel. On Harriet's return to Britain

in 1856, the Queen was keen to meet her. But advised against publicly associating with such a controversial figure, she had the palace arrange a supposedly chance rendezvous on a restricted platform area of King's Cross railway station.

Now, almost thirteen years on, Harriet had decided to make contact with another author much admired by the monarch – the great George Eliot. In 1869, Marian had yet to write *Middlemarch*, her most famous work, but she was already one of the Western world's most well-known and respected literary figures. Exercising even greater caution than she had with Harriet, the Queen would always make sure that she never came face to face with the unmarried Marian. Nonetheless, greatly taken by her first novel, *Adam Bede*, the Queen had commissioned the artist Edward Henry Corbould to paint watercolour images of scenes from the book.

Marian's sales figures paled in comparison with those of her American counterpart, but in 1862 she sold the exclusive serial rights for her novel *Romola* for a staggering £7,000. This was over three times the price of her impressive home, the Priory, which she and Lewes bought the following year.

Decades later, long after her death, Marian's preeminent biographer, Gordon S. Haight, would claim that Harriet's first letter to Marian was unexpected. But a careful perusal of Harriet's words, written in April 1869, reveals that they had not come entirely unbidden. A year earlier, Marian had hosted a visit from a mutual friend, the American writer Annie Adams Fields. Annie was married to James T. Fields, the editor of the *Atlantic Monthly* magazine, and a partner of the publishing firm Ticknor and Fields. Marian had given Annie a kindly message for Harriet, which she in turn had passed on.

A more conventional woman than Harriet might have kept her distance. The novelist and minister's wife, Elizabeth Gaskell, for instance – who'd been keen to get to know Charlotte Brontë and had also sought out Harriet's company during her first

British tour – would remain perpetually perturbed by Marian's unwed position and what she regarded as Lewes's 'soiled' morals. Though she'd written to Marian a decade earlier to express admiration for her fiction, the future author of *The Life of Charlotte Brontë* had steered clear of pursuing a friendship. And she had not been able to keep herself from lamenting to Marian, 'I wish you *were* Mrs Lewes.' The couple had been in what they regarded as a marriage since 1854, when they were both in their mid-thirties, but had never officially tied the knot. For Lewes was already wed to another woman – the mother of his children – whom he continued to support. As the success of Lewes and Marian's regular Sunday gatherings show, by 1869, the social frost suffered by her, in particular, had somewhat thawed. Nonetheless, many of these prejudices endured.

Harriet, despite her ardent Christianity, didn't much bother herself with the couple's unusual domestic arrangement. And yet, although she had intended initially to write at once, she'd ended up leaving it all these months. Intriguingly, she had found it necessary to embark beforehand on a literary marathon, carefully re-reading six of Marian's seven books in preparation for putting pen to paper. Especially given the heavy demands of her own writing schedule, and her tendency to be rather slapdash in the projects she undertook, the amount of energy Harriet put into this task was extraordinary – and her dedication points to a hidden motive for seeking out a relationship with Marian at this stage.

A date three weeks prior to Marian's arrival back in London marks the moment at which Harriet reached out in friendship across the waves. Four thousand miles away, she was staying at her Florida winter home surrounded by orange groves. In this idyllic spot in the rural community of Mandarin, the blue St John's River flowed by the front of her house – and future tourists would pay to take the steamer for a promised glimpse of the famous author sitting on her open porch.

Harriet dipped her pen into its inkwell. This letter would need just the right greeting. 'Dear Mrs Lewes' would be one possibility, as would the warmer 'My Dear Mrs Lewes'. But disregarding the British author's reputation for high-minded reserve, Harriet tossed aside any initial hesitancy and wrote the words 'My Dear Friend'. She had already sidestepped the awkward issue of Marian's marital status by deciding to refer to Lewes as Marian's husband, therefore thinking of her as a wife, like herself.

Over the following pages, in a more sloped hand than the upright lettering that flowed from Marian's nib, Harriet would launch into a review of Marian's published works. She'd even dare to make a candid appraisal of her recipient's '*thoroughly English*' personality, which Harriet felt she knew intimately through the page. Explaining that she had '*studied*' these books '*more*' than read them', Harriet praised Marian's originality and moral perception. Nonetheless, she went on to make several criticisms. Some of the strongest aspects of Marian's early stories, she wrote, had never been fully achieved in her novels. And she even dared to suggest that *The Spanish Gypsy*, a hit with the literary establishment of its day, would have been rendered better in prose than verse.

Harriet's considerable preparation faded into the background, the deeper she moved into the letter. Gathering pace, she began to drop punctuation and to leave sentences unfinished. She signed off by promising to send Marian a copy of her next book and inviting the British author to come and stay at her winter home in Florida, before also jotting down her permanent Connecticut address. Now, with her missive ready to seal up and send on its way, Harriet could only hope that Marian would be ready to look on its sender with generosity.

Harriet's letter had alluded to the heavy burden of writing *Oldtown Folks*, her new novel, due to be published in exactly a month's time. Work on this book, she said, was her reason for not making contact sooner. She didn't say that the decision to write to Marian now was motivated by nerves over its impending release, but reading between the lines of her first two letters this is the picture that emerges.

Harriet had high hopes but also fears for *Oldtown Folks*, a novel over which, unusually for her, she had laboured for several years. She had put her 'heart soul & life blood' into it, she'd say in her next letter to Marian, adding that it 'cost me more to write than anything I ever wrote'. Worried that delivering her story in instalments could dilute the impact of a book she regarded as her tour de force, she had insisted to her editor that serialisation in the *Atlantic Monthly* was not an option and that *Oldtown Folks* should appear from the beginning in book form. Harriet's tale chronicled the Massachusetts town of Natick and was inspired by the boyhood of her husband, who had experienced visions from a young age of what she called 'spiritualistic phenomena'. She'd begun the endeavour with all her usual enthusiasm, but now that the American and British publication dates drew near, she fretted that her huge overseas audience would struggle to engage with a work 'so intensely American' in character.

Finding an appreciative reader in someone as high profile as George Eliot could be a tremendous help and, given Harriet's sudden decision to get in touch at this time, it certainly seems that this had occurred to her. Little did she know that, by the time the early copy of the novel she'd promised arrived with her new friend, she would be looking to Marian for support on a rather more volatile matter.

Sensing nothing of this storm brewing, Marian simply rejoiced to receive that first letter. Three days after her return from her European travels, she wrote a response, addressing Harriet in kind as 'My dear Friend'.

Although Marian's tone was markedly more measured, she, too, wrote with a startling level of candour. Even in this initial reply she alluded to her frequent bouts of depression and talked – surprisingly to the modern reader aware of how her reputation has endured – of her uncertainty about the quality of her literary work. Harriet's letter, she said, made her 'almost wish' that her correspondent could have a fleeting sense of the 'paralyzing despondency in which many days of my writing life have been past', so that she might truly see 'the good I find in such sympathy as yours – in such an assurance as you give me that my work has been worth doing'. The Marian who appears in the pages of her letter reaches out to grasp Harriet's extended hand, recognising her correspondent for what she is – a 'fellow-labourer' and a woman with whom she has something unique in common. Despite marked differences in their temperaments – Harriet being the livelier and more impulsive of the two – their shared experiences as the most celebrated living female authors either side of the Atlantic immediately drew them close. That the pair shared this extraordinary status makes it all the more surprising that their friendship has not gone down in history.

The act of sitting down to write to Harriet would turn out to be the high point of a distressing weekend for Marian. Later that Saturday, her ailing stepson, Thornie, dramatically and unexpectedly returned home. The 25-year-old had been in South Africa for close to five years, hunting big game and seeking his fortune in farming, but his attempts had proved so unsuccessful that, not long before Marian and Lewes departed for their European trip, he'd written a pitiful letter to his father complaining of debilitating pains in his back and requesting funds to cover the return journey to London. Lewes had obliged at once, but with the health of his elderly mother to worry about too, and aware of Thornie's tendency to play fast and loose with the truth, neither he nor Marian seem to have recognised the extent of his son's ailments.

When, that day, the couple returned from paying a call on Lewes's frail mother, they were astonished to discover that Thornie had completed his voyage back to Britain weeks earlier than anyone thought possible. The spinal disease from which he was suffering now had such a grip on him that he had lost four stones in weight. His once strapping physique had wasted away, leaving him weak and gaunt. Still, he valiantly attempted to reassure them that all was not as bad as it seemed. Later, he would sit down with his father and Marian, giving the impression of pleasure as he listened to her play the piano. This was enough, for the moment at least, to convince Lewes to record in his diary that his son was in good spirits.

The next day, Thornie was far worse. The Priory was thrown into such disarray by his deterioration that Marian and Lewes scarcely had time to remember that Sunday afternoons were usually reserved for their popular gatherings. And so, hours later, and for the second time within a matter of days, an American author would make an unexpected appearance into the life of Mrs Marian Lewes.

The young Henry James, on his first overseas trip as an adult, had been persuaded to tag along with two American friends who'd previously visited in January. By this time, Sunday afternoons at the Priory had become so successful that – as Henry was to note in a subsequent letter to his father – to go accompanied with a 'received friend' was the only way for a stranger to gain entry, so 'hedged about with sanctity' had Marian become. Henry's female companions had perhaps already painted a picture of the Priory's artfully decorated drawing room, the theatrical sweeping curtains across its central archway, and the armchairs carefully arranged by Lewes and Marian in the hope that no one present should be seated less comfortably than anyone else.

Many famous personalities were said to have made appearances – over the years, Robert Browning, Lord Tennyson and Charles Dickens would be among them. And so, the young man must have arrived that day with more than a little trepidation. Little known though he was at this early stage of his career, Henry had written three reviews of Marian's work so far, both praising and criticising her writing. His verdict on *The*

Spanish Gypsy agreed with Harriet's assessment that poetry was not quite Marian's forte. If Henry fretted about such matters as he approached the house that Sunday, he would have soon learnt that he had no need to worry. The three friends were about to enter a moment in the life of George Eliot when her career and literary reputation could not have been further from her thoughts.

Inside the walls of the Priory that afternoon, there was much commotion. Thornie's back had begun to pain him so badly that, although he had dressed and come downstairs, he could do nothing but writhe in throes of agony on the floor. His frantic father – usually a gregarious presence at these Sunday gatherings – had gone out on a quest to purchase morphine, leaving Marian to tend to her stepson. The jangling gate bell, heralding the arrival of Henry and his friends, was a distraction, certainly, though hardly a welcome one.

It was perhaps a kind of crisis-induced numbness that encouraged Marian to allow her three American visitors into the house while her stepson still thrashed and groaned on the floor. Almost five decades later, when he wrote of the afternoon's drama in his memoirs, Henry would recall that, even in these extreme circumstances, Marian kept up polite conversation. If his word is to be believed, it seems that she felt compelled to go through the motions despite her distress, thereby rewarding the trio with the kind of learned talk that they had come here expecting.

During the gap in years between the day's experience and the writing of it, Henry had certainly added layers of varnish to his story. He embellished the cause of Thornie's suffering, for instance, by suggesting that his injuries stemmed from a past encounter with an angry bull. As an old man, Henry remembered his hostess's very human agitation, but her '*illustratively* great' demeanour, her black silk dress and lace mantilla covering her hair remained at least as strong in his mind. Even in a letter to his father, written the day after his visit in 1869, his chief impression, it seems, was that – despite the most taxing of circumstances – Marian remained a beguiling hostess.

What neither Henry nor his friends, nor perhaps even Marian and Lewes grasped at this point was the irreparable nature of Thornie's condition. But his torments that Sunday would merely mark the beginning of his decline. That evening, Queen Victoria's celebrated surgeon James Paget visited the house, and Lewes rose four times in the night to give morphine to his son. Marian, too, would soon be devoting much of her energy to caring for Thornie, who continued to suffer excruciating bouts of pain.

Under these heart-wrenching circumstances, she took some much needed cheer from Harriet's second letter, of late May. Having previously confided doubts about her own literary endeavours, Marian would have appreciated Harriet's description of writing a book as '*a hand* stretched forth in the dark passage of life to see if there is another hand to meet it'. Harriet's copies of Marian's books were full of annotations, she told her. If Marian could only see them, she would find 'how often the hand has met the kindred hand'.

While Thornie's health was steadily worsening in London, on the other side of the Atlantic Harriet had become embroiled in troubles of a very different nature. In the six-week gap between her first and second letters to her new friend, Harriet's thoughts had turned from *Oldtown Folks* to the prospect of writing another, shorter work – one that would soon eclipse public interest in the novel and mark a turning point in her literary reputation.

Within months, Marian would know all about this risky venture on Harriet's part, but this second letter from America gave the merest hint of what was to come. Harriet wrote only that she had returned from Canada, where she had gone to make sure she established copyright on *Oldtown Folks* for the lucrative British market. On her journey there, stopping at a

Boston bookshop, she'd happened on a much anticipated, newly translated title, just out in America. Harriet bought a copy of *My Recollections of Lord Byron*, written by the poet's last mistress, the Countess Guiccioli, and read it on her Canadian trip. What she found within its pages astounded her, and she'd returned to her home in the Connecticut city of Hartford burning with a sense of injustice.

During her first tour of Britain in 1853, Harriet had become close friends with the late poet's widow, Lady Anne Isabella Byron – a woman she believed to have shown a great capacity for love, charity and forgiveness. On her return trip, in 1856, Lady Byron had confided in Harriet a long-held secret and asked the American author whether she thought that this was the right moment to break her vow of silence. Lord Byron, his widow claimed, was guilty of an incestuous relationship with his half-sister. Though Harriet didn't doubt her friend's word, such was the scandalous nature of the accusation that she had urged Lady Byron to keep her 'sacred veil of silence' tightly drawn. But now, over a decade later, with the publication of the countess's book, Harriet was beginning to rethink the advice she had given.

Countess Guiccioli's memoir of the dead poet painted Lady Byron, now also deceased, as a cool, unfeeling woman, while Lord Byron came across as very much the wronged hero. Harriet, who had long harboured a deep resentment for her late friend's husband, was incensed by the thought that the British and American public, on reading this work, could come to regard the pair's marriage thus. Harriet knew that the rumour about incest gave a figure as influential as herself a potent weapon with which to counter the countess's claims. But she also knew that airing such matters in public could lead to her own censure.

Not long after her letter to Marian, Harriet began work on her rebuttal to the countess's book. Over three weeks in June, she toiled furiously on 'The True Story of Lady Byron's Life', an article that would in time be published in the *Atlantic Monthly*.

Her correspondence with another, long-established friend, the famous author and physician Oliver Wendell Holmes, hints that the unease Harriet felt about her endeavour was growing day by day. But, given what she saw as the unjust attacks on the memory of her friend, she still felt impelled to act. As she made clear in her letter to the doctor, she wanted his advice '*not*... as to whether the main facts shall be told, for on this point I am so resolved that I frankly say advice would do me no good'. Harriet hoped instead that he could take a look at the draft of her article in order to help her tell her story 'as wisely and well' as a story such as this could be told. Seeking this critique before she sent the manuscript to the *Atlantic Monthly*'s Boston offices was a good decision, for when the doctor returned it, Harriet discovered that he had corrected many errors in the writing – some grammatical, others caused by her tendency to exaggerate. Holmes predicted that her claims were bound to ignite an explosion of controversy never seen before. Yet he also let her know that he admired the substance of the article.

Harriet must have hoped that her British friend would be equally enthusiastic. Marian had by now received her copy of *Oldtown Folks* and, despite Harriet's fears expressed in her first letter that it wouldn't be understood abroad, had written back to let her know how much she'd enjoyed it. Given the frequency with which Marian wrote of past generations herself, she had unsurprisingly been drawn to the novel's evocation of what she described as an 'old-fashioned provincial life'. And as someone who had given up the ardent faith of her youth but remained deeply interested in religion, she'd warmed to the 'insight & true tolerance' with which the book's Calvinist characters were presented – especially since she knew that Harriet did not quite share their religious convictions. Rather than feeling excluded as a non-American reader, she appreciated Harriet's willingness to tackle a subject such as this – 'rare even among writers', and one missed 'altogether in English drawing-room talk'. On reading these words, Harriet perhaps dared to dream that Marian would look favourably on the Lady Byron article, too, and speak of it with equal admiration among the intellectual company within her own drawing room.

In August 1869, with the piece soon to be published simultaneously in the *Atlantic Monthly* in America and *Macmillan's* magazine in Britain, Harriet sat down once again to write to Marian. This letter, like her second missive of May 1869, is among that portion of the pair's correspondence that remains unpublished. To read it, researchers must gain access to the locked archive of the Henry W. and Albert A. Berg Collection at the New York Public Library, where we called up these neglected manuscripts. The 150-year-old sheets of cream-coloured paper hold Harriet's words of sympathy for Marian and her sick stepson. Her letter goes on to share with Marian her own sadness about her eldest living son. The 29-year-old, 'wounded and shattered' during the American Civil War, had been suffering physically and mentally for years – including with an alcohol addiction that preceded his army career, although Harriet didn't mention this. Knowing all about the emotional strain of constant care-giving, Harriet cautioned her friend to guard her own health.

Given Marian's circumstances, it would not do to make too much of the Lady Byron article, and yet Harriet could not quite let the opportunity pass. And so, she casually threw in the admission that she was enclosing two items that 'I thought might interest you': a sermon written by her preacher brother and her as-yet-unpublished piece for the *Atlantic Monthly*. In the letter's closing paragraph, she told Marian that she should not rush to answer this missive, adding the perhaps not entirely honest wish that her words should simply drop on Marian 'like a snow flake – melt & be gone'.

As Harriet guessed, the continuous upheaval of life at the Priory could not have made it easy for Marian to keep up with the daily ritual of dealing with the post. Thornie was growing ever weaker and suffering from attacks of paraplegia. The family had engaged the services of a nurse, but their growing sense of helplessness at the march of the disease had taken a toll on every one of them.

When she received Harriet's letter, the look of its first page must have been unexpected, her friend's writing appearing faint and frail. Unbeknown to her, Harriet too had been suffering in body of late, her fears about the possible public reaction to her Lady Byron article having apparently brought on a physical collapse during which she temporarily lost the full use of her arms and legs. As Marian continued to read, though, she would have witnessed Harriet's script growing visibly stronger as she hit her stride. Then, halfway through the letter, came the brief mention of the Lady Byron piece.

This probably made little impact at first. But it must have come as a shock when, having finished the letter, she began to read this accompanying article.

Whatever Marian was expecting, this could not have been it. In contrast to the lively flow of Harriet's correspondence and, indeed, the greater part of her published prose, the voice of 'The True Story of Lady Byron's Life' was trimmed of its author's pent-up emotions. Nonetheless, Marian baulked at the rumour about incest that Harriet was on the verge of making known to a far wider reading public.

Marian was no fan of Lord Byron. As it happens, she had recently re-read a significant number of his poems to try to ensure that she was being fair in her views, and had concluded that his writing was indeed repugnant. Be that as it may, this literary endeavour by Harriet appalled her too. She understood that Harriet wanted to defend her late friend, but felt certain that such a course of action could only make matters worse.

Another jolt was yet to come. Two thirds of the way through the article, Marian discovered what must at first have seemed a random mention of the author of 'the novel of "Romola"'

– a reference to her. Owing to her own socially precarious, unmarried status, Marian was someone who went out of her way to disassociate herself with unnecessary notoriety. So how disconcerting it must have been for her to find that Harriet had evoked the tragic relationship between two of that book's central characters to demonstrate 'the whole history of the conflict of a woman like Lady Byron with a nature like that of her husband'. This unexpected mention of such supposed similarities may have had an additional purpose. Given Harriet's anxieties about the public's potential response to the article, and its description of Marian as 'One of the first of living writers', these lines can also be interpreted as a pointed and thinly disguised request for endorsement.

Had Marian felt able to publicly support her friend, their relationship could perhaps have made it into literary legend. But the notion of defending Harriet's article was quite unthinkable to Marian, who felt at a loss even as to how she should answer this private letter. Against a backdrop of household anguish, she would keep mulling over its contents in the weeks to come, mentioning the piece when she wrote to other close friends and noting how much it had unsettled her. Nothing could outweigh 'the heavy social injury of familiarizing young minds with the desecration of family ties'.

Coincidentally, Marian had recently been working on eleven sonnets, entitled 'Brother and Sister'. The sequence was inspired by her early closeness with her own brother, from whom she'd been estranged for the past two decades – ever since he learnt of her relationship with Lewes. Though the poems, which portrayed the breakdown of their sibling relationship, were now finished, Marian would delay their publication for almost five years. Looking back on the writing of the sonnets some time later, she would recall in a letter to her publisher: 'This was always one of my best loved subjects. And I was proportionally enraged about that execrable discussion raised in relation to

Byron' – the implication being that Harriet's decision to write of such unsavoury things and drag her name into it could have led readers to misconstrue Marian's own work.

She was far from alone in her distaste for Harriet's article. The press would round on its author in condemnation. Despite her own misgivings, Marian worried about her long-distance friend. But with Thornie's health worsening by the day, she could not find a moment to pen what would be a difficult reply. And so, with the weeks passing, she could only trust that when at last she was able to send off such a letter, any hurt feelings on Harriet's part would not lead to a loosening of the clasped hands of their transatlantic bond.

~

CHAPTER 8

THE SPECTRE OF SCANDAL

As the summer of 1869 drew to a close, in a world unknown to George Eliot's reading public, Marian Lewes of the Priory, Regent's Park, girded herself for the worst. Behind the walls of her north London villa, the 49-year-old's sick stepson showed few signs of recovery. In fact, since his unexpected return in May, his symptoms had only deteriorated. In July, a glandular disorder, which the doctor feared might be tubercular, had added to the young man's suffering. By mid-September, Marian was recording in her journal that her stepson looked 'distressingly haggard'. Once a lively personality, he had lost his zest for life. Well-meant gifts of flowers from family friends brought him little pleasure and even conversation with his nearest and dearest often proved too great an effort.

Within this much subdued household, the scents of sickness and increasing desperation lent an unusual sourness to the closeted air. The new nurse was a constant presence, but Thornie's father and stepmother frequently took their turns at the young man's bedside. On at least one afternoon his mother came to visit, but Marian was the more frequent companion, sitting among medicine bottles inscribed with Latin names, quietly reading a book.

Her daily life bore almost no comparison to the hopeful new year she'd planned. Back on 1 January, she had cheerfully noted in her diary that she and her partner were well and that the 'many tasks' she'd set herself for 1869 included 'A Novel called Middlemarch'. Now, though, as the browning leaves beyond the window heralded the arrival of autumn, Thornie remained in grave danger, Marian's own health continued to suffer, and progress on this new book was arduously slow. Recently, the thought had come to her that 'I do not feel very confident that I can make anything satisfactory of Middlemarch'. Under normal circumstances, she might have written sooner to her American friend. But the pair's epistolary conversation had been on hold in the month since the British author received her copy of the Lady Byron article, and Marian would put off replying for several weeks more.

In mid-October, she recorded in her journal that her stepson was declining fast. Not long after, he would drop into a state of partial consciousness and on the early evening of the 19th, with his nurse and Marian at his side, he took his final breaths. Afterwards, Marian could at least console herself that his death had been peaceful. In the past, she had sometimes felt frustrated by Thornie's lack of self-discipline and few worldly accomplishments, but the last months had brought them closer and her bereavement was as genuine as his grieving father's. In a journal entry for that date when she was almost 50 years of age, she wrote 'This death seems to me the beginning of our own'.

While the Priory fell into deep mourning, across the ocean, the life of Marian's friend had been turned upside down following the piece she'd written for the *Atlantic Monthly*. As the author of *Uncle Tom's Cabin* – a book that remained controversial, particularly in the American South – Harriet had made the decision to publish 'The True Story of Lady Byron's Life' with some understanding of the risks involved. Indeed, anticipating that her revelations could ruffle feathers, the experienced 58-year-old had done her best to guard against public outrage by writing in a more restrained style than usual and seeking the support of important cultural influencers, such as Oliver Wendell Holmes, and, so it would seem, Marian herself.

But the sheer scale of the scandal unleashed by the magazine article had taken Harriet by surprise. After the story came out in the summer of 1869, the press attacked the accuracy of her account, questioning the credibility of her source, the late Lady Byron. What's more, Harriet's critics pronounced that, even if the allegations against Lord Byron were true, they were so obscene that Harriet should not have revealed them. A few voices, including that of Elizabeth Cady Stanton, came to Harriet's defence. As one of America's foremost female suffrage campaigners, she believed that the Lady Byron case illuminated the powerlessness of *all* women. But the majority of journalists, governed by Victorian ideas about decency, were indignant that a subject as shocking as sibling incest should have been made public under any circumstances.

A fighter by nature, Harriet refused to be cowed by her critics, setting her mind instead to turning her article into a book. She had adopted such a strategy in the past, with mixed results. When some readers had accused Harriet of vastly exaggerating the horrors of slavery depicted in *Uncle Tom's Cabin*, she'd written a work of non-fiction that provided documented proof of the underlying truths of her most famous novel. *A Key to Uncle Tom's Cabin* – a bestseller, like the work that preceded it – had its vocal supporters. Nonetheless, it had done little to change the minds of Harriet's most vehement opponents. Her critics accused her of cherry-picking the worst examples, claiming that the experience of most slaves at the hands of their masters was far better than Harriet would have it. Others attempted to shift the terms of the debate, shamefully putting forward the view that, even if her claims had merit, she was just as guilty as the perpetrators of such violence for bringing indelicate matters into the open. A similar argument was now being forcefully repeated by those who deplored the piece she'd written about Lady Byron. While Marian had applauded the power of *Uncle Tom's Cabin*, she was one of those raising such objections about the Lady Byron piece, albeit privately and in a gentler manner. Harriet, fuelled by the criticisms she had received, threw herself into writing this new book. If the varied responses to *A Key to Uncle Tom's Cabin* raised any doubts within her, she swept them aside, remarking to her publisher that this was '*war* to the knife'.

During the winter of 1869, while Harriet was so deeply embroiled in her work, across the ocean in London a bereaved Marian finally gathered the strength to respond to her friend's last letter. On 10 December 1869, she began with the usual heartfelt greeting 'My dear Friend', then an outline of Thornie's final months. 'I am recovering now from a very shattered state of health,' she told Harriet, but added that 'I cannot feel at ease without writing you a brief letter, first to tell you how my silence has been occupied… and next to thank you for all the helpful words that you sent me.' Marian knew from Harriet's letter of that May that her friend had lost a son of her own – a 19-year-old who'd drowned accidentally in the Connecticut river twelve years earlier, and whom she'd described as her 'silent blue eyed golden haired boy – who never gave me any sorrow but his death'. Knowing also of Harriet's troubles with her surviving veteran son, still suffering from the after-effects of war, Marian would have expected her recipient to understand the depth of her grief. On the tricky subject of the Lady Byron article, Marian tactfully wrote that, although she 'should have preferred that the "Byron question" should not have been brought before the public', she felt sure that Harriet had been 'impelled by pure, generous feeling'. Marian was careful to make it clear that she hadn't written to express a judgement, and that she was anxious only to convey to Harriet a sense of 'sympathy and confidence, such as a kiss and a pressure of a hand would give, if I were near you'.

Sealing up the letter, Marian could only wait to see how Harriet would respond. It was likely, of course, that Harriet might have felt some disappointment at the lukewarm response to her *Atlantic Monthly* article. But bearing in mind all that they had in common, Harriet was exceptionally well positioned to offer a unique kind of solace.

Marian would have sent her letter to her friend's main address in her Connecticut home at Hartford, unaware that Harriet was not there. Since making the decision that autumn to devote herself almost entirely to the research and writing of *Lady Byron Vindicated*, she had taken herself off to the New York clinic of George Taylor, well-known among the wealthy for his Swedish Movement Cure. This urban version of the better-known water cures of the era relied on a regime of massage and repetitive exercise instead of bathing rituals.

Boarding at Dr Taylor's facilities, Harriet had now established a regular daily routine. In the morning, she worked ceaselessly on her manuscript, putting a mental state already strained by the writing and reception of the *Atlantic Monthly* article under further pressure. Confined to her private room, she could at least be buoyed by the thought – as she would tell her daughters – that Lady Byron's voice would soon rise from beyond the grave, 'clear as the sun fair as the moon, & terrible as an army with banners'. Mindful of the need to keep up her strength, Harriet made it her afternoon habit to try to rid herself of pent-up anxiety by riding or walking in Central Park – a newly established oasis of luxurious calm within the bustling metropolis.

Here she cut a diminutive figure, making her way along the sculpted paths around the lake or by the sheep grazing on the Green. Passing the shadow outlines of bare winter trees, her small frame cloaked against the cold, she must inevitably have found that her thoughts kept returning to her anxiety-laden struggles to absolve Lady Byron's reputation. If only the great George Eliot had joined the small number of individuals to praise her *Atlantic Monthly* article. But Harriet was not the type to accept defeat easily, preferring instead to soldier on, focusing her energies on defending her cause.

Once the time for walking drew to a close, she could turn her mind to the more immediate prospect of her daily four o'clock appointment in Dr Taylor's Movement Room. There, she would be called on to perform a series of exercises with the clinic's gymnasium equipment. As Harriet had described it to her daughters, under the watchful gaze of the staff she could expect to be 'ribbed & stretched & otherwise operated on' until at last a sense of inner calm returned.

Dr Taylor's New York clinic was, in fact, not entirely unfamiliar to her British friend. In the same letter in which Harriet had enclosed the copy of 'The True Story of Lady Byron's Life', she'd mentioned that her older sister, Catherine, had been successfully treated by the doctor for a 'paralysis of the sciatic nerve which had crippled her for twenty years'. Knowing how Marian had also been suffering physically due to the strain of caring for poor Thornie, Harriet had explained that she was mentioning this 'philosophic system of exercising' in the hope that 'possibly in that way some avenue of relief may open to you'.

With the household now mourning her departed stepson, Marian – still struggling to muster much enthusiasm for *Middlemarch* – prepared to spend a sad and lonely Christmas in London. As she'd told Harriet when she wrote to her in December, even in the midst of her own misery these past months, she had often thought of what Harriet must be enduring, fearing that 'you were undergoing considerable trial from harsh and unfair judgements, partly the fruit of hostility glad to find an opportunity of venting itself, and partly of that unthinking cruelty which belongs to hasty anonymous journalism.'

There was a confidence to Marian's belief in her fellow writer's integrity and one which suggested that, from the eight months of their correspondence, she trusted she had a good measure of Harriet as a woman. In truth, even before the start of this epistolary friendship, Marian had formed a warm impression of the author of *Uncle Tom's Cabin*. She had gleaned such an image from Harriet's hugely popular publications, of course, but also from a private, though widely circulated, letter that had found its way into Marian's hands.

A decade and a half earlier, back in March 1853, Harriet's bestselling anti-slavery novel had already made her enormously famous. Marian Evans, on the other hand, though anonymously established as an assistant editor of the radical *Westminster Review*, remained largely unknown. An acquaintance of Marian's, the American abolitionist and author Eliza Lee Cabot Follen, on an extended trip to Britain, had recently written to Harriet Beecher Stowe, asking the lauded author to turn her pen to an account of herself. Harriet had obliged with a long letter and Eliza had enjoyed sharing its contents with her guests.

When the then 33-year-old Marian called one morning, she was treated, just like Eliza's other visitors, to a reading of the letter by her hostess. Seated on a drawing room chair, her skirts arranged neatly about her, Marian thrilled to the deeply personal voice of this author she so greatly admired. As she would remark at a future date, when the two had become friends, Marian thought how generous Harriet must be to put aside the busy demands of such a successful life to write at great length to this woman whom she didn't personally know. The Harriet that emerged from the pages of the letter was, in many ways, much the same as the one who would make contact with Marian sixteen years later – her tone serious and amusing by turns, her words brimming with emotion for the things that mattered the most to her. The jovial impression she painted of her husband Calvin Ellis Stowe – 'a man rich in Greek & Hebrew, Latin & Arabic, & alas! rich in nothing else' – would still reflect her feelings about her marriage in later life. She talked with passion of the faith in God that had burned so fiercely from the pages of *Uncle Tom's Cabin* and would continue to blaze throughout the years to come. Playing down the professional zeal that, in 1869, would lead her to Dr Taylor's clinic in order that she might preserve her strength for work, Harriet modestly presented herself as someone who became a famed author merely by chance.

A career in writing was all but forced upon her, she claimed, by economic circumstances and the expectations of a public clamouring for more stories. The thought of a proposed tour of England and Scotland raised the comment, 'It seems to me so odd & dream-like, that so many people want to see me – and I can't help thinking, that they will think that God hath "chosen the weak things of the world" when they do.' Harriet dwelt also on the death of one of her seven children – not Henry, yet to drown as a young man of 19, but little Charley, who had died of cholera as a baby in 1849. Looking back on scenes when she had sat beside his bed or stood mournfully at his grave, she drew the lesson that, from the experience of losing this little one, she had learnt the pain a slave mother must feel when forcibly separated from her children – a theme that remains one of the most powerful of *Uncle Tom's Cabin*.

Marian, who had read the ground-breaking novel when it came out in 1852, was interested, no doubt, in this hint at one of the seeds of its plot. Of the non-fiction follow-up on which its author was already working, Harriet had written in this letter that she had been deeply affected by the shocking true stories that her research had uncovered – many worse even than those featured in *Uncle Tom's Cabin*. 'It may truly be said I write with *heart's blood*,' she exclaimed.

What seemed to make the greatest impact on Marian, though, was the physical description that Harriet gave of herself. When Eliza reached the end of her reading, Marian asked if she might make a copy of something that was written on the first page. 'I am a little bit of a woman,' Marian's pen noted, 'rather more than forty, as withered and dry as a pinch of snuff – never very well worth looking at in my best days, and now a decidedly used up article.' Marian savoured these words. Why, she thought to herself, it 'makes one love her'.

There was something in this description particularly, that appealed to Marian. Though Harriet's prose was typically merry, this careful British reader thousands of miles away was able to peer behind their partial façade. And Harriet's comic portrayal of her own plain looks must have chimed with Marian, leading her to feel that she and the American writer, eight years her senior, shared a deeply personal affinity.

Born in rural Warwickshire in 1819, Marian's physical appearance had been a matter of family concern from an early age. Her father, fearing that his daughter stood little chance of securing a husband, had taken a similar approach to that of Reverend Brontë in the same period. He hedged his bets by investing in an unusually extensive education for a girl of the early nineteenth century. He sent Mary Ann – as she was known, before renaming herself Marian on her arrival in London in 1851 – to a series of local schools. After the death of her mother when Mary Ann was 16, he allowed the young woman to continue her studies independently, engaging tutors to teach her German and Italian, Greek and Latin. This way, at least, Robert Evans – an estate manager for a local landowner – must have reasoned that his clever young daughter would be equipped to support herself if his worries about her marital prospects were borne out.

On the other side of the Atlantic, and close to a decade before, the plain looks and bookish eccentricities of Harriet Beecher, too, had led her family to predict that she'd end up an old maid. Growing up in liberal Connecticut she, like Mary Ann, had benefited from progressive schooling. In 1824, when Harriet was 13 years old, she enrolled at the Hartford Female Seminary, founded by her older sister Catherine. After a successful career as a student, Harriet would later become one of the seminary's teachers. Unlike the constantly frustrated Charlotte Brontë, Harriet found her schoolmistress's job stimulating. Living among a group of other forward-thinking female tutors suited her, and, in her lessons teaching rhetoric and composition, she tended to have a good relationship with her students. The school was also perhaps a companionable environment for someone who, by her early twenties, seemed set never to wed.

Unlike Harriet, who distracted herself from the lack of romance in her own life by helping one of her brothers through the dramas of his turbulent courtship, Mary Ann felt humiliated by her likely unmarried destiny. Nonetheless, she was not prepared to wed just anyone.

In 1845, at the age of 25, she accepted a proposal from a local picture restorer. But she swiftly broke off the engagement, deciding that she could neither love nor respect him – his supposedly lowly profession seeming to have played a part. It wasn't only snobbery, though. She apparently felt that marrying such a man might hinder her ambitions, a friend of hers claiming at the time that Marian had felt it would prove 'too great a sacrifice of her mind and pursuits'.

When Mary Ann *did* fall for someone's charms, however, she could behave in ways that challenged accepted social norms and caused great consternation. Although she would later claim never to have felt anything for him – and to have been laughing at him in her sleeve all the while – a year or so earlier when she was almost 24, she had become friendly with the father of an acquaintance of hers, the 62-year-old Dr Robert Brabant. Mary Ann, who initially considered the doctor quite as learned as he did himself, went to stay with him and his wife. During her month-long visit, she spent hours reading to him in German – on occasion continuing for so long that she began to feel faint and had to lie down. He showed her his library, told her to consider it her own and talked of the great philosophical work over which he had been toiling for years – one he would never finish. At the time, the young woman exclaimed that she was 'in a little heaven here, Dr. Brabant being its archangel', but this was a paradise from which she would soon be cast out – ordered to leave by the doctor's wife, who grew suspicious of the pair's relationship.

In later years, she suffered two even more serious humiliations, inflicted by men to whom she had grown close. John Chapman, the owner of the *Westminster Review* with whose family Marian boarded when she first moved to London, toyed with her feelings by visiting her room, holding her hand and quite possibly having a short-lived affair with her. Mysterious symbols in his diary, similar to those he used when recording erotic encounters with other women, certainly suggest this. But with a watchful wife and jealous mistress – officially employed as the children's governess – also living under the same roof, he probably felt that he already had enough domestic drama to cope with and drew the line at pledging himself to Marian in any more meaningful way. Having rebuffed her, his assurance that he 'felt great affection for her', in contrast to his stronger feelings for his wife and mistress, caused her to break down in tears.

When working on *The Life of Charlotte Brontë* in the mid-1850s, Elizabeth Gaskell had felt the need to shield her deceased friend's true feelings for her married Belgian tutor from a respectable Victorian readership. Early biographers of George Eliot, writing soon after her lifetime, would be equally keen to gloss over the exact arrangements of Marian's stay in the Chapmans' home. The shocking revelation that she had allowed the man of the house to visit her private sleeping quarters would not be made known until the publication of his diaries six decades after her death.

Having got over this rejection, Marian's hopes were raised once again, this time by the philosopher and sociologist Herbert Spencer, a regular correspondent for the *Westminster Review*. He took her out to nights at the theatre and the opera, leading many to assume that he was all set to propose. But in an extraordinary show of courage and vulnerability that flouted the social conventions of the day, she was the one who ended up declaring the depth of her true feelings to him. Holidaying alone in the seaside town of Broadstairs, Marian wrote to confess that her whole life had begun to revolve around her love for him, although she knew that he did not feel the same way. If he would only have patience, she implored, he would find that she could be 'satisfied with very little'. The entreaty did nothing to sway him and can have served only to reinforce her self-image as someone unworthy of romantic love.

As with Charlotte Brontë – characterised as 'very ugly' by her school friend Mary Taylor – Marian's deep embarrassment at her appearance would last a lifetime. Two decades after this romantic rejection, when Harriet enclosed a photograph of herself with one of her letters, Marian would let her know that she'd treasure it, but claimed she could not reciprocate. Unable to bear having her own likeness captured on film, she said, she had no such pictures of herself.

But, in fact, Marian *had* sat for a few studio sessions – deeply unsettling experiences for her. As a young woman, she'd seen the results of what was probably the first-ever photographic image taken of her. Though its exact date remains unknown, a friend's more flattering pencil drawing of 1849, which looks as if it is a copy of the photograph, suggests that Marian is under 30. By this age, she would have been well aware of society's harsh judgement on her appearance. But it would have been one thing to have heard of her supposed lack of beauty, quite another to see herself for the first time shot from this unfortunate side-on angle. The cruel artificial light accentuated the hooked nose and pointed chin of a woman seemingly much older than her years. Metaphorically, and perhaps also literally, Marian would soon place the black-and-white picture out of her sight.

By the time Marian and Harriet became friends, contrary to the expectations of their families, each woman had long been in a partnership with a man who loved her. Calvin Ellis Stowe – characterised so amusingly by Harriet in her letter of 1852 to Eliza Lee Cabot Follen – had first declared his affection for the 23-year-old Harriet Beecher back in 1835, just months after the passing of his first wife, who had died of cholera. An earnest biblical scholar, though not without a sense of fun, Calvin, then in his mid-thirties, had got to know Harriet through the Semi-Colon Club, the literary society to which the two belonged. The group met at regular Monday evening gatherings, for readings and discussion, dancing and sandwiches, and Harriet and Calvin began to attend these occasions together. Their courtship culminated a year or so later in their marriage at the beginning of 1836.

When, soon afterwards, Harriet learnt she was expecting a child, her family, still unaccustomed to the notion that this highly educated, rather odd young woman might be marriage material, wondered exactly how she would cope with her new home life. Matters weren't helped by the fact that shortly after she became pregnant, her groom, still grieving his first wife Eliza, departed on an eight-month-long trip to Europe. There he planned to study the Prussian school system and buy books for the seminary where he lectured. It could hardly have brought the intended cheer when Harriet received these words by post shortly before his departure from America: 'I think all the time of you and Eliza, and hardly know which I want to see the most.' During his long absence, she dutifully followed his instructions to visit the grave of the first Mrs Stowe at times set by Calvin and synchronised with his own time zones overseas. On giving birth, she also honoured his wish to name

the baby Eliza. Unexpectedly, the labour didn't stop there and
the child was followed by a twin sister. When the news finally
reached her husband after his two-month return crossing to
New York, he insisted that his two daughters should be the
namesakes of each of his wives and that she must therefore
call the second child Harriet.

There was also another woman in the relationship between
Marian and George Henry Lewes, and her presence loomed
larger still: Agnes Lewes, the legal wife of Marian's partner.
Lewes had married Agnes in 1840, when he was in his early
twenties. Some years into their union, she had begun an affair
with his close friend, the journalist Thornton Leigh Hunt, after
whom Thornie had been named. After his birth and that of
two other legitimate sons, she had gone on to bear at least two,
probably four, children by her lover – though it was Lewes's
name that appeared on the birth certificate each time. Although
he apparently knew that he was not the real father, Lewes did not
wish to tar his wife and her offspring with the disgraceful brush
of adultery.

It was Marian's former flame, John Chapman, who had
introduced her to Lewes in 1851 – the same year as the publisher's
own dalliance with his boarder. Both Lewes and Marian were in
their early thirties, and Lewes had moved out of the home he'd
shared with Agnes. But the former couple would never make
their separation legal and, consequently, Marian had to risk social
exclusion if she wanted to share her life with Lewes.

In 1854, they 'eloped' to Germany, for a six-week 'honeymoon'
followed by several more months of study and work, leaving
behind concerned friends who were aghast at the rumours they'd
heard. On their return to London, Marian and Lewes would
announce their decision to live with each other. Such a departure
from recognised Victorian norms caused outrage. Even some
of Marian's closest liberal confidantes showed initial hostility,
and so, demoralised by this, she put off sharing the news with

her more conservative family. When, much later, in 1857, she eventually wrote to her brother to tell him the news, he swiftly disowned her and also persuaded their sister to cut off contact. Marian found herself barred from polite society and – especially in the early years of their relationship – when Lewes was invited to dine at the homes of his friends, the invitation was often not extended to her.

Though this state of affairs may well have felt inevitable, seeking a legal end to his marriage with Agnes would have been just about possible for Lewes. But to do so, he would have had to petition Agnes on the grounds of her adultery – something that in the past he had chosen to cover up. Neither he nor Agnes would have welcomed the publicity that such a claim would have brought. In Marian's case, by the time a change to the divorce laws in 1857 had made pursuing this a more viable possibility, her first stories were being published – initially anonymously and later as 'George Eliot' – in *Blackwood's* magazine. Now that she had found not just success as an author, but also the romantic partnership that had eluded her for so long, the prospect of a public shaming must have filled Marian with dismay.

Thanks to Harriet's willingness to ignore the unsanctioned nature of Marian's relationship – something perhaps made easier by their physical distance – the pair could share the kind of friendship on the page that might have been trickier if they had resided in the same country. The thousands of miles that separated them may, in fact, have allowed for some of the intimacy the two enjoyed. Unlike Arthur Bell Nicholls, the husband of Charlotte Brontë, who worried about the candour of letters she exchanged even with her mild-mannered friend Ellen Nussey, the menfolk of both Harriet and Marian positively encouraged the correspondence between them. Lewes and Calvin – a man Harriet called her 'Rabbi' on account of his long white beard and hair and the skull-cap that covered his bald spot – frequently appeared in the women's correspondence. Though most often through the thoughts each man conveyed to the other via their female partners, Calvin sometimes entered the conversation directly by sending his own notes to Marian.

The first of these dates from the spring of 1869, less than a month after Harriet's first letter to Marian. With a twinkling sense of humour, Calvin wrote: 'Since Mrs Stowe has spoken to you so freely about her reticent, introspective husband, I feel moved to say a word or two on my own account'. Harriet was apt to remark on his near illegible hand, but on this occasion, when writing to the great British author, Calvin made a special effort. When his wife had the chance to read this missive, she would find herself tickled not just by the 67-year-old's amusing self-description, but also the level of care he had taken with his usual scrawl. 'My Rabbi', she'd tell Marian in an appending note, 'has been moved to write to you the enclosed in his very best improved Arabic English characters', mischievously adding that since she knew Marian was a linguist, perhaps she would be able to decipher it.

In neat, forward-sloping black lettering, avoiding the looped flourishes that characterised Harriet's script, Calvin declared that he was an admirer of both Marian's and Lewes's work. Of all her fictional characters, he said, the female preacher in *Adam Bede* was the one that moved him the most, and he related that he had once believed Marian to be a preacher. In order not to stumble into difficult territory, Calvin would always keep the steadfast thought in his mind that – though his wife's friend might controversially have turned her back on the Church – she was a Christian at heart. As he would write to her on a future occasion, no one could conceive of a character like the Methodist Dinah Morris without 'a *Christ in dwelling*'.

In this first letter of May 1869, he talked of the strength of his own religious faith and his scholarly interest in the works of the German writer, Johann Wolfgang von Goethe, something he knew he shared with Lewes. Calvin also mentioned the visions of ghostly phenomena that he had been experiencing since he was a boy – a subject his wife had explored in her recently completed novel *Oldtown Folks* and written of in a separate letter to Marian, just five days before.

Spiritualism – the belief that the dead have the ability to communicate with the living, which grew rapidly in Victorian times – was a topic of great interest to Harriet. Her attraction to Dr Taylor's Swedish Movement Cure cannot be disentangled from her fascination with the practitioner's enthusiasm for spiritualism. During Harriet's time at his New York clinic, she would take part in several séances. These were not her first experiences of such practices either – for unlike her husband, naturally inclined to see visions since his boyhood, Harriet required help to summon the dead. As she had already claimed to Marian in her second letter, written in May 1869, she had been experimenting in this area for some time, and had even managed to contact the ghost of a famed female author.

Made unusually reticent perhaps by the newness of their friendship, or by Marian's reputation for rationality and measure, when Harriet initially brought up the incident she did not go into great detail. But even from two short paragraphs, Marian would have been able to gain quite a sense of this curious episode.

Harriet's words painted a picture of the darkened room in which she sat with another woman, a planchette placed on a surface beside them. Using this heart-shaped plank on castors, a pencil held in a hole at its tip, the spirit medium handled the wooden apparatus to channel the spirit of none other than Charlotte Brontë.

Harriet, who, like Marian, greatly admired the late author of *Jane Eyre*, had many things she wanted to know. For the next two hours, in the half-light of the séance, Harriet articulated her questions. And as she'd tell Marian in a later letter, via the moving pencil of the planchette, Charlotte answered her.

Harriet asked where Charlotte was residing now.

'Not heaven,' came the reply, 'but its antechamber.'

Charlotte described this as a place of 'Peace Calm – improvement. order usefulness. – the mistakes of life gradually being corrected the errors & frailties of life passing away.' Her fellow writer, William Makepeace Thackeray, was there too: 'The "slight savageness" is all passed away – he is perfectly lovely now.'

Charlotte talked also of her sister Emily, her husband Arthur, and that lingering sense of hurt that literary critics had characterised her work as '*coarse*' – a sentiment that Harriet knew all too well. With the wealth of evidence that emerged from the planchette – the personal details of Charlotte's life, the French words and '*wild* & Bronteish' language, Harriet felt certain that she and Charlotte had really been talking together. It stood to reason that there could have been no trickery involved, since the medium was a 'cool headed clear minded woman', and neither a French scholar nor poet. Later, though, to make absolutely certain, she would verify the authenticity by comparing the various things transcribed by the planchette to incidents in *The Life of Charlotte Brontë* by Elizabeth Gaskell – the author who had sought out Harriet's company on her first trip to Britain in 1853.

Prior to Elizabeth's death in 1865, she had met with Harriet twice more and the two had kept up a letter-writing friendship for several years. It must have gratified Harriet to read in the *Life* that Charlotte had been interested in hearing about the author of *Uncle Tom's Cabin*. It had also perhaps amused her that, on asking of Harriet's appearance, Charlotte was pleased to learn that – like her – Harriet was small in stature.

On that first occasion in May 1869 when Harriet mentioned her encounter with the dead British author, Marian felt sceptical. But, using the method that Harriet adopted to deal with Marian's unwed status, she tactfully chose to ignore these references to Charlotte. On the other hand, bound by politeness and probably some genuine interest too, Marian could not completely disregard the many paragraphs Harriet had devoted to talk of spiritualism. Both she and Lewes, she told Harriet in July 1869, were 'deeply interested' in Calvin's 'peculiar psychological experience', and would 'feel it a great privilege to learn much more of it from his lips'. In this letter, Marian wondered if the recent fervour for spiritualism in her friend's home country – so recently ravaged by civil war – could be regarded as a kind of outpouring of grief 'towards the invisible existence of the loved ones'. Perhaps also recalling that Harriet had suffered the death of two sons, Marian let her know that she found such an interpretation 'deeply affecting'. Nonetheless, while carefully avoiding speaking directly of Harriet's communing with Charlotte Brontë, Marian remained resolute in the strength of her opinion that – at least from her own experience on the other side of the Atlantic – 'spirit communications by rapping, guidance of the pencil etc.' had always appeared to her as 'degrading folly, imbecile in the estimate of evidence, or else as impudent posture'. But concerned that Harriet might take offence, she assured her correspondent that 'my deep respect for you' compelled her to be truthful, and that she would still gladly read anything that Harriet sent her on the subject.

Walking this tightrope between blistering honesty and at least lukewarm encouragement seemed to do the trick. In her next letter, Harriet would leave the theme of spiritualism alone. At a later date, though, she brought up the Charlotte Brontë episode again, furnishing her friend with many more details about what had happened. On this occasion, Marian was firmer still, letting Harriet know that 'whether rightly or not' the story struck her as 'enormously improbable'.

Marian, then, could at times be sternly frank with Harriet. But in her closing communication of 1869 – that 10 December letter, which told of the passing of her stepson – she would open herself up with the greatest intimacy.

Death had been a stranger to her for two decades, she would tell Harriet, ever since – as an already motherless young woman of 29 – she'd lost her father. Talking of the great privilege of ministering 'comfort through love and care', Marian was quick to acknowledge that Harriet's experience in this area was far greater than hers. And so, she surely assumed that Harriet would soon send a sympathetic response.

During the last weeks of the year, Marian and Lewes prepared for a sad Christmas in London, when, on 25 December, they would walk to Highgate Cemetery to spend some time by Thornie's grave. Little kindnesses, recorded in their letters and journals, brought some cheer to the dark days of their bereavement: a basket of gifts from a friend of Marian's, which brightened a foggy winter's morning; Christmas dinner with two of Lewes's children; the prospect of a possible trip to Germany if Lewes's mother's health held out.

As the clinging winter frost eventually made way for the spring flowers of a new decade, it also heralded the approaching first anniversary of Marian's literary alliance with Harriet. Through their regular and affectionate exchange of post, the pair had steered each other through their mutual experience of fame and notoriety as well as sharing intimate reflections on their private lives. But now it looked as if their friendship was not so secure: Marian's last letter had specifically requested some contact from her 'sister woman', and yet the weeks continued to go by and by and still there came no response.

CHAPTER 9

AN ACT OF BETRAYAL

More than two years would pass before Marian Lewes at last received an explanation, of sorts, for the silence of her faraway friend. During the many months since she had poured out her grief on paper, sharing her deep feelings of loss over the death of her stepson, she had not forgotten Harriet Beecher Stowe. Now at last, in early 1872, a letter arrived at the Priory. But when Marian sat down to read, its contents would fall far short of her hopes.

In the chill of her north London home, Marian surveyed the day's post laid out before her. As was his usual habit, the man she called her husband, George Henry Lewes, had already vetted her correspondence. Having effectively taken on the role of Marian's literary manager, for some years now he had been weeding out anything that he deemed unworthy of her attention and dealing with it himself – an intrusive, though well-intentioned, act meant to save Marian the pain of seeing upsetting reviews of her work. A non-critical letter from a literary friend such as Harriet would have made the cut, but if

Lewes lingered over the American woman's words, he too may have wondered at what she said to Marian.

'Dear Friend' the first line read, the familiar greeting offering cold comfort, for it was followed by Harriet's paltry excuses for her failure to write. Her letter claimed that she would have been in touch sooner if only 'two years of constant and severe work' had not 'made it impossible to give a drop to any thing beyond the needs of the hour'. As Marian read on she found no belated condolences; not even a mention of her bereavement; no acknowledgement of that plea in her own last missive when she'd reached out across the waves in her anguish. In December 1869, Marian had written that she would not 'be so unreasonable as to expect a long letter', but that 'some brief news of you and yours will be especially welcome just now.' And yet even this simple request had remained unanswered by Harriet.

Now, at last there *was* news from her, but it could hardly have brought Marian much cheer. The pages she grasped in her 52-year-old hands were largely taken up by a long commentary on the work of several spiritualists known personally to her friend. Harriet talked of George Taylor, the doctor who held séances by night, and at whose New York clinic she'd been residing while working on her book about Lady Byron. She also mentioned the social reformer and author Robert Dale Owen and lavished his books, *Footfalls on the Boundary of Another World* and *The Debatable Land Between this World and the Next*, with the strongest praise. Harriet said he was a great admirer of Marian's and planned to send her some of his writing in order to seek her opinion.

As Marian continued to leaf through the paper sheets, embossed with Harriet's personal seal – a creeping branch S for Stowe sprouting leaves from its bark – how could she not lose heart? A single moment was the letter's saving grace, and to this Marian grasped hold. She would mention it in the opening paragraph of her own otherwise understandably curt reply, sent off promptly within days despite her own demanding schedule.

Harriet, who had written from her winter home in Florida, had painted a picture of her surroundings, so ripe and vivid that – in spite of everything – Marian could briefly leave behind the wallpapered rooms of the Priory, fires burning in the grates at this time of year, and go out into the sunshine of this rural idyll.

Following the trail laid by her friend's words, Marian could breathe in the fragrant air of the distant orange orchard. Within the wooded land surrounding Harriet's house on the banks of the St John's River, she could take in the sight of the glittering water, and, as Harriet had described them to her, 'the waving of the live oaks with their long, gray mosses over head & the bright gold of oranges looking thro dusky leaves around'. Here, Marian felt she could 'bathe in that quietude'. Within this landscape of creeping vines and flowers, Harriet had told her that the pressures of the world receded. Here, there was 'no winter' and it was warm enough to spend one's days outside in a tent: writing letters, reading books and 'spinning ideal webs' for stories as yet unwritten.

Harriet's letter had also mentioned that she'd ordered copies of *Harpers Weekly*, the American magazine in which *Middlemarch* was now being serialised. This continued literary engagement must surely have appealed to Marian despite the personal sense of having been badly let down by her friend.

In the two years since December 1869 when the pair had stopped corresponding, Marian's attitude towards the manuscript of what would become her best-known novel had moved from a state of utter despair, to one of hopefulness and eventually great activity. In December 1870, many months since she started the book, she'd recorded in her journal the seemingly unconnected entry that she was now experimenting with a different story, which she had first begun 'without any very serious intention of carrying it out lengthily'. This was to be 'Miss Brooke', the imaginary account of a passionate, deeply pious young woman – strikingly similar to the young Marian – who becomes the wife of a fusty, petty-minded clergyman. This tale of the undermining and eventual triumph of Dorothea Brooke would ultimately break through the constraints of the short story form originally envisioned by Marian. In time, she would stitch Dorothea's tale into the fabric of *Middlemarch*, where it would become, for many readers, the most memorable part of the book.

At the beginning of December 1871, the novel's first substantial volume (of a planned eight) was published in Britain, followed swiftly by its release in weekly instalments in America, much to the chagrin of Marian's British publisher who feared that 'bits will be published right and left in this country in spite of our teeth'. By the time that Harriet wrote in February 1872 to let Marian know that she had 'sent north' for copies of *Harper's Weekly*, she was already several issues behind. But being able to receive post only once or twice a week in her remote home in Florida, she could at least claim honestly that arranging for the magazines to be sent was no straightforward matter.

As usual, Harriet had travelled down to Mandarin in November, to avoid the coldest Connecticut months. More than ever this winter she must have felt that she needed this annual escape. In February 1871, her troubled son Fred, whose alcoholism had already caused her so much heartache, had announced his intention to go away to sea. His parents would learn that he made it as far as San Francisco, but on disembarking there he disappeared, never to be heard from again. With no body, and no final communication from him, Harriet still held onto the hope that Fred might be found alive. Although, in the past, she had opened up about some of her son's troubles to Marian, she could not bring herself to mention him at all in this letter, perhaps mindful of her own neglect during her friend's time of need.

The year preceding Fred's disappearance had also been one of stress, this time from a professional point of view. Harriet's book, *Lady Byron Vindicated*, over which she'd been labouring so madly when Marian last wrote, had been rushed out, just a month later, in January 1870. Rather than serving to restore the reputations of either its author or aristocratic subject, so badly shredded by Harriet's *Atlantic Monthly* piece, this longer-length work did more harm than good. The *Nation*, a northern American magazine, criticised Harriet for failing to supply the reader with any substantial new evidence and damningly likened her account of the Byrons' marriage to that of a 'drawing-room scandal'. The *Charleston Daily News*, and several other southern papers, gleefully reprinted the words of the *New York Sun*, which had called the book a 'weak and trashy production'. Similarly, the Virginia-based *Richmond Dispatch* decried Harriet's intended vindication as 'a turning over again of the offensive mass of scandal, whose exhalations can have no effect but that which is bad'.

Marian's last letter of two years earlier, mostly filled with her palpable sadness over the death of Thornie, had also summarised her disapproval of Harriet's Lady Byron article. Unfortunately, this criticism would have arrived with Harriet during the sorry aftermath of her new book's publication. This meant that the timing of Marian's words, measured though they were, would have sharpened their impact.

Though this catalogue of sorrows and disappointments cannot excuse Harriet's failure to write earlier, they do at least offer an explanation for her delay. What's more, Marian's grief perhaps brought back memories of Harriet's own son – the 19-year-old who, well over a decade earlier, had drowned in the Connecticut River. Rather than making her well placed to empathise, as Marian might reasonably have assumed, this sad news could have brought up buried sorrows which Harriet, as a twice – possibly thrice – bereaved mother herself was still not ready to face.

Marian's decision to forgive, if not forget, cannot have been easy – something that was more than hinted at in her response of March 1872, written while she was still only about halfway through the concerted labour of producing the eight volumes of *Middlemarch* promised to her publisher. With a frostiness that had never entered her conversation with Harriet before, her letter began: 'I can understand very easily that the last two years have been full for you of other & more imperative work than the writing of letters not absolutely demanded by charity or business.' As to her friend's lengthy discourse on spiritualism, although she told her that she would 'certainly read Mr. Owen's books if he is good enough to send them to me', Marian was unequivocal in her view that, in terms of what she had seen for herself, 'spirit-intercourse' seemed to her to be 'the lowest form of charlatanerie'. She signed off by saying, pointedly, that she wrote 'very imperfectly, for my letters are always written in shreds of time'. Nonetheless, she added that she was, and would always be 'Yours with sincere affection and gratitude'.

This initial reply was notably shorter than usual, but during the coming months the pair swiftly steered their relationship back on course. Other women, though more reliable than Harriet, could not share such personal insights into both literary challenges and the experience of notoriety. Marian's own history of ostracism, too, may have played a part in her generosity. Having known what it was like to be shunned herself, she understood the suffering that Harriet had endured at the hands of the press during her period of silence.

Marian's prompt reply resulted in another letter from Harriet, this time sent within a couple of months. Treading carefully for now, Harriet began by offering another vivid description of her Florida home: an entrancing place of labyrinthine creepers, swinging draperies of moss and yellow jessamine climbing 'into & over every thing with fragrant golden bells & buds'. Despite Harriet's continued entreaties that her British friend should come and stay, Marian did not feel that travelling such a distance from London was a possibility. Lewes's health had suffered terribly following the death of his son, and Marian's constitution remained as easily upset as ever. So she must have particularly appreciated Harriet's efforts to sketch out the scene in such detail, offering her the opportunity to visit 'in spirit if not personally'. If Marian were here with her, Harriet wrote, she would take her 'in heart & house & you should have a little room in our little cottage'. They would go out gathering flowers and, for the length of her enchanted stay, they could forget the worries of the world.

After the warmth of the letter's beginning, it might even have amused as well as exasperated Marian that the following pages were stuffed, once again, with Harriet's usual outpourings about ghostly phenomena. But her following letter, written in September 1872, would present something else entirely.

Since the revival of their correspondence in the spring, it had seemed to Harriet that she'd been involved in two distinct conversations with her British friend: one within the pages of their letters, and another in the instalments she had seen of *Middlemarch*. After leaving sunlit Mandarin behind, she had been away for much of the summer, first staying at a resort in New Hampshire – escaping the heat this time – and then giving a series of readings in cities around New England. As a consequence, she'd only been able to read *Harper's Weekly* on and off, but moments from the novel, reimagined by her, had kept playing over in her mind. And now, today, though she was presumably still mid-tour, she found herself suddenly overcome with an urge to write Marian another letter.

There was a line she believed to be spoken in the book by Dorothea's suitor, 'Ladislaw or whatever his name is'. Being away from her papers, Harriet was unable to look it up, although this may hardly have been the best way to put it to the meticulous Marian. According to Harriet, the young man said something to the effect of 'whatever is honestly & purely attempted for good becomes part of the great force that is moving for good thro the universe'. This struck her as such a wonderful notion that she declared it 'one article of my creed'.

The worlds of their published works and their personal letters provided a space in which these literary legends could come together. But the ocean that parted them could also exacerbate misunderstandings. The unintended friction soon to follow could perhaps have been avoided had the pair been able to sit together, sharing confidences on the veranda of Harriet's Florida home.

Presumably not realising that Lewes vetted at least some of Marian's post, Harriet wrote, 'My darling I confess to being very much amused & sympathetic with Dorothea's trials with a literary husband.' And then, 'Now, dont show this to Mr Lewes, but I know from my own experiences with my Rabbi that you learned how to write some of those things by *experience*. Don't these men go on forever getting ready to begin – absorbing learning like sponges – planning sublime literary enterprises which never have a *now* to them.'

Like Mr Casaubon, the husband of Dorothea in Marian's novel – forever buried in his *Key to All Mythologies* – Calvin Ellis Stowe had made a lifelong habit of researching ad infinitum without completing several of the ambitious books he planned to write. What's more, Harriet seems to have sensed that her well-meaning attempts to chivvy him along had often served only to slow his progress. By sharing this part of her marriage with Marian, Harriet was offering her the chance to take their friendship to a new level of closeness. But, removed as Harriet was from Marian's life in London, she hadn't allowed for the reality that her friend – who remained controversially unmarried to Lewes – would never have felt able to engage with this line of conversation.

Resolute in the need to steer clear of scandal and present her 'marriage' as an entirely unblemished union, Marian would write back, telling Harriet in no uncertain terms that it was:

'Impossible to conceive any creature less like Mr. Casaubon than my warm, enthusiastic husband'. In fact, when he failed to get down to work, Lewes himself joked that the 'shadow of old Casaubon' hung over him. Nonetheless, he hardly resembled Harriet's characterisation. Even now that his management of Marian's career took up so much of his days, he continued to publish books. In his time, he'd turned his hand to subjects as varied as the theatre, philosophy and the natural world. His sociability, too, made him a very different personality from the cold, mean-spirited Mr Casaubon.

But Harriet – who, in any case, had only been focusing on the tarrying side of Mr Casaubon's nature – was talking of her own partner as much as Marian's and had seemed keen to admit as much to her friend. Even if Lewes did not entirely fit the bill, there were figures in Marian's past – most notably the overbearing Dr Brabant of her youth – who likely did mix with her rich imagination to help create Mr Casaubon. The pair might indeed have been able to discuss such former associations if Marian hadn't felt bound by then to present such a chaste version of herself. But since Marian remained reluctant to divulge such details, she rejected the opportunity to deepen their bond in this way.

To make matters worse, Harriet unwisely fired off another missive to her friend even before she'd received Marian's strongly worded response. The fact that both letters must have arrived at the Priory in quick succession can only have worsened the damage already caused.

On receipt of this second letter, Marian learnt that Harriet was staying at the home of the author Annie Adams Fields – the 38-year-old wife of Harriet's publisher James T. Fields, and the woman who had first put them in touch with each other. Usually, such news would have brought Marian pleasure. But when Harriet told her that the by-now precarious subject of

Mr Casaubon had dominated recent conversation with Annie, too, her happiness must have been somewhat soured.

Harriet's letter invited Marian to envisage the two women huddled together in the dove-like Annie's 'sweetest little nest' of a house, where the sound of the sea could be heard from the back rooms and the sights of a busy Boston street seen through the windows of the front. Framed pictures crowded the walls of Annie's elegant parlour and, as could be expected for a literary home such as this, there were shelves of neatly bound books. In light of the recent comparisons Harriet had made between Casaubon and Lewes, Marian surely felt alarmed when Harriet declared the younger Annie and herself both 'out of our senses with mingled pity & indignation at that dreadful stick of a Casaubon – & think of poor Dorothea dashing like a warm sunny wave against so cold & repulsive a rock'.

To add insult to injury, though Harriet remained gripped by *Middlemarch*, she had already – part way through the serialised novel – come to some conclusions about where its author was going wrong. And she didn't hold back on telling Marian where the issue lay, namely the story's lack of 'jollitude'. Harriet claimed that 'You write & live on so high a plane – it is all self abnegation – we want to get you over here, & into this house where with closed doors we sometimes make the rafters ring with fun – & say any thing & and every thing no matter what & won't be any properer than we's a mind to be.'

In Marian's swift reply, she was firm in her guarantees that her partner was nothing like Mr Casaubon, but when it came to this appraisal of her lack of fun, she fell back on the technique of simply ignoring the words in question. Harriet, for her part, held off on answering for several months and eventually wrote back with the insistent assurance that there had been a misunderstanding: 'Dear Love, did you think for one moment that I fancied a resemblance between Mr Lewes & Casaubon? – Oh thou of little faith!'

Despite Harriet's feelings about the lack of 'jollitude' that she perceived in *Middlemarch*, Marian would remain keen to explore her work with her friend. Over three years later, in 1876, Marian's eagerness to discuss her next novel with Harriet shows the premium she placed on her fellow writer's opinions.

Unlike *Middlemarch*, set in the era surrounding 1832's Great Reform Act – the political event that had so excited the young Charlotte Brontë and Mary Taylor a generation before – *Daniel Deronda* would take place in contemporary times. This was unusual for Marian, whose fiction tended to focus on the recent past. What's more, this new work would take a further unexpected turn when, part way through the novel, its titular protagonist turns out to be Jewish. Within the context of the English literary world of the time, this felt revolutionary indeed.

Since her early days as an editor and writer for the *Westminster Review*, Marian had rated the creator of *Uncle Tom's Cabin* as an author of 'rare genius'. She admired Harriet's ability to weave a story that could hold her audience in thrall, while also raising important social issues. Just as Harriet's best-known novel had sought to open the eyes of her readers to the evils of slavery, Marian now hoped to encourage her audience to ask themselves difficult questions about their own deeply engrained prejudices against Jewish people. Her praise for Harriet's talents was not without limits: she disliked what she termed the 'feeble' travelogue *Sunny Memories of Foreign Lands* and, more recently of course, she had expressed her disapproval of Harriet's writings on Lady Byron. Overall, though, she felt that her friend's best work assured her a place 'in that highest rank of novelists'. Regarding Harriet – discomfitingly for a modern reader – as someone who had '*invented* the Negro novel', she understandably desired her friend's thoughts on the subject of racism in her own new book.

When *Daniel Deronda* came out in America in 1876, Harriet and her husband read it faithfully in serial form each month –

with Calvin, now in his seventies, staying up well past his usual eight o'clock bedtime in order to finish the latest instalment. Harriet, whose own public battering in recent years had led to her fatigue with the literary world, found herself stimulated, right from the start, by this new tale from Marian.

In Florida, it was orange blossom time once again. Bees were roaming about the white-flowered branches, filling the air with their humming. In the fruit tree, just beyond the window where Harriet sat, a red cardinal was singing with such sweetness that she almost broke off mid-flow. Glancing out at the sunny scene, pen and paper before her, Harriet wrote of her wish that she could really send some of this southern winter weather to her British recipient. But, as ever, she had to rely on her words to do the job, transporting rays of light and warmth across the waves.

She could tell Marian, for instance, all about this 'easy undress, picnic kind of life, far from the world & its cares', where, now that she had reached her mid-sixties, her twin daughters, aged almost 40, relieved her entirely of former domestic chores. It was as well, really, for – though she could not describe it with any more clarity than this – a strange feeling had been coming over Harriet recently. It was, she confided in the privacy of her correspondence with Marian, as if she had 'been playing and picnicing on the shores of life' and now woken with a start from an afternoon's dream to find almost all of her companions gone and the few that remained 'packing their trunks & waiting for the boat to come & take them'.

But their later years nonetheless offered Harriet and her husband some pleasures. They continued to read the instalments of *Daniel Deronda*, and Harriet would ultimately proclaim it 'a splendid success'. Literary critics of the day, however, would be more divided in their opinion, particularly regarding what Marian termed 'the Jewish element' of the novel. Even before publication, her editor had expressed concern that the Jewish characters were the least well-drawn of her cast. Later, in the pages of the *Atlantic Monthly*, Henry James – no longer the relatively inexperienced writer who'd made his way to Marian's front door, but a published novelist himself – complained that neither the hero, Deronda, nor his love, Mirah, were remotely convincing. According to Henry, they had 'no existence outside of the author's study'. On the other hand, Marian was pleased to receive a letter from a London rabbi, who – writing within an age of pervading anti-Semitism on both sides of the ocean – let her know of his 'warm appreciation of the fidelity with which some of the best traits of the Jewish character' were illustrated in her novel.

Yet some of Marian's subconscious prejudices – the stereotyped Cohen family, with its oily-skinned pawnbroker patriarch and his vulgar-looking mother, whom the hero supposes sleeps in her jewellery – are troubling to today's reader. By contrast, the object of Deronda's affections, Mirah, also Jewish, embodies an all-encompassing saintliness. In this way, she may bring up similar feelings of frustration to those so often triggered by Harriet's hero, the pious and long-suffering Uncle Tom, whose story had so profoundly moved and influenced Marian.

In late 1878, Harriet sent her friend the gift of a new edition of her most famous book. This time, it would be Marian who delayed responding, since the package arrived in the middle of a difficult period. She and Lewes had bought a second home in the Surrey countryside two years earlier, and were still deep in renovations. As they had with the Priory, they spent considerable money doing the place up, overhauling the plumbing, the poky butler's pantry and the kitchen. Here, they were planning to spend many more happy summers together.

Sadly, this was not to be. By 1878, Lewes was suffering so greatly with his health that a friend of Henry James had recently remarked unkindly that it looked as if Lewes 'had been gnawed by the rats – and left'. In November of that year, the couple returned to London and, while their servants hurried ahead to open up the Priory, they went to stay at a hotel. Lewes had been complaining for about a week of what he believed were haemorrhoids. But when James Paget, the family's long-serving doctor, was summoned, he pronounced the condition considerably more serious, describing it ominously but mysteriously as 'a thickening of the mucous membrane'. On the 30th of that month Lewes died at home at the Priory, plunging Marian into a period of deep mourning.

Separated as they were by the Atlantic Ocean, it must have been some time before Harriet learnt of Marian's sorrow. For a week, the grieving woman did not leave her room. Below stairs, the servants could hear her anguished cries, which rang throughout the house. It would be several months before Marian replied to Harriet to acknowledge the gift of *Uncle Tom's Cabin*. And so, this new edition of the book would have been Marian's main way of communing with Harriet for the time being. Attired in mourning clothes, turning the pages of the novel, Marian must have found the lively voice of its narrator a touching reminder that its story was her first introduction to this dear, literary friend.

When, in April 1879, Marian at last wrote to tell Harriet of her loss, there would be another significant gap – of a year – before Harriet answered. This certainly firms up the impression created in the aftermath of Thornie's death that, when confronted by events that mirrored her own worst fears, Harriet responded by retreating within herself. This time, though, her letter – which, unknown to either woman was to be the last between them – acknowledged the real reason behind her lack of action. Marian's missive, she said, was 'so deeply hopelessly sad' that it had made her feel 'a sort of despair'. Unable to find the right words, she had delayed replying, reassuring herself that she would write when her orange trees blossomed again, 'but the time came & passed'. She was always busy now, she continued, caring for her elderly husband. Calvin was aging fast and, although his mind remained 'yet as clear as ever', his physical strength was ebbing away, so that Harriet could no longer hide from the fact that their time of 'earthly companionship' was 'drawing to a close'.

Given the warmth of Marian's and Harriet's enduring feelings for each other and their hard-won capacity to face difficult truths, it seems strange that neither woman took the opportunity to speak publicly about their relationship – a silence that Harriet would maintain even once their correspondence was brought to an abrupt end.

At the close of 1880, eleven years after they first began writing to each other, the 61-year-old Marian fell unexpectedly ill. Sitting in the audience of a Greek-language performance of *Agamemnon*, she'd felt the stirrings of a sore throat. By the next day, her condition had grown drastically worse, much to the distress of her new partner, John Walter Cross, whom she had married earlier in the year – in fact on the same May date of Harriet's letter. His age, at two decades her junior, had set people gossiping about her once more. But at least this man – who'd seemingly been a confirmed bachelor – was someone she could legally wed. When her husband sought medical assistance, a first doctor suspected laryngitis, but Marian was eventually diagnosed with heart problems brought on by kidney failure. She declined quickly, and, three days before Christmas, slipped away from life.

Not long afterwards, a sad Harriet spoke with the publisher husband of Annie Adams Fields about the possibility of bringing out an article, in the *Atlantic Monthly* again, commemorating her friend. Her collection of letters from Marian, she wrote, showed her to be 'so fine and noble'. Harriet's only hesitation was 'one of delicacy'. Although Marian had been able to officially call herself Mrs Cross in that last year of her life, any biographical piece would have to acknowledge her longest romantic partnership, which had lasted until Lewes's death. Harriet feared that even the American public, less bound by formal conventions than the British, would find Marian's conduct anything but 'fine and noble' in a woman. Harriet asked whether James T. Fields knew if 'any marriage ceremony of *any* kind' had taken place between Marian and Lewes. As neither he nor his wife were able to give such a reassurance, Harriet quietly let the subject drop.

Just as Harriet's own epistolary boldness had once given Marian permission to express herself candidly, so Harriet in turn seems to have learnt from Marian when it was better to keep quiet. In doing so she honoured the spirit of her friend. But in remaining silent, Harriet would leave their relationship at the mercy of biographers.

Unlike in the days of Jane Austen, the male relatives of this pair felt under no compulsion to hide their pioneering alliance. In his three-volume work, *George Eliot's Life*, Marian's widowed husband included several of her letters to Harriet. And one of Harriet's sons published a memoir of his mother. He wrote it during her twilight years, a period during which her mind became increasingly confused – moments of lucidity, as his sister put it, coming and going 'like falling stars'. Charles Edward Stowe devoted a whole chapter of his book to the women's bond, calling it one of the 'most delightful' experiences of his mother's life. But – perhaps because of the divergence in the authors' future reputations – later researchers would show little interest, their failure to value the friendship's historical importance, leaving it to become all but forgotten.

PART 4

KATHERINE MANSFIELD AND VIRGINIA WOOLF

~ The queerest sense of echo coming back to me
from her mind the second after I've spoken

Diary, Virginia Woolf
25 August 1920

~

CHAPTER 10

FRIENDS OR FOES?

Virginia Woolf stepped out of her Richmond townhouse one April afternoon in 1917, embarking on her mission without feeling assured of success. The 35-year-old author, of just one novel to date, was on her way to see Katherine Mansfield – a writer who, despite being six years younger, had carved out rather more of a literary name for herself. Although Virginia tentatively considered Katherine a friend, she still regarded the charismatic New Zealander as an 'utterly unscrupulous character'. Despite this ambivalence, Virginia knew that the proposal she intended to put to Katherine would have the power to draw them into a close alliance.

The unlikely pair had first met the previous year, introduced by Virginia's flamboyant friend, the bearded and bespectacled Lytton Strachey. He had come across Katherine at Garsington Manor in Oxfordshire, where the literati flocked to salons hosted by the aristocratic Ottoline Morrell. During this time, Lytton was hard at work on *Eminent Victorians* – the biography that would make his name. But Katherine's attention was on *The Voyage Out*,

Virginia's recently published first novel, and she told Lytton that she wanted to get to know its author more than just about anyone else. He promptly wrote to Virginia, suggesting that she consider meeting this young woman whom he found so intriguing. With a cattiness characteristic of the set of writers who congregated at Garsington, he sniped that, despite potentially warranting friendship, Katherine had 'an ugly impassive mask of a face – cut in wood, with brown hair and brown eyes very far apart; and a sharp and slightly vulgarly-fanciful intellect sitting behind it'.

As was her wont, Virginia had attempted to match his gossipy tone in her response: 'Katherine Mansfield has dogged my steps for three years,' she claimed. Yet such haughtiness was contradicted by her evident keenness to get to know this woman, who had brought out dozens of short stories in magazines as well as a book-length collection.

Through Lytton, the pair arranged to meet at Garsington, where a poker-faced Katherine would sit ramrod straight at the very edge of the sofa, regaling her fellow guests with witty tales. Her talk transported Virginia to worlds so different from her milieu among the London intelligentsia: a far-flung childhood in colonial New Zealand; tours in Scotland with a travelling light opera company; early employment as an entertainer at private parties, offering mimicry, recitation and music.

Nine months later, Virginia had read Katherine's writing, admiring its extraordinary evocation of the sensory world. Although it had been two years since the New Zealander had published any significant new work, Virginia's esteem for these stories had prompted her mission today.

Her walk from her elegant Georgian home took her along the edge of the squash courts on Paradise Road, where balls rifle-cracked against rackets, and next past the public house at the corner – a male refuge of smoke and warm beer. During her uphill climb to the railway station, she would have had the chance to stretch her limbs for the first time in days. Since the delivery of her new printing press earlier that week, she had been happily ensconced in her dining room, setting up the machine. Virginia and her husband Leonard had purchased the hand-operated press in the hope that an involving and physical occupation would alleviate the stresses of his work with the Women's Co-operative Guild. More important still, Leonard believed that the press might ward off the debilitating bouts of depression and mania from which his wife had suffered intermittently from the time of her adolescence. Since the arrival of the machine, Virginia's attention had certainly been absorbed by the task of separating the blocks of type into piles of each letter and font before storing them into their correct compartments – a time-consuming job made more laborious still by her failure to distinguish between the h's and the n's.

The task complete, and her health currently on an even keel, Virginia was ready to venture from this sleepy, outlying suburb of Richmond to London's bohemian quarter of Chelsea. Here, she would visit Katherine – whom she'd first met while emerging from her most recent and protracted mental breakdown. Four years earlier, when Virginia was finishing *The Voyage Out*, she had begun to experience headaches, insomnia and a revulsion to food – all symptoms of an impending crisis. Sure enough, from 1913 to 1915, she had endured a series of deep depressions interspersed with spells of violent hallucination. Up to four live-in nurses treated her with a regimen of enforced bed-rest, overfeeding and a ban on writing fiction or journalism, which were considered dangerously stimulating. During the following months and years of recuperation, Virginia was once more making her creative work central to her life.

As the train trundled eastbound, she left behind leafy Richmond, whose tranquillity Leonard insisted was essential for his wife's continued well-being. Her journey took her from the royal parkland and military hospital of her own locale towards the artists' clubs and colleges of Katherine's home in

Chelsea. Along the way, she passed close to streets that had been devastated by the previous year's Zeppelin raids. Although the ongoing war with Germany had inevitably caused Virginia much anguish – the air raid sirens frequently sending her from her bed to seek shelter down in the cellar – she had not lost a close relative in the bloodshed. Katherine, however, hadn't escaped with such good fortune. Her beloved brother had died in the trenches two years earlier, and none of her friends who'd departed for the front had returned.

On arriving at Katherine's studio flat, Virginia found herself in cramped, damp-ridden quarters that could not have been more different from her own spacious residence of Hogarth House, or, indeed, her secluded country home on the South Downs. Despite the talk that had circulated about Katherine's relationship with the small-time magazine editor and writer John Middleton Murry, this modest space betrayed no sign that she could currently be 'living in sin'. Murry, as he was known, was in fact residing in his own rooms nearby, for he and Katherine had recently parted ways.

If there was hardly sufficient room in Katherine's studio for a couple, there was certainly none for a live-in servant. Virginia may well have found this aspect of Katherine's lifestyle oddly enviable. She had fraught relations with both her parlourmaid, the passionate foundling Lottie Hope, and Nellie Boxall, her affection-starved cook. Katherine would, in fact, soon squeeze a second occupant into this flat – someone whose role in her life was crucial yet unconventional. But Virginia had yet to encounter this companion.

So much here was hidden from view: a mattress stowed in the minstrels' gallery created a secret sleeping area, and a curtain drawn across the studio concealed another bedroom plus a kitchenette where Katherine kept her saucepans, nutmeg grater and coffee mill. The unsightly makeshift furnishings were a perpetual source of frustration for Katherine, who fended for herself without the assistance of a husband. How she longed for a maid, but she could afford only a charwoman. Someone of Katherine's genteel colonial upbringing would never have expected to lug heavy buckets from the coalhole, wash her own dishes or empty her bedpan.

Despite drab surroundings, Katherine had long found innovative ways of entertaining company, on occasion donning a kimono and instructing guests to sit upon floor cushions while she served up tea in bowls. Her conversation could be equally surprising, frequently turning to stories of her youth: expeditions into Maori country; sailing in a cargo ship from New Zealand to Britain; playing the cello for the local factory girls during her stint at a boarding school on London's Harley Street, where she was sent at 15 years old. Such tales must have seemed extraordinary to Virginia, who – though given free rein of her editor father's well-stocked library – received little formal education, and whose childhood holidays were spent in the Cornish fishing town of St Ives, just a day's journey south-west of London by rail.

Katherine had never before shared a bond with a woman she considered her intellectual equal. Despite her early publication successes, the New Zealand banker's daughter felt very much the outsider in literary London – ill-equipped to decipher its unwritten rules. On this spring day in Chelsea in 1917, Virginia steered the conversation to her new printing press, sharing her hopes of starting her own small publishing house. In so openly setting herself up as an editor, she would be overturning outdated Victorian ideals of womanhood. Even George Eliot had felt compelled initially to hide her professional identity, by working anonymously as an editor within the male coterie of the *Westminster Review*. The social changes of the past half century, however, had opened up chances for female writers to work together – but with them came the prospect of new kinds of professional rivalries. The scheme that Virginia planned to suggest to Katherine could offer both women just such opportunities, but it was also rife with risks.

Virginia hoped Katherine might consider submitting her work to the newly formed Hogarth Press. Aside from planning to bring out one short piece of her own and another by Leonard, Virginia had not sought stories from anyone else. She was pinning all her hopes on convincing her new friend to provide the imprint's very first commission.

Katherine's keen acceptance not only established a professional alliance between the two women, it also deepened their personal relationship. Within a few months, Virginia would invite Katherine and Murry (who were back together once more) to dine with her and Leonard at Hogarth House, where they could take a look at the new printing press.

The evening left a strong impression on both women, whose memories have been handed down through correspondence from Katherine to Virginia, and from Virginia to her artist sister, Vanessa, who called by during the evening.

Katherine recalled sitting alone, hearing the sounds of Virginia and Vanessa chatting outside in the garden. The night, thus far, had been free of the sinister gleams of airships and subsequent flashes of shells, which so frequently forced the Woolfs' household to congregate in the basement kitchen – the servants huddled on one camp bed, Virginia on another, and Leonard under the table. During these hours of peace, Katherine breathed in the scents of the coffee and strawberries that the two couples had been enjoying. The men had gone off to examine the handle and cylinder of the printing press, and so, when Vanessa left and Virginia returned inside, the two writers were free to converse undisturbed.

Falling back on one of her longstanding techniques for winning over female friends, Katherine confessed to Virginia some of her seamier stories, but history leaves us to guess at which ones: her marriage to an older bachelor, which lasted just one night but still prevented her from marrying the young and handsome Murry; her unwanted pregnancy that ended in miscarriage; a regrettable liaison in a German boarding house; or the erotic encounters of her youth, more taboo still.

Such talk would have caused Virginia some distress, for her own earliest sexual experience had been intensely traumatic, occurring back in 1889 when she was a very young child. At the family's holiday home in the seaside resort of St Ives, her 18-year-old half-brother had lifted her onto a stone slab in the hallway. Reaching beneath her skirt, ignoring her resistance, his hands had firmly and steadily explored her body, insistently, intimately, touching her. Almost thirty years later Gerald now owned a leading publishing company, and Virginia had felt forced to rely on him to bring out her first novel and only short story to date.

By her mid-thirties, Virginia had long since learnt to hide her vulnerability behind an armour of aloofness and arch asides. And so, her friend's contrasting boldness would lead her to remark that Katherine 'seems to have gone every sort of hog since she was 17, which is interesting'. For all the attraction and repulsion that Virginia simultaneously felt about Katherine's sexual escapades, she couldn't help but take unalloyed pleasure in the unusually insightful literary conversation she also offered.

For her part, Katherine so needed a creative ally that her longing brimmed into gush. 'My God, I love to think of you, Virginia, as my friend', she declared in a letter of that summer of 1917. 'Dont cry me an ardent creature or say, with your head a little on one side, smiling as though you knew some enchanting secret: "Well, Katherine, we shall see"…'

A flurry of visits between the new friends ensued, with Virginia regularly calling on Katherine at her studio in Chelsea, and Katherine repaying the compliment by journeying out to Virginia's Richmond home. The talk between the two women would meander from literature and politics to news of their respective acquaintances. In this way, the pair managed, for a while, to nurture their fledgling friendship. In between visits, Katherine wrote to Virginia, urging her to 'consider how rare is it to find someone with the same passion for writing that you have', and expressing a desire 'to be scrupulously truthful with you'. Had they both maintained this dedication to honesty, perhaps they could have protected themselves from the dual threats of literary rivalry and Garsington gossip. But it would only be a matter of time before their two shields would clash.

The first blow was delivered later that same summer by a group of Virginia's Bloomsbury friends who had not fully welcomed Katherine into their ranks. The name for this loosely defined group harked back to their pre-war Thursday night meetings in the Bloomsbury area of London. The male-dominated crowd would gather at the home that Virginia shared with her siblings. There, over cigarettes, buns, coffee and whisky, they would debate questions of philosophy, religion and art, as well as egg each other on with ever inflated gossip. Virginia enjoyed such banter, treating the wielding of insults like a competitive sport, and sometimes expressing her affection through eye-wateringly cruel teasing.

In early August 1917, Virginia had certainly carped to one friend about Katherine's days as a chorus girl, her overuse of make-up and her tendency to frequent low-class teashops. But the particular incident to which Katherine took umbrage has been passed down to us only through asides in surviving diaries and letters. By piecing them together, however, a picture begins to appear.

Virginia's male friends congregated at Hogarth House, surrounded by the paraphernalia of the Woolfs' publishing venture – inking discs and blocks of wooden typeface. In between mouthfuls of such meagre treats as Virginia's ration book could supply – plain buns, perhaps, filled with sugar plums; cups of weak tea powdered with Nestlé's dried milk – the men divulged the latest gossip. There were so many salacious stories to choose from, but it appears that the Bloomsbury men accused Katherine of conducting a flirtation with the mathematician and philosopher Bertrand Russell, a feminist and philanderer who was by now accusing Katherine of being poisonous and untrustworthy, consumed with envy for other women. Among her old friends, Virginia was known to shed her aloofness and become quite the raconteur, her quick wit frequently causing the rest of the company to collapse in laughter. As the conversation progressed, it would have been in character for her to serve up salacious titbits about Katherine's sexual encounters with travelling musicians, older bachelors and impoverished Poles, and to succumb to snobbery, telling her friends that the New Zealander surrounded herself with unsavoury characters, that she was part of a shadowy underworld.

The men had to head off before nightfall, when searchlights would comb the sky for German airships, and the mean-spirited talk would be replaced by the ghostly wails of sirens. At some point before they took their leave, Virginia mentioned that she and Katherine made unlikely comrades: the 'Chaste & the Unchaste,' she joked.

The gossip inevitably got back to Katherine via Garsington. Some of the crowd that descended on the Elizabethan manor of literary patron Lady Ottoline Morrell were old friends of Virginia's from Bloomsbury days. But others, like Katherine, moved in slightly less privileged circles. Here, all sorts of artists and intellectuals, shirkers and genuine conscientious objectors escaped war-torn London for weekends of whisky and wine, dips in the ornamental pond, parlour games, love affairs and endless conversation.

Windswept guests would roar on motorbikes through Garsington's imposing gates while others arrived more sedately by train, all of them glad to immerse themselves in the peacefulness of the Oxfordshire countryside. The Battle of Passchendaele must have seemed impossibly distant when the kitchen here supplied plentiful provisions of ham, eggs and scones, and the household staff catered to each guest's every whim.

It was probably through Garsington's host herself that Katherine heard of Virginia's rumour-mongering. In the summer of 1917, Katherine returned to Ottoline's home, where she threw herself into the weekend's activities, cultivating a mysterious air in her voluminous cloak, her face partially hidden by a small black fan. Pacing the paths between the topiary by moonlight, she paused now and then to rub between her fingers here a spike of rosemary, there a spear of lavender. She often seemed cold and inscrutable but she came alive in the gardens at Garsington, enchanted by the Chinese lanterns; the still, dark ponds; and the talcum-powder scent of stock flowers – a perfume released only at nightfall.

Katherine wandered around the garden with the six-foot, flame-haired Ottoline, filling a basket with a potpourri of fresh rose petals, sweet geranium and verbena, which they'd scatter on a sheet, ready to dry when the sun rose the next day. Katherine's thoughts sometimes turned to Virginia, who had not joined them on this occasion. 'I do like her tremendously,' Katherine would tell Ottoline, following this visit. 'The strange, trembling, glinting quality of her mind.'

On Katherine's return to London she wrote to Virginia, sharing her recollections of the gardens at Garsington. The description clearly made quite an impact, since Virginia recounted it in a letter to Ottoline on 15 August: 'Katherine Mansfield describes your garden, the rose leaves drying in the sun, the pool, and long conversations between people wandering up and down in the moonlight.' This is the only glimpse we have of Katherine's exchange with Virginia, because Katherine's original letter has never been found. Such an omission is unusual, for Virginia was always fastidious in cataloguing her correspondence – a habit that would stand her in good stead during later years when she had more reason to believe that there might be posthumous interest in her life and work.

However, on the very same day that Virginia's pen had turned to the gardens at Garsington, Katherine also described them in her own missive to Ottoline, suggesting that the location would make an ideal setting for a piece of creative work. Given what would happen next, it seems likely that Katherine's conversation with Virginia had also turned to this idea. In *her* letter to Ottoline, Katherine began by asking herself '*who* is going to write about that flower garden' – a question that appeared perfectly innocuous, but had the potential to ripple beneath the surface of her friendship with Virginia for years to come.

The golden oranges and reds of the zinnias germinated in Katherine's imagination, the snapdragons and sunflowers, the pale pinks of the stocks. 'It might be so wonderful, do you see *how* I mean?' Katherine went on in her letter to Ottoline, describing the approach she might take if she were to write a story inspired by Garsington's lawns and ponds. She would focus on 'people walking in the garden – several *pairs* of people – their conversation their slow pacing – their glances as they pass one another – the pauses as the flowers "come in" as it were.' Her words failed to form into full sentences as her ideas seized her more swiftly than her ink could flow. She likened the composition of such a work to that of music: a 'conversation *set* to flowers'. Knowing that someone ought to write about this symphony of sight and scent, she proclaimed that 'it's full of possibilities', vowing to 'have a fling at it as soon as I have time'.

This idea, it seems, was also blossoming in Virginia's mind. Her health was continuing to improve, and she relished the chance to return to her desk. She could not have asked for a timelier gift than the seed Katherine had planted in her mind. As Virginia wrote, a new kind of rhythm made its way from her pen to the page; a fresh view on the world. She transposed the setting from Garsington to the botanical gardens at Kew, which she could see through the rear windows of Hogarth House.

Once Virginia had finished her draft of *Kew Gardens*, she took steps to deepen her friendship with the woman who'd surely inspired it. Their mutual friend, Lytton Strachey, would be spending a few nights at Asheham, the Woolfs' country home in the South Downs, and Virginia hoped that Katherine might also come to stay. The invitation arrived at just the right moment for Katherine, who was feeling despondent because of the recurrence of rheumatic pain – a symptom that had intermittently flared up over the previous seven years, ever since her sexual liaison with a Polish man in a German boarding house, which had perhaps left her with gonorrhoea.

The lengthy delays to Katherine's rail journey from London on 18 August 1917 could not have helped to improve the state of her body or mind. Those who had known Katherine as a plump child would have been hard-pressed to recognise the gaunt woman Virginia greeted off the train at the county town of Lewes. Virginia's arms were laden with the lily roots and red-leaved plants that she'd bought while she was waiting. This set the tone for the coming days since the fine weather would allow for many pleasurable hours out of doors: strolls along the lane, the air thick with thistledown; the sighting of a caterpillar turning into a chrysalis, aeroplanes as well as butterflies on the wing overhead; the planting of crimson-petalled flowers in the walled garden's overgrown beds. Such pursuits were fitting, since it was during this stay that Virginia, anxious to gauge her reaction, would show Katherine her draft of *Kew Gardens*.

It wouldn't have been hard for Virginia to get Katherine on her own. Leonard had various commitments in London that week and Lytton was dividing his time between Asheham and Charleston, inhabited by Virginia's sister. Confronted with the garden story, on top of her knowledge of Virginia's backbiting talk, Katherine's behaviour was guarded.

She could be forgiven for feeling aggrieved. She was already suffering bodily pain, and now her friend had taken up her story plans almost wholesale: pairs of people talking in a flower garden, slowly pacing, glancing at each other as they passed – the conversation just as musical as she had envisaged it. It would be only natural for her to have envied Virginia her creative industry since the lethargy, pain and ill temper brought on by Katherine's recurrent rheumatism frequently forced her from her desk. At some point, however, her garden idea did eventually migrate from notebook jottings to a poem entitled 'Night-Scented Stock'. Its lines, just like Virginia's story, featured people talking in a flower garden, pacing its length, casting sidelong glances. But it would not find a publisher. After a promising start to her career, Swift & Co., which had brought out her first collection, had gone bankrupt. Most of the magazines that had run her early work had since folded, and her first champion, the editor of the *New Age*, had fallen out with her when she'd dared to sell her stories elsewhere.

Virginia's ownership of the Hogarth Press freed her of such publication concerns. Aware of this difference in their situations, and now back at home in London, Katherine mulled over both the short story and the gossip. She had quite a tendency to go on the defensive when she felt under attack, becoming spiteful when afflicted by jealousy. On this occasion, she had an arsenal of weapons at her disposal if she chose to use them. She could pretend to feel unaffected by the rumours spread by her friend or expose this fellow writer as a filcher of ideas. She could even demand the return of her story commissioned by Virginia for the Hogarth Press – a radical redraft of a much longer work begun in 1915.

How different life had been back then, when she'd written the first draft of this story about colonial family life in the years preceding the Great War. Her younger brother, Leslie Heron Beauchamp, had not yet left for the front and Katherine, too, had seemed invincible, her work almost guaranteed publication. Less than a year later, Leslie's death had made her keener still to 'make our undiscovered country leap into the eyes of the old world'.

By Katherine's return from Virginia's country home in late August 1917, she'd decided that it would be far more important to her future as a writer to maintain their friendship than become distracted by literary possessiveness or embroiled in Garsington affairs.

Sitting down to write Virginia a letter, Katherine's eyes came to rest on the gladioli in her studio, which she considered 'very proud & defiant, like indian braves' – qualities that could just as easily have described the behaviour of Katherine herself. Pausing for just one moment to admire what she would call the 'green gage light on the tree outside', she reminded her friend of their literary ties. But she couldn't help wryly alluding to the similarities in their work, remarking that it was curious they 'should both quite apart from each other, be after so very nearly the same thing. We are you know; there's no denying it.'

In this letter, Katherine found it in herself to be magnanimous indeed – a strategy that would prove tough to maintain – praising *Kew Gardens* and noting her particular fascination with the 'still, quivering, changing light over it all and a sense of those couples dissolving in the bright air'.

Thinking of the gossip that had got back to her, she let her pen race ahead, unhampered by punctuation: 'But dont let THEM ever persuade you that I spend any of my precious time swapping hats or committing adultery – I'm far too arrogant & proud.'

When Virginia received this impassioned plea, she wrote up her version of events in a letter – justifying her part in the gossip. But she hesitated before posting these words, wondering whether such a strategy could do more harm than good. And she wasn't quite sure what to make of Katherine's proud denial. After all, her impetuous friend had already confided her history of sexual affairs, and, given that she was still legally married to someone else, even her relationship with Murry officially counted as adulterous. But, mostly, Virginia felt keenly aware of all that she stood to lose. She would shield their friendship from the Bloomsbury men in future. Surely it was strong enough to withstand this difficulty. And so, Virginia tore up her note and penned an invitation instead, asking Katherine to come over to dinner when, as she would confide in her diary, she knew that, 'many delicate things fall to be discussed'. In the meantime, she devoted her afternoons to setting the type for the first page of *Prelude*, Katherine's story for the Hogarth Press, the idea that its author might hold a grudge against her for writing the flowerbed story hardly likely to have crossed her mind.

By the time the date of the meal came around, the path was scattered with acorns and there was sufficient bite in the air to warrant a fire in the grate. But although the year had now reached October, the leaves had not yet yellowed or fallen, and Virginia clung to the hope that her fragile friendship with Katherine might also be graced with extension.

When the host and her guest sat down together in the panelled dining room, the tension was surely palpable. As well as the issue of the gossip, Katherine felt anxious about Virginia's opinion of *Prelude*. In such situations, Katherine tended to protect herself with a show of impassivity.

The Woolfs were known among friends for the paltry refreshments they served to guests, but the success of the evening wouldn't be so much reliant on the quality of the meal as on the women's capacity to chew the fat. With the fire spitting from the range, Virginia expressed her genuine admiration for the sensory richness of *Prelude*, which she considered to have 'the living power, the detached existence of a work of art'. Katherine was especially appreciative of Virginia's praise, since the story had become for her a way to resurrect her brother and their pre-war idyll. The change of title from its original, 'The Aloe', to *Prelude*, as suggested by Murry, would subtly remind readers that the world of the story would soon change irrevocably, for war lurked on the horizon, just out of sight. Astounded by the depth and sincerity of Virginia's words, Katherine couldn't help but feel gratified, later telling a friend that she imagined these accolades being served up to her in a golden bowl.

As the evening unwound, both women began to relax, their conversation turning to their shared opinions on the ponderousness of the work of Henry James, who had recently died at the age of 72. And, as the hours passed, Virginia eventually acknowledged that she had played a part in the unkind gossip. But she was quick to claim that it had all been wildly exaggerated, that she absolutely, categorically, did not say *quite* what she was alleged to have said: something about the 'Chaste & the Unchaste'.

According to Virginia's diary entry, at the end of the evening a woman showed up to accompany Katherine back home. This was Ida Constance Baker – the friend who had moved into the cramped Church Street studio at around the time that Virginia had called in to commission a story. Katherine had first met Ida, a fellow daughter of Empire (in her case Burma and later Rhodesia, as they were then called), back when they were both adolescent students at Queen's College boarding school, and they had grown unhealthily dependent on each other over the years. Unlike the self-absorbed Murry, Ida couldn't bear the thought of Katherine alone in her Chelsea studio, racked with pain and afflicted by night terrors during the pitch-dark hours. But when Ida moved in, Katherine, who often found her an infuriating presence, forbade her from returning before nine o'clock in the evening. Should she be around when Katherine was receiving a guest, Ida had to keep herself concealed by lying in her makeshift bed up in the minstrels' gallery, still and silent. Her presence didn't always go undetected, however. The author, Aldous Huxley, for instance, was rather taken aback when, halfway through a visit, he heard someone coughing from behind the curtained-off mezzanine.

On this autumn evening in 1917, Virginia, falling back on her habitual snobbery, treated the cheery Ida with condescension, writing her off as lower class and coarse. The privileged author noted nothing of Ida's appearance beyond the sallowness of her complexion, nothing of her life other than her war work at a munitions factory, and did not give her another thought.

Virginia would soon tell Ottoline that the falling-out was 'formally buried'. Unbeknown to her, however, Katherine had not quite laid it to rest. Over a month after their supposed rapprochement, in mid-November 1917, Katherine wrote to one of Ottoline's guests, saying: 'I am sorry the Wolves are at Garsington. There will be a rare bone dragged into the light before they are gone –'. Yet, deep down, Katherine knew that she could be just as indiscreet as Virginia, that, as fiction writers, they were both natural gossips of sorts – trading in stories passed back and forth. For all their hostility and half-truths, the pair did manage to negotiate an uneasy truce.

During the rain-sodden summer of the following year of 1918, Virginia devoted her mornings to completing her second novel, *Night and Day*, and her afternoons to working on the publication of Katherine's *Prelude*. While hailstones the size of pigeon eggs hammered against the windowpanes, Virginia laboriously set the type for her friend's lengthy story, placing each and every letter on a composing stick, face up and upside down, then tightly packing each line with blocks of spacing.

Once all 68 pages were produced, the couple was ready to bind them within covers. But herein lay a potential pitfall. Katherine was a friend of the Scottish artist John Duncan Fergusson, who had designed a linocut for the cover. It featured a simple outline of a woman's head surrounded by aloe flowers, such as those in *Prelude*, which bloom just once every hundred years. Virginia took an instant and intense dislike to the design, and, although she included it on the first few copies, she couldn't help but tell Katherine that she did not rate it. Her preference, she explained, would be to feature only the story's title and the author's name on Persian blue covers.

Fortunately for Virginia, Katherine was gracious indeed, backing down straight away and bowing to her friend and publisher's apparent better judgment. She did let herself vent about it to Murry, though, exclaiming: 'To Hell with other people's presses!'.

The matter of the design apparently settled without rancour, Virginia holed herself away for days on end, turning down tempting invitations from the likes of Ottoline. Behind the closed doors of Hogarth House, Virginia filled her days with folding, stapling and gluing sheet upon sheet of her friend's words, binding them within the plain blue covers that she considered so stylish. Pleased with the professional appearance of their work – despite misnaming the title on several pages – the couple then readied themselves to parcel up each of the 300 books.

The more immersed Virginia had become in typesetting the story, the more sisterly she'd felt towards its author. Virginia and Leonard harboured high hopes for this book, which had cost them such time and effort to produce. Buoyed up by their enthusiasm for the work, they committed to a print run of about 300 copies – at least double the amount of their first publication, which had contained two of their own stories. And yet, in the run-up to publication, they'd managed to secure only six or seven orders. When Virginia admitted this, Katherine had felt understandably mortified. 'I shall have to come back & persuade you & L. to let me sell it on a barrow', she wrote in response, 'customers to bring their own wrappings'.

When the story finally winged its way into the world in July 1918 – three years after Katherine began writing it and fifteen months since Virginia first commissioned it – both women eagerly anticipated its reception. The Woolfs sent copies for review to several magazines and newspapers, and then waited to see what the critics would make of it – a wait that was largely in vain. Only two of the publications considered it worthy of review, and even they pronounced it unremarkable.

Virginia continued to champion Katherine's story, undeterred by the scarcity of critical attention and its lack of popularity among some of her friends. She defended *Prelude* when one of the original Bloomsbury-clique gossips sneered that it 'Doesn't set the Thames on fire', and assured another that 'Katherine is the very best of women writers – always of course passing over one fine but very modest example.' Buried in Virginia's droll aside was the knowledge that shared artistic aspirations could easily descend into dangerous envy. And yet, for now, Virginia and Katherine had managed to rise above their feelings of envy to support each other's literary careers. At their best, both women recognised that when 'afflicted with jealousy', as Virginia would put it, 'the only thing is to confess it'. This lesson allowed these two ambitious women to benefit from their creative competition – a process that proved as valuable to their shared art as that experienced by better-mythologised male writing duos. But history has found it far more difficult to weave Katherine and Virginia's rivalry into the fabric of their relationship, too often mispresenting these literary friends as merely bitter foes.

~

CHAPTER 11

CAT AND MOUSE

Despite working so closely with Katherine Mansfield to bring *Prelude* to press, Virginia Woolf still found her fellow writer fascinatingly 'marmoreal'. But she felt that the two had come to 'an oddly complete understanding' based on their shared love of literature. At the beginning of 1918, back when Virginia was embarking on typesetting the first pages of Katherine's story, its author had headed off to the south of France. This trip, taken on medical recommendation, could not have appeared anything more than a minor interruption in the progression of their relationship. Since Katherine behaved as if she were simply keen to catch some winter sun, Virginia could hardly be blamed for failing to appreciate the poor state of her friend's health and well-being.

But, in fact, Katherine felt lonely and frightened. The War Office had forbidden her on-off partner John Middleton Murry from accompanying her to the Côte d'Azur on account of his new post as Chief Censor, and Katherine's live-in friend Ida

Constance Baker had failed to get permission to leave her job as a tool setter at a West London aeroplane factory.

On 7 January 1918, Murry and Ida waved off Katherine as she staggered onto the boat train alone. She was suffering from a spell of pleurisy in addition to the rheumatism that intermittently plagued her, and the three-day-long journey weakened her further still. Neither food nor hot drinks were served on board the French locomotives, and Katherine had to sit for hours on end beside a broken window, which let icy air into the carriage, snowflakes soon covering the large fur muff that Ida had insisted she must wear.

The test of Katherine's endurance didn't end there. On arrival in war-weary Bandol, she found a destroyer anchored in the harbour, the patisserie closed down, the shops bare of tobacco and short on meat. The Hôtel Beau Rivage, where Katherine had booked a room, stood almost empty, a cold wind blowing through its halls. It was here, under these conditions, that Katherine would write the ironically titled 'Bliss' – a story that would later cause Virginia much distress.

By the time Katherine began to work on this piece, however, she was no longer alone. Ida, concerned by Katherine's despairing letters, had wept before a government official, who relented and belatedly granted her request for leave.

'What *have* you come for?' Katherine asked incredulously, when the exhausted woman showed up beneath the mimosa trees that lined the courtyard of the hotel.

What a welcome for poor Ida, whose journey had hardly been less gruelling than Katherine's own. But both women knew deep down that she would be grudgingly allowed to stay. Katherine planned to write intensively, and, for this, she was reliant on Ida's ministrations.

Ever since their boarding school days, Ida had willingly taken on Katherine's chores, thus freeing up the writer to pursue her creative endeavours. Falling back into their well-established routine, Katherine soon enjoyed a sustained '*state of work*', as she put it in a letter to Murry: 'dead quiet and spinning away'. While working on 'Bliss', she tended to rest in bed throughout the morning, lunch with Ida, write industriously each afternoon, and then take supper with fellow guests in the hotel's salon. Her reliance on her old friend engendered in Katherine a swollen sense of hatred. When a sugar-starved Ida dared to delight in Bandol's plentiful supply of bananas and Medjool dates, for instance, Katherine could not disguise the force of her revulsion. But, egged on by Murry, who recommended she treat Ida as an 'abject slave', Katherine stomached her loathing – which was always combined with a contrarian kind of love. Claiming to 'use her as a walking stick', Katherine produced reams of writing, leaving her companion to build the fire in the grate, buy supplies from the local shops and liaise with the doctor.

Katherine may have been making great progress with her writing during the period when Virginia was delivering *Prelude* into the world, but she was still confined to the literary wilderness. As far as either woman knew, the Hogarth Press could well prove little more than an enthusiastically pursued hobby, and, in any case, there was no guarantee that the couple would seek any more of Katherine's work. She wrote in Bandol without any guarantee of publication, while Virginia, at home in Richmond, could bring out her stories through her household printing press.

Anxious for Katherine's literary future, not to mention his own, Murry hatched a plan to set up a rival press. Before Katherine had completed the enjoyable toil of drafting 'Bliss', Murry was already negotiating with his brother about the joint purchase of a handpress, imagining the sensation of the sheets of paper, bright and clean between his palms. Just over a week after first mentioning the idea to Katherine, Murry wrote again, insisting that his ambition to establish their own publishing house was not just a passing phase. This time he tried to convince her of its good sense by sending financial projections.

He had published a thinly disguised autobiographical novel with Constable & Co. two years earlier, which had been a critical and commercial failure, resulting in a net loss. He had come round to the idea that he could not hope to profit from publishing in the conventional manner. The same, he suggested, might well be true of Katherine. By following the subscription method the Woolfs had instituted – whereby customers could pay in regular instalments to receive each title the Hogarth Press brought out – he and Katherine could anticipate an annual profit of £300. She didn't take much persuading. This was hardly a sum to sniff at, given that she managed largely on an allowance from her father of just over £150 per year – sufficient to live off but only with frugality. 'It's the soberest sense I'm talking,' Murry insisted. 'I haven't got a bee in my bonnet or a maggot in my brain. It's a chance of real salvation.' They would surely have no problem producing beautiful books, he assured Katherine. 'Think of that *tripe* of the Woolves!'

While Katherine was beginning to share in Murry's dreams of setting up a press, her chest was causing her increasing pain, and she yearned for his company. Such privations would cause her to feel increasingly envious of the Woolfs. It was no wonder that Virginia could write so freely, Katherine later exclaimed in a letter to her partner: 'her roof over her – her own possessions round her – and her man somewhere within call'. Over the other side of the English Channel, Virginia was indeed enjoying a much-needed period of well-being, while, in France, Katherine's health was about to take a turn for the worse.

Insisting that a spot of exercise would do her no harm, Katherine tramped with Ida through feathery fronds of undergrowth, leading the way through the slate-blue olive groves that lined the heat-soaked hillsides. Nestled among banks of blue violets, she spotted an empty house, its stones a yellowish shade of pink, white hyacinths growing in between the cracks of its veranda. She let herself imagine making a home here with

Murry, just as Virginia and Leonard had their creative haven at Asheham. But the impossibility of her dream soon crashed over her, and, before long, Katherine felt too weak to continue the steep climb. Despite taking a shortcut back, she returned to the hotel physically exhausted and emotionally drained.

On waking the next morning, she got up to open the shutters, admiring the plumpness of the rising sun. Her situation brought to mind a line from Shakespeare, which she felt compelled to recite aloud: 'Lo! here the gentle lark, weary of rest'.

For lack of a sofa or armchair, she bounded back onto her bed. But the energetic leap brought on a coughing fit. Her saliva tasted strange, and, as the coughs continued to rack through her thin frame, she spat into a handkerchief. When she looked down, she saw that the cotton was stained with blood.

Although it would be a few months before her tuberculosis was officially diagnosed, the possible seriousness of her condition had already struck home. She was overcome with anxiety that she might die, leaving just snippets of work – her best as yet unwritten.

She already regarded 'Bliss' as representing a new direction, and she longed for the chance to write more in this vein. Katherine was not the only one to hold this story in high regard. For five years she had failed to secure significant publication by anyone other than Virginia, but now 'Bliss' was picked up by *The English Review*, a prestigious magazine, which offered to run it in its August 1918 edition, alongside a poem by William Butler Yeats.

Its readers would be treated to the story of naïve, 30-year-old Bertha Young and her husband, who 'got on together splendidly and were really good pals'. The passionless yet jovial couple can afford an 'absolutely satisfactory house and garden', entertaining 'modern, thrilling friends' and employing a new cook who 'made the most superb omelettes'. The authorial irony is tinged with longing for elements of such a life – sentimentally so, as Virginia would soon have it.

The story is set on the day of a dinner party thrown by the Youngs, to which they have invited a guest named Pearl Fulton. Bertha has 'fallen in love' with this striking and enigmatic character, just 'as she always did fall in love with beautiful women who had something strange about them'. Pearl's arrival fans within Bertha a 'fire of bliss'. Although she herself does not fully comprehend her own erotic stirrings, she senses that they are silently shared by her guest. In the dark of the garden, beneath the blossoming boughs of the pear tree, Bertha feels in perfect communion with Pearl, both of them containing 'all this blissful treasure that burned in their bosoms'.

This moment of silent desire is interrupted by the voice of Bertha's husband – a scene curiously similar to one that Virginia would include in *Mrs Dalloway* several years later. In Katherine's story, when Bertha joins her husband back inside, the feelings she has experienced for Pearl begin to transfer towards him. 'For the first time in her life,' the reader learns, 'Bertha Young desired her husband'. But, no sooner does she long for the dark warmth of her marital bed than she spies him following Pearl into the hallway. Thinking himself unobserved, he holds their guest in his arms, whispering plans for an assignation the following day.

The August 1918 issue of *The English Review* containing this new story would come out at around the same time as a scheduled visit from Katherine to the Woolfs' country home. Now that she had returned to Britain for the warmer months, Virginia and Leonard had invited her and Murry to come to stay at Asheham. There were multiple reasons for celebration. Not only had the Hogarth Press published *Prelude*, but Katherine's divorce from her short-lived first marriage had finally come through, allowing her and Murry to wed. Virginia, whose partnership with Leonard formed the bedrock of her existence, knew that Katherine made out that 'marriage is of no more importance than engaging a charwoman'. But she put Katherine's nonchalance down to 'the obligation she is under to say absurd things'.

Here, on the South Downs, Virginia envisaged the two going off for walks along the windswept cliffs, inhaling the salty air, and invigorating their minds with free-roaming conversation. During this time together, Virginia had good reason to assume that she would, as usual, 'get down to what is true rock' in her friend.

A few days ahead of their guests, the Woolfs had travelled by rail from suburban Richmond – finding it almost miraculous that their various connections all left and arrived on time. The sharing of tea and sandwiches in the train carriage created the feeling of a family outing, the motley crew consisting of a Jewish businessman, who took charge; an injured soldier, whose kneecap and foot arch had been fashioned of nickel; and a gaggle of children with their mother, who steadied her nerves with sips of whisky.

On arrival, and with much assistance from their two servants, Lottie Hope and Nellie Boxall, Leonard and Virginia set about opening up Asheham for their guests. They aired the rooms, unlocking the latticed windows to let in the summer breeze and rid the place of the small frogs and black beetles that had found their way in from the neighbouring field. On the table, Virginia set a vase of carnations that she'd brought with her from a recent trip to Garsington Manor, their petals still pleasingly bright, and Leonard harvested beans from the overgrown garden, the smoke from the nearby farm settling in a haze on the meadows beyond.

But the warm spell failed to hold, succeeded by mornings of black skies and torrential rain. This downpour augured ill for the much-anticipated visit, and Virginia predicted that the Murrys might not manage the tortuous excursion by train. Her fears proved well founded. As Katherine explained to her would-be host, she had been beset by a 'beastly attack' of rheumatism. 'The sofa leg has got me & I cant move from it,' she wrote in her short, apologetic letter. 'My right wing is playing up, too,' she added, referring to her lung, 'so that altogether the machine is a thoroughly unsound machine and wont stand a journey.'

On this occasion, Virginia did not stew on possible unvoiced reasons for the last-minute cancellation. She was well placed to sympathise with the Murrys' predicament since she knew at first hand the privations of ill health. When Katherine played down her ailments by exclaiming, 'Its the devil of a blow – but there you are!', and sent them up by signing off 'Yours funereally', she did not fool Virginia. Recognising the falsity of the cheer and darkness of the comedy, Virginia guessed that her friend 'may be rather hopelessly ill'. But she naturally believed Katherine's claim to feel 'horribly disappointed' that the pair couldn't walk together by the sea 'with sudden immense waves of conversation scattering us, or flinging us together'.

On the same day that Katherine wrote this message to Virginia to call off her visit, however, she also penned a note to their mutual friend, the literary hostess, Ottoline Morrell. And, here, she put a rather different slant on her decision. 'We are supposed to have fought our way over to Asheham today – hung with our own meat and butter,' she complained, 'but I couldn't face it.' Virginia's request that the Murrys brought along their own provisions must have seemed stingy indeed to Katherine, who coveted the unattainable comfort enjoyed by her friend. Katherine was currently staying in Murry's rented bedsit in Chelsea, and Ida, who had returned to work at the aeroplane factory, was living in one of its hostels. Katherine positively relished the seediness of Murry's building and its inhabitants, enjoying the everyday pleasures of boiling her own egg or running her own bath. But it was so much easier for Virginia to keep producing high-quality creative work, having a maid and cook on hand.

Virginia had no inkling of Katherine's growing resentment, and she would have felt aghast had she known of her friend's peevish complaint. As Virginia would admit to one of her house guests, her weekly pat of rationed butter 'merely greases the top of one's toast at breakfast, and leaves one to dry bread at tea'.

True, Virginia's inheritance yielded about four times Katherine's allowance. But the Woolfs' annual expenditure in 1918 came to double Virginia's income, and, like Murry, Leonard was not of moneyed stock. The couple kept careful accounts to ensure that they could afford to remain warm, fed and watered. Especially during the threadbare war years, they laboured to maintain their enviable way of life, which Leonard considered necessary for Virginia's health. Plus, they had to keep a contingency fund for her costly and unpredictable medical expenses. Unlike Katherine, who hardly received a penny from Murry despite his well-paid job at the War Office, Virginia had insisted on a joint budgeting system with Leonard, pooling most of their income for shared costs and keeping some aside for individual treats. The Woolfs worked hard to earn their required additional £400–500 per year, toiling at the handpress and each aiming to write 1250 words per day – an ambitious and unremitting output. As with Katherine and Murry, much of their time and intellectual energy went into journalism, which, in the early decades of their marriage, brought in far more money than their books.

In August 1918, it did not occur to Virginia that Katherine might have reasons other than ill health for choosing to cancel her visit. Deprived of literary debate and lively company, Virginia indulged instead in a quiet weekend, foraging for mushrooms; spotting the first ripe blackberry of the season; and enjoying the sight of a hare loping through the long grass. The tranquillity was interrupted only by a Silver Queen from the nearby airship station, which floated in the blue skies above.

But an intrusion a few days later would truly unsettle Virginia. As she would recount in her diary and letters during the days, weeks, months and even years to come, it was Katherine, towards whom she had been feeling so fond, who created the source of her disquiet.

The return of her servants, Nellie and Lottie, from the nearby town seemed at first a cause for celebration, since they carried with them a stack of political books for Leonard and a copy of *The English Review* for Virginia. After days hidden away in her secluded home, with little more to note than the price of eggs or the squashing of a caterpillar, the prospect of a new work by her friend offered Virginia a diversion. She wasted no time in settling down, opening the teal covers of the magazine in which she would find 'Bliss', Katherine's story of female desire and betrayal.

As Virginia began to read, her friend's words gradually infected the peacefulness of this summer's evening. The deeper she immersed herself in these pages, the more violently she reacted, Katherine's writing working on her on a deeply intimate level. Virginia recoiled from this fictional world. She could not judge 'Bliss' purely on its literary merit because Katherine herself kept springing into Virginia's mind. This story, she felt, unmasked its author's 'callousness & hardness as a human being'.

When Virginia reached the final line, she threw down her copy of *The English Review*. 'She's done for!' she exclaimed out loud. The mind of such a writer, Virginia would conclude in her diary the next day, 'is a very thin soil, laid an inch or two deep upon very barren rock'.

In the moment, Virginia felt compelled to rinse her own mind by soaking herself in the words of a very different type of author. She rushed to the bookcase, scouring the spines of her books, which were rotting in the damp. First she searched for one of the plays of William Shakespeare, next a novel by Joseph Conrad, even her own book *The Voyage Out*. But her gaze ended up alighting on her copy of Lord Byron's *Don Juan*. Given the infamously erotic nature of the poem, this choice of reading material could hardly be more ironic. But it did the trick, and she soon found herself musing on the surprising ease with which she could imagine the effect that the Lothario Byron must have had on women.

Virginia had yet to acknowledge what she would come to call her 'Sapphic' desires, but 'Bliss' had clearly touched a raw nerve, vivifying something that she could not yet name. It was hardly surprising that she should have taken the story personally, since the character of Pearl Fulton shared some of her own most prominent qualities.

Back when Katherine had first shared a draft of the story with Murry, she'd admitted to basing some of the characters on people they both knew, warning him that he would recognise them as 'fish out of the Garsington pond'. She had insisted, however, perhaps protesting too much, that Pearl Fulton was her 'own invention'. And yet Pearl and Virginia were strikingly similar, sharing the quality of icy aloofness. Like Pearl, Virginia was one of those pale, slender, 'beautiful women who had something strange about them', capable 'up to a certain point' of rare and wonderful candour, though 'the certain point was there, and beyond that she would not go'. Even Pearl's way of smiling and holding her head 'a little on one side' is reminiscent of Katherine's earlier depiction of Virginia in one of her letters to her friend: 'your head a little on one side, smiling as though you knew some enchanting secret'.

Virginia would remark in a note to her sister that she felt 'a little disturbed' by Katherine's story. Just like Pearl, though, Virginia could not bring herself to open up further. 'Its –' she wrote, before clamming up, 'well I wont say'.

These kinds of silences had never deceived Katherine. Reading between the lines of Virginia's appearance and behaviour, the younger writer had revealed to Ottoline in 1917 that she put Virginia's fragility down to her being 'one of those Dostoievsky women whose "innocence" has been hurt'. Such an insight was astute. Not only had the very young Virginia endured the molestations of her half-brother, Gerald, she had later also been abused by her other half-brother, George. It would take Virginia until 1921 to admit this to fellow members of the Bloomsbury Memoir Club. As Virginia would explain to her memoirist friends, the death of her mother had precipitated her first mental breakdown. During this time, when she was 13 and George was 27, he had taken advantage of her grief-stricken vulnerability. A period of almost a decade was tainted for her by his habitual tapping on her door in the dead of night. He would then fling himself onto her bed, 'cuddling and kissing and otherwise embracing' her.

No wonder, then, that the pleasures of the Woolfs' marriage appear to have been more gentle than rambunctious. As Virginia confided in her diary, their deep tenderness found expression in such private everyday rituals as 'sitting on the green smoking, taking the letters out of the box' or 'making an ice, opening a letter, sitting down after dinner, side by side, & saying, "Are you in your stall, brother?"'. Not so very long into their marriage, they stopped sharing a bed, but their unwavering love for each other found expression in their pet names ('Mandril' for Virginia and 'Mongoose' for Leonard); intimate games (alone, they'd talk of indulging in something they called 'airing the marmots'); and, during uninterrupted spells, they enjoyed the 'space & quiet thats rather favourable to private fun'.

Some in their circle wrote off Virginia as frigid, her own sister telling the newly wed Leonard that her sibling 'never had understood or sympathised with sexual passion in men', and Virginia's brother-in-law maliciously claiming in 1919 that her husband 'fucks her once a week' but 'It gives her very little pleasure.' Katherine, however, had never turned her cruel tongue to criticising the Woolfs' marital relations. And so, it must have felt appallingly exposing for Virginia to read her friend's fictional depiction of a couple whose private life resembled that which she shared with Leonard. Like Bertha, Virginia had once told her husband that she loved him deeply but that she did not desire him, and, like her, she had understood that he felt differently.

Despite the erotic adventures of Katherine's youth, she was better placed to empathise than Virginia could have realised. Following her daring early encounters, she had chosen in Murry a man who was sexually naïve. Leading a rather less liberated private life than the gossips at Garsington and Bloomsbury had assumed, Katherine compared her marital interactions to the joshing of two young boys. Such a characterisation fails to convey the pain she must have felt at Murry's aversion to touching her for fear of tubercular contagion. In his memoirs, which he would publish in 1935, Murry claimed that their intimate relations had always been inadequate, admitting that throughout their long partnership, he never truly 'made love to her'.

During her unwed years with Murry Katherine had longed to be married, for all her disdain for bourgeois domesticity. Knowing of his revulsion at the idea of same-sex relationships, she had hidden from him the experiences she'd previously enjoyed with women – more intimate than any she ever shared with men. Her infatuation with Maata Mahupuku, a Maori princess, was more than simply a schoolgirl crush, and Katherine had continued to explore this side of her sexuality.

Back in 1907, when she was 19 and reluctantly living once more in New Zealand, she'd befriended the 27-year-old artist, Edith Bendall, for whom she'd confessed in her journal to feeling 'more powerfully all those so termed sexual impulses with her than I have with any men'. She'd invited Edith to join her for a sojourn at a seaside bungalow on the far side of Wellington Harbour in Day's Bay, away from her family's prying eyes. Here, as Katherine continued to record in her journal, she lay with her head on Edith's breast, 'clinging to her hands, her face against mine', feeling like a 'child, woman, and more than half man'.

But of all Katherine's formative relations with women, it was her ties with Ida that would prove the most complex and enduring. During their youth, the pair had caused such consternation that, in the summer of 1909, Katherine's mother had separated them to prevent the development of what she regarded as their unwise friendship. Years later, Katherine's first husband had even cited a supposed lesbian affair with Ida as his reason for finally seeking a divorce. Poor Ida Constance Baker claimed to have no idea what was meant by a lesbian affair, but she had proven a constant friend indeed. If Katherine did harbour any secret sexual longing for the woman whose friendship would become for her 'every bit as sacred and eternal as marriage', it was masked by the intensity of her feelings of revulsion at her dependence on this devoted companion.

The two authors ganged up against Ida, with Virginia following Katherine's example by referring to her as 'the Monster' and excluding her from their conversations. Half a century later, Ida wrote up a detailed account of what she remembered as her only visit to Virginia's home. The recollection in Ida's memoir differed significantly from Virginia's mention of her in her autumn 1917 diary entry. Here, Virginia wrote of Ida fetching Katherine. But Ida described a much fuller visit.

She recalled waiting for Virginia in the Woolfs' sitting room, Katherine whispering that their host was a famed beauty. Their attention was diverted by a stray handkerchief, which they spotted stuffed into the edge of the armchair's seat. Katherine, who was fastidiously tidy, remarked with some amusement that 'If Virginia was carrying a jelly to the supper table and had dropped half of it, I can see her picking it up and dreamily putting it back on the dish as she went on into the room'.

When Virginia eventually made an appearance, Ida found her as enchanting as she'd been led to expect. This tall, slender woman, her face long and fine-featured 'as in a nineteenth-century portrait', greeted both guests but then immediately swept Katherine off to the study, where they could talk undisturbed.

Katherine's embittered reliance on Ida continued to increase even once the Murrys experienced a dramatic improvement in their fortunes. After the War Office awarded Murry a pay

rise, the couple took out a lease on a spacious villa in leafy
Hampstead and employed two maids and a cook. Deep down,
Katherine knew that she could not survive without Ida, and so
she persuaded her reluctant companion to give up her much-
loved job at the factory and leave her dear friends at the hostel
to join the new household. Feeling disempowered by illness,
Katherine admitted that she would find it difficult to share her
home with Ida, regarding it as her entire world and wanting to
make it *'mine beyond words* – to express myself all I can in the
small circle remaining'. For her part, Ida felt utterly unequipped
for her paid role as housekeeper. She knew nothing of cooking,
cleaning, shopping or management of domestic staff. Despite
her reservations, however, she never seriously considered
denying Katherine her desire. And so, by autumn of 1918,
Katherine, Murry and Ida established their unconventional
living arrangement at 2 Portland Villas, the house boasting views
across Hampstead Heath to the city spread out below.

Virginia could not keep herself away from Katherine's new
residence, despite her continuing disgust whenever she thought
of 'Bliss'. As for Katherine, now that her domestic set-up rivalled
Virginia's own, she warmly greeted her friend's offer to make the
long trip across London – a far greater distance than that from
Richmond to the old studio in Chelsea. But Katherine was not
motivated simply by a desire to show off. Virginia's letter had
found Katherine bedridden, although she explained in her reply
that she tried to behave as if she 'were there for pleasure & not
from necessity'. Since the current highlights of her days involved
listening to the wind whistle up the chimney, the roar of the
fire and the rustle of the beech leaves tied to her bedpost, she
especially welcomed the chance to talk over 'a power of things'.

When Virginia paid her first visit, Katherine was lying on
the sofa, a glass of milk and a medicine bottle beside her. At
the sound of her friend's voice, Katherine drew herself up, her
movements like those of some suffering animal. But over the

coming hours, the literary conversation distracted her from the worst of her pain. And by 11 November 1918, when the armistice was forged across the Channel, the two authors had already brokered their own kind of peace.

It was a fragile sort of harmony, though, requiring continuing work on both sides, and, within only a month, it would be put to the test. On 10 December, Virginia sensed a tense atmosphere within the Murrys' grey-painted drawing room. Murry had not gone to the office, and he sat with the two women, brooding and silent.

Virginia tried to inject some cheer by rustling up stories as bright as the greens and oranges of the curtains. She put his stiff attitude down to shyness, perhaps assuming that the tempestuous nature of the Murrys' marriage contributed to the ominous mood.

Murry finally admitted that he had a confession to make, directing his words at Virginia. He then went on to explain that he had bought his own hand-operated press, which he'd installed in the basement. Making out that it was really his brother's project, he talked about producing beautiful volumes inspired by the Arts and Crafts movement. Murry told her that they were intending to bring out some of his own poetry with Heron Press, which they had named after Katherine's late brother, Leslie Heron Beauchamp. But he was quick to reassure Virginia that she and Leonard might still do as they pleased with a long poem of his that he had recently submitted. Virginia had already agreed to publish it, despite secretly finding his work laborious and crass.

Virginia took Murry's revelation in her stride. Everyone seemed to be setting up presses these days, and she prided herself on having been one of the first. She was not convinced that Murry and his brother had the skills required to produce artful printing, but, by all means, let them try.

For all her mixed feelings about Katherine's work, Virginia was coming round to the idea that it was absurd to be afflicted by jealousy. Literary competitors were entirely different from romantic rivals, she told herself, the two kinds of relationships having nonetheless become entwined in her mind. In the realms of art, she decided, 'there's room for everyone, unlike love' – a thought to which she would keep returning as her feelings for Katherine grew ever stronger and more complex.

While Katherine had put aside her lesbian desires by this stage, Virginia had yet to embrace this aspect of herself. This, then, was a space in time when both women were repressing the element of their identities that would prove especially fascinating to later biographers. Virginia's subsequent friendship with the popular novelist Vita Sackville-West – which included a short period of sexual intimacy – has become integral to the mythology that has grown up around her. This has overshadowed Virginia's more physically inhibited relations with Katherine, her literary equal.

Throughout the winter of 1918, Virginia called on her friend once a week, and in the years to come she would often reflect on these visits, which merged in her memory.

On arrival at the imposingly tall house in Hampstead, Virginia would be ushered inside by a nervous Ida, who'd direct the guest up to the study. On days when Katherine's health allowed, Virginia would find her friend working away at a yellow-painted table, her feet in a muff to keep them warm. Katherine loved to write up here, admiring the afternoon light, which she likened to the colour of 'a pale shell'.

On seeing her visitor, she would fling down her pen and plunge into a literary discussion, dismissing Ida out of hand. Katherine and Virginia enjoyed literary debate, each woman fighting her corner at times and, at others, backing down, both speaking with animation and ease about their own work.

When Ida returned with a tray of tea, or to check that the room was sufficiently warm, the conversation between the other two women would become stilted. Ida assumed that their tartness was nothing to take personally. But there was likely rather more to their reaction. Ida's wifely role in Katherine's life, and the rumours that had circulated about a lesbian attachment, seem to have informed their discomfort. Now that Katherine had married Murry, Virginia regarded Ida as a woman spurned. Whenever she came in, it seemed to Virginia that the room became infected by Ida's 'lacerated feelings'. Since both Virginia and Katherine were, at this stage, repressing their desires for women, Ida's supposed wounds bled into their own confusing bond.

But Ida carried on her household chores in oblivion, assuming that she was hardly being excluded from a chat between friends: Katherine and Virginia were just meeting as writers, their talk formal and erudite. But Ida could not have been more wrong.

Behind closed doors, Virginia and Katherine became increasingly trusting of each other, their conversation drifting towards their own lives. Virginia would later recall being fixed by her friend's gaze, Katherine insisting that she cared for her. Virginia would never forget those words or that lingering glance, recording in her diary years later her memory of those 'beautiful eyes – rather doglike, brown, very wide apart', looking as if she'd 'like always to be faithful'. Virginia would long treasure the sensation of Katherine's kiss: a gesture of warmth that perhaps contained a silent frisson, stirred up by traces of her friend's abandoned past and her own unanticipated future.

CHAPTER 12

LIFE AND DEATH

The year of 1918 culminated for Virginia Woolf in a delightful balance of seclusion and festivity. Especially pleasurable, she and Leonard had Asheham House to themselves for a week while their domestic help took a well-earned break. During this time, Virginia read through the manuscript of her second novel, *Night and Day*, to work out her approach to the next draft. This delicious solitude was followed by a gratifyingly sociable time. During the period around the birth of her niece on Christmas Day, Virginia gladly helped her sister, Vanessa Bell, by taking in her beloved nephews for a fortnight. The boys celebrated with Virginia and Leonard in the South Downs, with a few old Bloomsbury friends joining the gathering for tea. Amid all this activity, Katherine Mansfield continued to occupy her thoughts.

Both women took the time to pick out cheerful presents for each other, parcelling them up, and carefully timing their arrival for 25 December. Virginia also sent warm and lengthy letters to the Murrys' villa in Hampstead, which arrived, along with her package, to scenes of wine-fuelled fun: the wearing of red and yellow paper hats; exchanging of stockings under a decorated tree; dressing up in makeshift costumes; playing charades; eating pudding, and crackers and cheese.

No record remains of the exact nature of the gifts the pair exchanged. Katherine regularly destroyed great stacks of her correspondence, and so Virginia's accompanying letters have not survived. What's more, on this occasion, Katherine sent no word of thanks. Virginia received neither a reply to her enquiries after Katherine's health, nor a response to any of her offers to visit. By mid-February 1919, this wintry silence had left Virginia feeling hurt and confused. But, unwilling to extricate herself from their habitual game of cat and mouse, she eventually resorted to contacting Katherine's husband, John Middleton Murry, who insisted that his wife would love to see her.

And so, on 17 February, Virginia readied herself to meet her friend again. At about eleven o'clock on the morning of her planned visit, the telephone rang through Hogarth House. It was the voice of Ida Constance Baker, Katherine's loyal companion, which reached Virginia through the crackled line. Katherine's health was not up to a visit, Ida explained, without going into detail or suggesting an alternative time.

Unlike Virginia's reaction to the postponement of the Murrys' trip to Asheham the previous summer, this time she disbelieved the excuse. After all, she too had been bedridden for the first weeks of the year – in her case with toothache and headaches.

Knowing that Katherine and Murry now owned Heron Press, and that he had just been offered the prestigious editorship of the *Athenaeum* – a position once held by Virginia's father – she must have wondered whether her friend had simply used her as a means to publication. Later, in her diary, Virginia asked herself whether their relationship had been built on nothing more than 'quicksands', and, to her sister, she accused Katherine of being 'brittle as barley sugar'.

While Virginia was getting feverish about the abandonment, it turned out that Katherine was suffering from actual fevers. Desperate to try any new treatment for her tuberculosis, she had agreed to a course of injections that brought on a high temperature for 48 hours each time. Several days after cancelling on Virginia, she sent a letter explaining that 'Alas – I have just had another inoculation and by tea time tomorrow I shall be sailing on tropic seas –'. She extended an invitation for the following week and even told Virginia that Murry would love her to write for the *Athenaeum*, leaving Virginia feeling rather foolish for assuming that her friend had set out to hurt her.

The weekly visits to Hampstead reinstated, Virginia would often arrive at the front door, her arms laden with gifts: a freshly baked loaf; the Hogarth Press books typeset by her own hand; sprays of flowers to brighten the mantelpiece; a columbine plant, its deep purple petals aflame. The pair plunged right back into both their literary and more intimate conversations. Katherine was especially keen to hear Virginia's views on Dorothy Richardson, whose pioneering stream-of-consciousness technique would end up profoundly influencing them both. Virginia soon learnt that her friend had pulled together enough new stories to fill a collection. Heron Press was still too small to cope with a book of this length, and even Hogarth had yet to bring out anything so ambitious. Besides, Katherine had set her sights on William Heinemann, the British publisher of Joseph Conrad and Fyodor Dostoyevsky – two writers she much admired. She was also keeping busy as the new fiction reviewer at the *Athenaeum*, hired by her own husband to write about as many as four books per week.

Still not entirely trusting the resurrected friendship, Virginia hoped that Katherine would not review her novel when it was eventually ready for publication. Virginia was dividing her time between redrafting *Night and Day* and preparing an essay to mark the centenary of George Eliot's birth. Over the coming months, she would read every work by and about the great author, starting with one of the first biographies, by the novelist's later-life husband John Walter Cross. In a letter to a friend, Virginia claimed 'that no one else has ever known her as I know her', wishing that the novelist had lived and loved in the early twentieth century when she could have 'been saved all that nonsense' surrounding her unmarried life with George Henry Lewes. After all, Virginia had witnessed first-hand the experience of Katherine, who, during the early years of their friendship, had lived unwed with Murry. While cutting a bohemian figure, and enduring the disapproval of her family, Katherine had never been subjected to the level of ostracism suffered by their literary forebear.

Through their discussions about writers such as these, Virginia rediscovered the rare quality in Katherine that she had long admired: 'a sense of ease & interest', stemming from 'her caring so genuinely if so differently from the way I care, about our precious art'. Virginia grew to enjoy Katherine's inscrutability, her lack of 'apologies, or sense of apologies due', and began to wonder whether 'its I who live in the suburbs & think it necessary to answer letters'.

By Easter Monday 1919, the two writers and their husbands were strolling together in the sunshine across Hampstead Heath. Although Katherine was more heavily made-up than Virginia and had more outlandish taste in clothes, it was her older friend who tended to attract the attention of passers-by. It wasn't so much Virginia's widely admired beauty that drew their stares, but something odd and other-worldly about her movements. Strangers often found her appearance faintly ridiculous, reducing them to awkward laughter and leaving poor Virginia in great distress. Distancing themselves from the crowd, the two couples sat on a hillock, watching the far-off children play on canary-coloured swings and a pair of dancers performing to a barrel organ's repeated song.

Both women professed a snobbish disgust at the throngs of people on the grass, and Virginia's repulsion was directed towards Katherine too. In her diary, a few days later, she couldn't resist making barbed remarks about the commonness of Katherine's prose, and her 'haggard & powdered' appearance. And yet, throughout the entire summer of 1919, the strength of the two women's friendship helped them to keep their demons at bay: Virginia's haughtiness; Katherine's capriciousness; their mutual literary envy.

During this period of apparent calm, an incident occurred that should have raised alarm bells for Virginia. Just weeks after that bank holiday walk on Hampstead Heath, she had eventually self-published *Kew Gardens* – the story that was so strikingly similar to Katherine's own idea. Assuming that it would not attract many readers, the Hogarth Press printed little more than half the 300 copies they had produced of Katherine's *Prelude*. At first, their caution appeared to have been wise. During the month after its release, they sold fewer than 50 copies.

On 3 June, however, when Virginia and Leonard returned to Hogarth House from a stay at Asheham, they found the hall floor carpeted in postcards, the table stacked high with letters, the sofa strewn with envelopes, all containing orders from booksellers and individuals the length and breadth of Britain. This surge in interest had resulted from a review that the *Times Literary Supplement* had run a few days earlier, as Virginia and Leonard had been whiling away some unusually drowsy days surrounded by the buttercup-gilt fields of their country home. The critic's description of the story as 'a thing of original and therefore strange beauty' had resulted in this towering pile of book orders, which the Woolfs opened over dinner. The couple hardly paused to celebrate. That evening they set about trimming covers, printing additional pages, gluing backs and packaging the books for immediate dispatch. As they worked, they wondered how they could possibly produce and send out all these books in good time. Growing increasingly aware of the impossible magnitude of their task, their anxiety caused them to bicker.

Such intensity was not sustainable, they quickly realised. They simply could not hope to meet such demand themselves. Taking on the services of a professional firm, they ran a second print run of a further 500 copies. These sold at such a rate that the Hogarth Press's net profit on *Kew Gardens* ended up almost doubling that of *Prelude*.

Katherine could have been forgiven for having felt that her friend was receiving the recognition that rightly belonged to her. While the *Times Literary Supplement* lauded Virginia for taking the short-story form in a pioneering new direction, its editor had not deemed *Prelude* worthy of review, and 'Night-Scented Stock' – Katherine's flowerbed poem, probably of the same germination as *Kew Gardens* – remained in hibernation within the covers of her notebook. What's more, Katherine had recently heard back from William Heinemann with a rejection of her new collection, *Bliss and Other Stories*.

On the day following the deluge of book orders, Virginia would receive a letter from Katherine. As fiction reviewer for the *Athenaeum*, she had written a piece on *Kew Gardens* and wished to apologise to Virginia in advance. 'You must forgive the review – I cant hope to please you – tho' I wanted to –', she protested. 'For one thing I hadn't enough space.'

Wrapped up in the unexpected success of her story, Virginia was focused on negotiations with London-based printers about its second edition. Among this flurry of excitement and industry, she thought only of the possibility that the prospective review in the *Athenaeum* might further increase her sales, hardly allowing herself to feel the apprehension that Katherine's note should perhaps have provoked.

When the piece came out almost ten days later, Virginia was still so fixated on her triumph in the *Times Literary Supplement* that she failed to notice anything untoward. Although Katherine had

bemoaned the lack of space afforded to her in the *Athenaeum*'s
review pages, she had used up almost half of her not ungenerous
allowance of over 1000 words on exploring a matter seemingly
unrelated to her friend's story: the tendency of the era's writers to
satisfy themselves with notebook jottings instead of refining their
prose into works of art. 'The note-books of young writers are
their laurels', she complained: 'they prefer to rest on them.' It was
advice she knew she herself should heed, her own journal full of
self-chastisements for failing to maintain a strict writing routine.

The author of *Kew Gardens*, Katherine opined, set an example
for all dilettant notebook scribblers: here was a writer with the
stamina to draft and redraft. This praise was highly charged, but
Virginia failed to spot its undertones of resentment. 'She begins
where the others leave off', Katherine claimed; her work was
infused with a sense of 'leisure' and 'poise'. Virginia's privileged
lifestyle had afforded her the luxury to lift ideas high above the
level of the notebook. Although Katherine had managed to
write sufficient stories to fill a new volume, she still struggled to
match Virginia's productivity. Katherine's writing was hampered
by the draining effects of persistent ill health, and she did not
have the support of a steadfast husband like Leonard.

Far from picking up on the backhanded nature of the
review's compliments, Virginia blithely continued her visits to
Hampstead. She called in on the Murrys on 14 June 1919, just
the day after the publication of Katherine's article, and two
days after the *Times Literary Supplement* ran a biting critique of
Murry's book-length poem, which the Woolfs had reluctantly
brought out with the Hogarth Press.

Virginia entered a depressing scene at 2 Portland Villas. An
emaciated Katherine was irritable, and defensive about her own
writing, and, as Virginia would note in her diary, Murry behaved
like a schoolchild who insisted that his recent caning hadn't hurt.
Tellingly, Virginia took away an abiding image of the Murrys
with 'nothing seeming to grow or flourish round them; leafless

trees'. That night, Virginia confessed in her diary to feeling 'gorged & florid with my comparative success'. But she was to ignore Katherine's frustration at her peril.

Throughout the rest of the summer, Virginia continued to make the long journey across London to her ailing friend without picking up on any latent resentment. These visits were terminated only when Katherine, following her doctor's advice, headed off to the Italian Riviera in September 1919. Virginia found the time to write to her friend in between working on *Night and Day*'s final tranche of edits. But Katherine retreated once more into silence, leaving Virginia to agonise over what had gone wrong this time. The talk in literary London was that the balmy Mediterranean air had been beneficial to Katherine's physical health, so this time Virginia suspected a psychological motivation for her friend's sudden remoteness. Had Virginia unwittingly offended her, or could Katherine have felt jealous about the progress of *Night and Day*?

During the autumn of 1919, though, Virginia had other things to distract her from Katherine's abandonment: both her domestic staff resigned; she and Leonard were considering purchasing Hogarth House from their landlady; American publishers made offers on both Virginia's novels; and the British publication of *Night and Day* elicited a surge of letters, phone calls, invitations and reviews. When, in the midst of this especially busy period, her November 1919 issue of the *Athenaeum* arrived, Virginia discovered between its covers an article that partially explained her friend's withdrawal. Without letting Virginia know in advance, Katherine had now reviewed her novel, *Night and Day*. This tale, while more conventional in form than Virginia's later work, explored the lives of modern women: Katharine Hilbery, an aspiring mathematician, and Mary Datchet, a campaigner for women's suffrage.

The review of this, her second full-length book, would affect Virginia's work for years to come. Surrounded by piles of typeface

letters – which, just a year and a half earlier, she had arranged
into each word of *Prelude* – she came across Katherine's criticism
of her novel. It read like 'Miss Austen up-to-date', Katherine had
claimed. She, like Virginia, was a huge admirer of Jane Austen.
When reading the work of her forebear, she especially cherished
the sensation of having become the novelist's 'secret friend'. But
her review went on to explain that 'whereas Miss Austen's spell is
as strong upon us as ever when the novel is finished and laid by',
in *Night and Day*, 'Mrs Woolf's loses something of its potency'.
Ultimately, Katherine claimed, it 'makes us feel old and chill'.
Virginia closed the covers of the *Athenaeum*, feeling desolate and
confused by the spitefulness she detected in Katherine's words.

In the immediate aftermath of this experience, Virginia
rashly issued Murry an invitation. As both the magazine's editor
and Katherine's husband, she expected him to be able to offer
an explanation. What she didn't know, of course, was that Murry
had encouraged his wife to be as scathing as she liked about
Night and Day, reminding her that, 'We have no right to require
truth from others if we don't exact it from our friends'. And
he did indeed class Virginia as a friend, telling Katherine that
he considered her the woman with whom they had the most in
common, admiring 'something hard & definite & self-contained'
about her.

Only a week after the review's publication, Virginia and
Murry sat down to dinner in the high-ceilinged dining room
of Hogarth House. The occasion fell during a brief lapse in
Virginia's diary entries, but Murry would write up his account
the following day in his letter to Katherine, who was still in Italy.

Just as he had predicted she would, Virginia mustered the
courage to ask what Katherine had really made of her novel.

'She thinks that you make an abstraction from life, that you
left one important element completely out of account, or rather
withered it,' he explained, referring obliquely to *Night and Day*'s
omission of the Great War.

Hardly reassured by his reply, and still none the wiser, Virginia comforted herself by telling him, 'Katherine's review shows that she's not interested in novels.'

With this dismissive statement, she swept aside the difficult subject of the article, asking instead what was happening with Katherine's collection. Just seven months earlier, the pair had been on such good terms that Katherine had confided in Virginia about William Heinemann's rejection. Now, Virginia asked Murry whether she might read the manuscript, for – despite her disgust at 'Bliss' – Virginia remained interested in publishing her friend's work.

In the days and weeks that followed, she kept turning the review over in her mind, suspecting that spite must have had its way with her friend's pen. What was the source of Katherine's malice, Virginia wondered.

Certainly, Katherine bore a grudge against Virginia, considering *Night and Day* full of intellectual snobbery. 'Virginia's cry that she is the flower, the fair flower of the age – that Shakespeare & his peers died that she might be saved that she is the result of God knows *how* many hours in a library,' Katherine complained to Murry, 'is becoming a mania with her.'

What's more, Katherine despised *Night and Day's* failure to acknowledge the changes wrought on the world by the war. In her article, she had compared the novel to a ship returning from 'a perilous voyage' with a curious 'absence of any scars'. Privately to Murry, she'd described the novel as 'a lie in the soul'. Writers are under an obligation, she'd continued, to incorporate the new world order into their work, finding 'new expressions new moulds for our new thoughts & feelings'.

Virginia herself also appeared to have emerged from the war unscathed, while the battlegrounds of Europe had affected Katherine so deeply. During a reckless visit to the front in 1915 for a tryst with a lover, she had seen the casualties first hand: French soldiers with bandaged limbs; trainloads of German prisoners of war, one with a torn ear, another with blackened hands; cemeteries filled with line upon line of young men's graves. And, of course, her own brother had died in the trenches that year.

Over the next six months, Katherine did not send a single letter from the Italian Riviera to Hogarth House; nor did she receive one. Detecting anger in the reciprocal silence, tangible from across the waves, she forbade Murry from sharing her short stories with Virginia.

Back in Britain, Virginia found it crushing that Katherine's early promise to be 'scrupulously truthful' had culminated in this. Still immersing herself in the life and works of George Eliot, Virginia grew painfully aware of her predecessor's good sense in refusing to read reviews of her work. Virginia had often felt staid and suburban in comparison to Katherine's wilder approach to life, but the review's criticism had stung her so keenly that she perceived herself as 'a decorous elderly dullard'. And it seems she couldn't help but wonder whether Katherine had been right about the failings of *Night and Day*.

Katherine's words continued to gnaw at Virginia long into the new year. That Easter, far from whiling away the holiday with the Murrys, she now shuddered at the high praise Katherine's writing was garnering under Murry's editorship of the *Athenaeum*. And yet, at her most self-aware, Virginia knew that the value placed on Katherine's work was not merely nepotistic. And so, in May 1920, about six months after the publication of Katherine's review, when Virginia got wind of its author's return from warmer climes, she immediately began to wonder which of them would make the first move. She vowed to wait for Katherine to initiate contact, and yet, within a fortnight, Virginia, as ever, was the first to get in touch.

Katherine eventually penned a short reply to her request for a visit, agreeing to meet but failing to suggest a date. 'I am grown *very* dull,' she warned. Virginia, ever sensitive when it came to her friend, considered the letter stiff and formal. It seemed to Virginia that Katherine was behaving as if *she* had been the one snubbed.

But Katherine's response had, in fact, largely sprung from her continued ill health. In time, Virginia would come to understand this, well placed as she was to sympathise with bodily torment. She still suffered intermittently from headaches, insomnia and aversion to food – symptoms related to her depression. She never seriously considered refusing to make the familiar journey from Richmond across town to Hampstead Heath.

On a cool day in late May 1920, Virginia arrived at Portland Villas to a reception from Katherine so frosty that she would later puzzle over this visit in her diary, quoting their conversation from memory.

Katherine asked after the cottage that Virginia and Leonard had purchased in Rodmell the previous summer, their tenancy of nearby Asheham House having expired. There was no pleasure in these enquiries, no excitement in Katherine's eyes.

It struck Virginia that her friend had a feline quality: 'alien, composed, always solitary & observant.' No sooner had this thought crossed her mind than Katherine raised the subject of solitude. Gradually, it began to feel to Virginia as if she were hearing her own feelings expressed as never before. Despite her initial apprehension, she was ultimately reminded of the 'common certain understanding between us – a queer sense of being "like" – not only about literature – & I think it's independent of gratified vanity. I can talk straight out to her.' Their conversation flowing more easily, it soon seemed to her as if '8 months were minutes'. They spun gossip about their male friends, and then spooled back to the subject of their literary work.

Now that the women had fallen back into step, Katherine surprised Virginia by asking whether she might commission her to write some stories for the *Athenaeum* – the very same magazine that seemed to have published her criticism of Virginia's novel.

'I don't know that I can write stories,' Virginia said, voicing the sentiment that she felt Katherine had articulated in her review of *Night and Day*.

But Katherine countered: 'No one else can write stories except you.' *Kew Gardens*, she tellingly suggested, marked a turning point.

'But *Night and Day*?' Virginia heard herself say, although she had not meant to speak of it.

'An amazing achievement!' Katherine replied. 'Why, we've not had such a thing since I don't know when –'

'But I thought you didn't like it?' asked Virginia, oblivious to the implicit criticism that her work was old-fashioned.

'I could pass an examination in it!' Katherine insisted, her tendency to dramatise taking hold.

Although Katherine had not actually disowned her original feelings about *Night and Day*, she had become haunted by her review. Feeling that they needed to talk about the book at greater length, she invited Virginia to Portland Villas again, for lunch the following week.

It was an invitation that Virginia readily accepted. And so it was that one early June day in 1920, while high society congregated beneath a burning sun at Epsom Races, Virginia returned to Katherine's home. This time, they dived straight into talk about books.

'*Night and Day* is a first-rate novel,' Katherine announced, but she knew that she could not brush off her friend so easily. 'The suppression is puzzling,' she admitted, obliquely alluding to the book's omission of the Great War.

Virginia found such an appraisal refreshing. 'You've changed,' she told her friend. 'Got through something.' And she savoured in silence the relief that they had now progressed beyond the need for subterfuge.

Certainly, recent developments in Katherine's own career seemed to have dampened her scorching resentment. A few months after her review of Virginia's novel, Katherine had eventually experienced the satisfaction of seeing *Prelude* praised in the *Times Literary Supplement* in a piece that also applauded the innovation of her latest work, *Je ne parle pas français*. The Murrys had brought out this long story themselves with Heron Press. Like 'Bliss', it explored a triangular relationship and Virginia secretly felt that it breathed 'nothing but hate'. Katherine had now received better news even than the positive review: her collection had found a publisher. Constable & Co. would soon bring *Bliss and Other Stories* to press, finally ending her nine-year hiatus between books.

The conversation turned towards Katherine's private life, and she admitted to Virginia that she felt badly let down by Murry, claiming that he had failed to support her financially or emotionally during her illness. By the time Virginia took her leave, making her way past walls covered in ivy and gardens planted with tobacco flowers, she sensed as acutely as ever that she shared with Katherine something more fundamental than what she enjoyed with many of her Bloomsbury friends. Far from all the backstabbing, half-truths and downright lies for which history would remember the two women, Virginia deeply appreciated their rare sense of communion. With her literary friend, she could talk without altering her thoughts – an uncensored conversation that she experienced with no one else other than Leonard.

Virginia, in fact, owed a huge debt of gratitude to Katherine. Her friend had delved into her own intellectual reserves to work out the source of her intolerance for *Night and Day*, thereby offering Virginia one of the richest, if most unpalatable, of literary gifts. In the months following Katherine's critique of *Night and Day*'s muteness on the terrifying repercussions of worldwide combat, Virginia set to work on a war novel. *Jacob's Room*, as it would become known, ended up tracing the life of young Jacob Flanders, whose surname presages his death on the Western Front.

Unlike time spent with other writer friends, after which Virginia sometimes found it difficult to re-submerge herself in the world of her novel-in-progress, visits to Katherine stimulated her creativity. And so, throughout the summer of 1920, the pair enjoyed yet another rapprochement. Blessed by a reprieve from the worst ravages of illness, Katherine was even able to attend a luncheon hosted by the *Athenaeum*, at which she sat opposite Virginia. But most of the time the pair met behind the closed doors of Katherine's Hampstead home, Virginia travelling there all the way from the South Downs.

During this period, Virginia was working on her experimental third novel and still basking in the praise generally heaped upon her more conventional second. Katherine, who was anxiously awaiting the publication of *Bliss and Other Stories*, asked Virginia to consider reviewing it. Given her own article on *Night and Day*, her request was audacious indeed.

Virginia's gut reaction was to refuse. Reviews detracted from the pleasure of reading, she insisted, and she could tell that Katherine had picked up on the deeper reasons buried beneath the excuse. *Bliss and Other Stories* did contain some pieces that Virginia rated highly, but to others – the title story especially – she had responded with such vehemence that she could not have trusted her pen.

The piece on *Night and Day* had prompted Virginia to think long and hard about the ethics of literary criticism. She acknowledged her inability to respond fairly to the fiction of her contemporaries – especially that by women – finding herself at times looking for faults, hoping even to find some. She couldn't help wondering whether there was only so much space at the top, but she knew it was ludicrously illogical to think that 'If she's good then I'm not.'

And yet, Virginia wavered. In late August 1920, the 38-year-old would make another trip from Sussex to Hampstead to bid farewell to her 31-year-old friend, whose health had taken a turn for the worse, forcing her to cancel her planned visit to the Woolfs' new cottage in Rodmell. The wheezing of Katherine's breath and the aching of her limbs had now convinced her not simply to winter in the Mediterranean but to stay there for a full two years. As usual, Murry would remain in London, leaving Ida to take care of his wife.

That summer afternoon, Virginia found Katherine reclining on the sofa, her sharp nose and thin lips illuminated by the summer light streaming in through the nearby window. With her thick fringe cut blunt across her forehead, she reminded Virginia of a Japanese doll, and the brightness and tidiness of the room made her feel as if they inhabited a doll's house. As usual, they talked about writing, and Virginia felt the familiar yet nonetheless odd sensation of an 'echo coming back to me from her mind the second after I've spoken'. In this atmosphere of camaraderie, she found herself revoking her initial refusal to write about *Bliss and Other Stories*. But even as she did so, she no longer felt certain that Katherine really wanted her to review it.

The pair continued to talk for hours, steering clear of gossip as they tried to cover as much literary ground as possible. But beneath the surface of their conversation lay the blankness of their imminent separation, the sense that so much remained to be said.

When Virginia finally took her leave – the train she'd planned to catch long since missed – both women promised not to forget each other.

'We will write,' said Virginia, knowing that she would keep her word but unsure – even now – whether she could rely on Katherine to reply.

But Katherine surprised her with a pledge of greater intimacy still: 'I'll send you my diary,' she declared.

'Our friendship is a real thing,' they assured one another, holding each other's gaze. 'Whatever happens, it will always go on.'

Over the coming years, the bond between the two writers would endure, but hardly in the form that they'd envisaged. As Virginia had feared, Katherine did her usual trick of retreating into silence the moment she'd left Britain's shores. Her arrival in the south of France marked a four-month period of intense productivity. During this time, Virginia did not hear anything from her, not a single letter – let alone any of the promised entries from her diaries. But word of her absent friend was everywhere: review upon review of *Bliss and Other Stories* piled on the superlatives; Katherine's own well-regarded literary articles continued to come out in the *Athenaeum* each week; and she was publishing new short stories at an impressive rate. Virginia finally decided not to add her own voice to the mix. Instead, she penned a short 'insincere-sincere' note, the writing of which excised her envy of her friend and renewed her fondness. The message, which arrived on Christmas Day 1920, let Katherine know 'how glad and indeed proud I am' of the book's success. It was perhaps the four-month silence and the leagues of sea separating them which deterred her from asking whether, like her, Katherine ever doubted the merit of her own work – a question that she had kept circling ever since the *Athenaeum* review of *Night and Day*. But Virginia ended up saying only that it was a shame that the author of *Bliss* was not in London to enjoy her triumph.

Katherine replied swiftly and was far more honest than she had been in some of her previous correspondence – although she couldn't resist sarcastically passing comment on the brevity of Virginia's letter. She cast off embarrassing talk of 'triumph', admitting instead to thinking often of her friend and yearning to meet up again. Perhaps she might visit her here in France? Virginia was, Katherine admitted, 'the only woman with whom I long to talk *work*. There will never be another.' Here in Menton they could sit on the stone terrace overlooking the garden while the cloud and light shifted in the sky above, and the breeze trembled the cups of the wild orchid flowers. Despite all Virginia's loyalty over the past five years, Katherine signed off her letter with 'Farewell dear friend' but then felt obliged to ask 'May I call you that'.

It would have been in character for Virginia to respond promptly, but it is impossible to know for sure since Katherine continued to destroy much of her post. The next surviving letter took two months to reach her hands. Virginia wrote in February 1921, spurred on by motives very different from the congratulations of her previous note. She had been at Murry's farewell dinner in London, for he finally planned to join his wife abroad – at least for a while. The pair talked about Katherine, of course, and he ended up confiding in Virginia that he had recently strayed from his marriage. His affair with Princess Bibesco, an aristocratic contributor to the *Athenaeum* magazine, was the talk of the town, and Katherine had already learnt of it from the Princess herself, who wrote to accuse the ill and absent author of cruelly refusing to relinquish her hold on Murry.

Virginia felt for Katherine, whom she knew must be suffering intense jealousy and isolation. When she returned to Hogarth House, she put pen to paper. Letting down her guard, she confessed to Katherine that, bereft of their weekly meetings, she'd resorted to jotting in her diary those things she longed to talk about with her. The missive was full of praise for the transparent quality of Katherine's work; reflections on the importance of writing by women; and even an anecdote about E.M. Forster's recent claim that Virginia and Katherine were the two leading fiction writers of their time. 'Damn Katherine!' Virginia joked; 'why can't I be the only woman who knows how to write?'

The peal of Richmond church bells interrupted Virginia from her correspondence, reminding her that she and Leonard must soon crack eggs into a frying pan, it being their cook's day off. They would stand side by side at the gas stove, their rashers of bacon rippling with the heat. She had just enough time to finish up her four-page letter with a plea to stay in touch: 'Please Katherine,' she begged, 'let us try to write to each other.'

Predictably, Katherine failed to respond. Over on the continent, her health appeared to improve and she was enjoying a sense of renewal with Murry, whose empty affair with Princess Bibesco had ultimately taught him to value his marriage. Katherine was finally getting to experience some of the harmony that she had long envied in the partnership between Leonard and Virginia. Like their counterparts in Britain, the Murrys worked industriously and discussed their writing with each other. But this idyllic period would not last, Katherine's health and marital problems inevitably rearing up once more. Fearing that she was destined to die young, Katherine spent as much time as possible writing fiction: failing to mend frayed clothing, putting off visitors, feeling that she should leave letters unanswered.

This time, Katherine's abandonment pained Virginia more profoundly than ever before. Still, over the course of the year, she continued to think of things that she'd like to share with her writer friend. If she were to travel to France, as Katherine had suggested back at the cusp of the year, she predicted that their conversation would kindle within just three minutes. But she could not countenance making such a journey after all 'the small lies & treacheries, the perpetual playing & teasing'. Besides, she, too, was deeply immersed in her work. Despite its more experimental structure, the drafting of *Jacob's Room* was far swifter and more pleasurable than that of her previous two novels. She nonetheless worried that it might seem to her 'sterile acrobatics' by the time it came out – a fear exacerbated by the spring 1922 release of Katherine's third collection, *The Garden Party*. Virginia noted in her diary that the book 'soars in the newspapers, & runs up sales skyhigh', causing her to feel so consumed with envy that she tried to persuade herself that anything so popular could hardly be much good.

By mid-August, after her two-year absence, Katherine came back to London. She stayed at the Hampstead home of a friend, Dorothy Brett, spending much of her time shut away in her room, a card hanging on her door to inform prospective visitors that she was working and did not want to be disturbed. During free hours, she attended lectures about achieving harmony between heart, body and mind.

Although Katherine did not get in touch directly, a mutual friend let Virginia know that she was back in town and Dorothy contacted Virginia to invite her to one of the regular Thursday evening salons she held at her house. Virginia agonised over the invitation, trying to calculate the effect of such company. It was a particularly unsettling time for her. Having now completed *Jacob's Room*, she was anxiously awaiting its launch. She identified 'a certain instability' in her character (although she preferred to think of it as a 'generosity of temperament'), which led her to 'extremes of passion and repulsion'. Right now, she felt wary of the Murrys. But, if she saw them again, she knew she would warm to them once more. Was yet another reconciliation worth the pain, and would it affect her writing?

Her latest novel would be self-published by the Hogarth Press, marking, finally, her liberation from the publisher half-brother who had abused her. Virginia was now working on a new short story, 'Mrs Dalloway in Bond Street', which she was considering expanding into a novel. After a positive start, she was struggling – a problem Katherine was far better acquainted with than her. Virginia blamed intrusions from the outside world for her inefficiency, and worried that should she enter 'the heart of the enemies camp' she might find herself 'rasped all over, or at any rate dulled & blunted'. On the other hand, she worried that surrounding herself only with old Bloomsbury pals might cause her mind to 'soften and rot'.

Weighing up which was the better of these two evils, Virginia decided not to visit Katherine at Dorothy's house. She simply assumed that they would meet again the following summer, when they could start afresh.

It was a choice that Virginia would live to regret. Katherine was far from cured. Her return to Britain had, in fact, been prompted by a flare-up in her lung disease. Increasingly desperate for a cure, she had come back to London for a course of newfangled radiation treatment. And when that began to take a toll on her heart, she sought more extreme treatment still. The lectures she'd been attending in London confirmed her belief that her physical ailments stemmed from her diseased spirit – a theory that most of her nearest and dearest could not abide. But the opinions of friends and lovers were of little interest to Katherine, who had decided to break free from old relationships in order to embrace a new way of life.

At the beginning of October 1922, she returned to France, this time to join the ranks of self-appointed guru George Gurdjieff, a Russian of Greek and Armenian descent, who'd set up a commune in Fontainebleau. Here, he was putting into practice the theories espoused in the lectures that Katherine had so recently attended. She bid farewell to both Murry and Ida, telling them that she must tread this path alone. Yet she nonetheless attempted to stage-manage their lives from afar, suggesting that the pair could set up a farm together in Ditchling – a village just across the chalk hills from the Woolfs' new cottage in Rodmell. This outlandish plan stemmed from her own eccentric regimen at the Institute for the Harmonious Development of Man. Here at Le Prieuré, pupils and patients engaged in a combination of manual labour and artistic pursuit. Katherine escaped the most punishing tasks on the institute's farm, being set to work instead in the kitchens, scrubbing and peeling vegetables, and helping with the butchery of pigs. This work was interspersed with mandatory hours spent sitting in a draughty hayloft, whose ceiling was decorated with paintings of the community's members. Here, Katherine put her faith in the dubious health benefits of inhaling the breath and aroma of cows. Come the evening, she would join the vodka-fuelled dances, drama or operatics, which continued late into the night before finally retiring to her stark, icy room.

Communication between Katherine and Virginia had become so sporadic by this stage that little had got back to the British writer about the New Zealander's perilous state of health. It therefore came as a great blow in January 1923 when Virginia's maid, Nellie Boxall, greeted her at breakfast with some startling news.

'Mrs Murry's dead!' Nellie informed her. 'It says so in the paper!'

Katherine's obituary run by *The Times* on the 12th of that month announced with regret that this writer of short stories and 'witty and penetrating novel reviews' had died suddenly three days earlier. Murry, to whom Katherine had issued an unexpected invitation to Fontainebleau, was with her during her final hours. That afternoon he'd found her positively glowing, but, at about ten o'clock, when she headed upstairs to bed, she suffered a pulmonary haemorrhage, blood pouring from her mouth. Murry was quickly ushered to one side by the doctors. But, although Katherine beseeched him with her eyes, she would die with her husband looking on, incapable of taking her in his arms.

Katherine's death would come as a 'severe shock to her friends', her obituary said, on account of the apparent improvement in her tubercular condition. When Virginia heard the news, she felt overwhelmed by confusion. As the day progressed, the sensation ebbed into a chasm of emptiness and regret. When she tried to embark on her usual morning routine, sitting down at her desk, she found herself unable to write. What was the point, she wondered, without her one-time friend to read it? They had shared something of deep importance, which she expected never to find in anyone else.

An image of Katherine kept intruding into her mind: the 34-year-old reluctantly lifting an icy, white wreath to her head, before slowly turning her back on Virginia, taking her leave with dignity.

In her diary, a week later, Virginia would bring herself to admit that Katherine's prose was 'the only writing I have ever been jealous of'. Virginia's despair at her untimely loss continued to brew. Although ink eventually flowed from her pen once more, for weeks she felt as if she wrote into a void. 'There's no competitor,' she lamented, feeling, as she put it, like a lonely cock of the walk: 'For our friendship had so much that was writing in it.'

In the mid-to-late-1920s, when Virginia completed two of her most lauded works, *Mrs Dalloway* and *To the Lighthouse*, she wondered on each occasion what Katherine would have made of them. On completing the last words of *Mrs Dalloway* – a novel about a party thrown by an upper-class woman, which is disrupted by the death of a shell-shocked man – she allowed herself to fantasise that, had her friend lived and continued to write, 'people would have seen that I was the more gifted'. And yet, for all Virginia's celebratory egotism, she knew deep down that she owed a debt of gratitude to this fellow author who had pushed her to find new forms for the novel in the wake of the war. Early biographers of Woolf, though, would be reluctant to admit that this leading female modernist might have been so deeply influenced by a lesser-known writer such as Katherine Mansfield. But the evidence had to be studiously overlooked. Throughout the rest of Virginia's life, references to Katherine continued to litter her letters and diaries. And Virginia's fiction regularly revisited scenarios that her late friend's stories had first explored.

Katherine's death ruptured the natural course of their relationship, ending as it did during one of their estrangements, and so Virginia would remain haunted by the spectre of her bitter opponent and beloved friend – unrivalled by any other. Over the decades to come, and especially during her richly mythologised love affair with Vita Sackville-West, Virginia's thoughts would frequently turn to her complex bond with Katherine. 'What odd friends I've had – you and she –', Virginia wrote in a letter to Vita in 1927, having just read the *Journal of Katherine Mansfield*.

Although Katherine was never a consistent diarist, Murry had brought together any notebook jottings he could date, publishing them in one volume – a laborious endeavour that was expressly against his late wife's wishes. He did not include any entries that explicitly referred to the Woolfs. When he later brought out a volume of Katherine's letters, he presented his late wife as a matchless genius who relied on no one other than him for literary advice, excising several of the missives she had written to Virginia.

Murry's editorial choices, combined with the attitude of Woolf's early biographers, resulted in a misleading and incomplete public record of the tempestuous friendship between these two deeply ambitious women. Virginia herself, however, did manage to forge a resolution of sorts with the inscrutable Katherine, whose true feelings she had been left forever trying to read.

Eight years after Katherine's death, in the early summer of 1931, the late author appeared to Virginia in a dream. Even in her sleeping state, Virginia knew that her old friend was dead, but the words of the apparition offered her comfort nonetheless. Katherine said 'something by way of explanation' – which Virginia considered a 'curious summing up' of 'what has passed since she died'. And, before waking, Virginia reached for her rival's palm one last time, responding to the hand of friendship that Katherine seemed to have extended from beyond the grave.

EPILOGUE

A WEB OF LITERARY CONNECTIONS

We began with a simple aim: to find the literary women on whom our four authors relied. But one of the unexpected pleasures of researching this book has proved to be the discovery of a wider web of threads that linked these writers across generations, and vast expanses of land, sea and time.

Four decades after the death of Jane Austen, George Eliot read the work of her forebear before embarking on her first novel. Some seventy years later, Virginia Woolf's book-length essay *A Room of One's Own*, published in 1929, acknowledged the debt she owed, not just to Jane, but also to Charlotte and Marian. And they, in turn, she said, were indebted to the great female writers who preceded them.

Virginia wondered on the page about the sheltered existences of the women who came before her. Understandably, given the sanitised images of each author painted by their earliest biographers, she regarded Jane, Charlotte and Marian as isolated individuals, each set apart from the society that surrounded her. In Virginia's imagination, Charlotte languished in a moorland parsonage, 'without more experience of life than could enter the house of a respectable clergyman'. Marian, thanks to her frowned-upon relationship with George Henry Lewes, endured a lonely existence, tucked away in a corner of north London. Jane was a bookish spinster aunt – so shy she hid her manuscripts even from the relatives with whom she shared her tiny domestic sphere.

In the memoir of his aunt, Jane's conservative nephew inevitably failed to mention the Austens' governess. His complete disregard for Anne Sharp, whose friendship Jane had placed above the loyalty she owed to her brother, represents the snapping of an important thread in the literary web that might otherwise have inspired future generations of female authors.

Long after Jane had gone to her grave, other women who forged an independent path through their writing continued to unsettle the established social order. But if they appeared only to scribble between household chores, their endeavours could be presented as more eccentric than subversive. Elizabeth Gaskell's portrait of Charlotte as a devoted daughter and sister hardly posed much danger. The real Charlotte, though, a woman with strong convictions of her own, who chose a friend as radical as Mary Taylor? That would have been beyond the pale.

Far from the image of the closed community of Brontë sisters shut away in their father's parsonage, Marian is remembered as a particularly cerebral writer with little need for female company. To many critics, it has long seemed impossible that someone with such supposedly masculine qualities might have shared a sisterly bond with Harriet Beecher Stowe, whose novels are often now dismissed as overly sentimental. But – like Charlotte Brontë, born three years before her – Marian had greatly admired the anti-slavery novel *Uncle Tom's Cabin*. Interestingly, when she aired her affectionate feelings for its creator in a letter to a friend, back in 1853, her thoughts flitted between Harriet and Charlotte. 'Villette – Villette,' she wrote with endearing urgency, '– have you read it?'

The kinds of fascinating conversations shared between female author peers of the past continue, of course, to this day – as does communication, through the written word, across great distances or generations. Yet, well into the twentieth century, the creative relationships of male writers still overshadowed those between women. Virginia Woolf may have been the high priestess of Modernism, occupying her dais alongside a group of celebrated literary men, but the myth goes that there could only have been room for one woman at the top. And so Katherine Mansfield was branded Virginia's enemy, and another literary thread was swept away.

Since Virginia's time, many more pairs of female writers have spun similar threads of their own. Like us, her first biographer, the novelist Winifred Holtby, and the wartime chronicler Vera Brittain met when they were in their twenties. In their case, though, their first encounter was marked by mutual distrust.

After suffering what she took to be a humiliation by Winifred during a college debate in their days as undergraduates at the University of Oxford, Vera went out of her way to avoid the company of her fellow student – a frostiness that would be repaired when Winifred called on Vera, who'd been fighting a cold, with the unexpected gift of a bunch of grapes. Once they'd got over their initial wariness, they realised that – despite any outward differences – they had a great deal in common. Winifred was tall, blonde and gregarious, whereas Vera was small, dark and more reserved. But they bonded over their experiences of service during the First World War, as well as their mutual aim to become professional writers. After university, they decided to move in together, so that they could encourage each other in their ambitions. They even lived together in later years when Winifred joined the family home that Vera shared with her husband and two children. During their sixteen-year friendship, the two actively supported each other's careers and, despite the soar-away success of Vera's book *Testament of Youth*, this would always remain a friendship between equals.

We find ourselves especially drawn to this pair who met when they were close to the beginning of their literary journeys and – as Winifred put it – became for each other a 'travelling companion', never afraid to acknowledge the depth of support they had given each other. After Winifred's early death at the age of 37, Vera would go on to immortalise their alliance in her book *Testament of Friendship* – a fitting tribute from the woman she once described as the person who 'made me'.

During these interwar years, two other female authors were beginning to make their way. Long before Jean Rhys published *Wide Sargasso Sea* – her prequel to Charlotte Brontë's *Jane Eyre* – she got to know Eliot Bliss. Both women were white writers from the Caribbean, living in London at the time. During the summer of 1937, they began to see each other every fortnight for what Eliot referred to as 'delightful West-Indian suppers', washed down with vast quantities of wine. Such was Jean's ability to drink that her poor friend – whose adopted pen-name was inspired in part by George Eliot – always felt ill after these meals. Jean, too, sometimes ended up so drunk that her husband would have to put both women to bed. On such occasions, Jean would sometimes angrily accuse Eliot – the daughter of a colonial army officer – of looking down on her. But when Jean was sober, she was, according to her friend, always kind-natured and full of fun.

In the winter of that year, Eliot left for America. But they continued to write to each other during the decades to come, Eliot sharing in her correspondence, her knowledge of the Sargasso Sea. Their warm and sometimes humorous letters, which Jean joked she would one day frame, challenge the common perception of her as a volatile character, unable to make friends with other women.

In Florida at about this time, a rather more unlikely friendship was being kindled between two other female writers. Zora Neale Hurston, the author of *Their Eyes Were Watching God*, grew up in an all-black town, her father a former slave. Marjorie Kinnan Rawlings, a Pulitzer Prize winner, was married to a man who owned a white-only hotel. They met at a time when their home state was a Ku Klux Klan stronghold and Jim Crow racial segregation laws were harshly enforced.

When Marjorie gave a guest lecture to Zora's students at the all-black Florida Normal and Industrial College in 1942, she was so taken with her host that, despite the many social barriers to friendship, she invited Zora to tea the next day at her husband's hotel. Prejudice and conformity ran deep, however. Marjorie, fearing the reactions of other guests, arranged for the bellboy to whisk Zora up to their private apartment to get her out of sight. Such precautions, however, would prove unnecessary. Zora, knowing that her presence would prove sensitive, entered through the kitchen and up the back stairs, allegedly dressed as a maid. Remarkably, such squalid moral compromises failed to hinder their enjoyment of each other's company. 'I've never had so much fun,' Marjorie told her husband. For her part, Zora, quick to realise their many similarities, would soon refer to Marjorie as a 'sister'.

Their mutual admiration might have been assured, but the ethical dilemmas didn't stop there. When Zora visited Marjorie's country residence, they talked, laughed and got tipsy together on the porch. But when it became clear that Zora was in no fit state to drive, Marjorie felt she had to send her friend to sleep out in the black servants' quarters, although there were plenty of spare bedrooms in the main house.

Once again, Zora didn't seem to hold her friend's cowardice against her. But Marjorie subjected herself to tough questions about her behaviour. And, on a second overnight visit, she insisted that this time Zora stay with her in the house. Marjorie went on to speak out against racial segregation, and showed solidarity with her friend by putting in a good word for her with her own esteemed editor, who had also commissioned famed literary comrades F. Scott Fitzgerald and Ernest Hemingway.

The multi-talented Maya Angelou was no stranger to the sort of racial prejudices writ large in the friendship of Marjorie and Zora – something she explored in a series of memoirs. Growing up in the town of Stamps in Arkansas, the young Maya read the novels of Jane Austen and Charlotte Brontë, and was entranced by the unfamiliar worlds of British nineteenth-century manners and moorland passion. Much later in life, well after the enormous success of 1969's *I Know Why the Caged Bird Sings*, Maya would find herself sharing the bill at a literary festival with fellow legend Toni Morrison. In the Welsh village of Hay-on-Wye, Maya and Toni were in strikingly similar circumstances, each far from home at a time when their mothers were ill. They were, as Maya put it, 'just two Black ladies who were missing our mothers'.

In the following years, they would go out of their way, time and again, to show each other support. In 1993, when Toni won the Nobel Prize in Literature, Maya threw her a party, because as she would later recall, she felt it was something that the United States should have done. When Maya was honoured at the 2013 American National Book Awards, it was Toni who presented her award. And as Toni's tribute speech made clear, her respect for Maya went far beyond professional admiration. Having just praised her friend's culinary talents, she spoke, with clear emotion, of the sustenance she received from Maya during a particularly dark time. When Toni's son died one Christmas, Maya, she remembered, was the very first non-family member to call on the phone, 'that unmistakable voice of sheer balm' offering comfort from afar.

By poignant coincidence, Toni, in her eighties by then, would find herself back at Hay-on-Wye in 2014 on the day that

Maya died. Months before, when we'd heard that Toni would be speaking at the festival, we had eagerly bought tickets for the event. And so ours were among the shocked gasps that rippled through the draughty tent when Maya's death was announced. As Toni articulated her deep grief, we found ourselves saddened by her loss. Sitting side by side, many rows back from the stage, we imagined how one of us would feel, some future day, left without her friend.

But there is so much more that we can learn from Toni and Maya, as well as the other literary pairs in this book. In stark contrast to our early fears about the threat of literary envy, the bond between Jane and Anne shows that friends can indeed overcome any friction caused by differences in worldly success. The example of Mary, whose hectoring did such a lot to encourage Charlotte's ambitions, suggests that the willingness to speak uncomfortable truths is sometimes the hallmark of a real confidante. Marian's forgiveness of Harriet's neglect is testament to the power of letting go of past grievances. And the friendship of Virginia and Katherine, those supposed arch foes, demonstrates that professional rivalry can actually fuel a female literary alliance.

Vera and Winifred, more recent friends who supported each other's early ambitions, will doubtless always remain a particular inspiration. And Maya and Toni reinforce our belief that it is important to celebrate the lives of those closest to us, not just in fine tributes when they are gone, but also when they are still here.

These lessons have had a special relevance to us in recent times. By 2015, we'd spent a decade-and-a-half labouring over several books that remained unpublished. On a wintry evening, descending the escalator of a crowded London Underground station, our conversation turned to the latest writing competition that we had each entered – for 'new' and unpublished authors. Neither of us felt very optimistic. Remembering that long-ago meal in a Japanese shopping mall, Emily wondered whether we'd have embarked on this literary journey at all had we known how little further forward we'd have come by now. Though equally downcast, Emma reminded us both that it wasn't the writing itself that was getting us down, but the lack of improvement in our writerly prospects.

Before the month was out, though, Emily would receive a message that she'd been shortlisted for that competition. She immediately thought of Emma, hopeful that she too had heard good news. But when she picked up the phone, she discovered this was not the case. And though she'd been given a guest ticket to the prize dinner, she wondered whether it would really be an act of generosity to offer it to her friend.

In early spring, having in fact jumped at the chance to come along, Emma sat at the judges' table alongside those on the shortlist. Despite her pride in Emily, the evening would not be without awkwardness. Over dinner conversation, Emma studiously avoided mentioning that she too had entered the prize, indeed keeping quiet about her novel altogether. This, the second she'd written, had racked up its own rejection slips. But against the banqueting-hall soundtrack of clinking cutlery and glassware, she felt grateful to be experiencing this evening with her friend.

When Emily's name was announced as the winner it brought sheer joy to us both. The official photographer took a picture that captured the moment, a split-second later, when we'd throw our arms around each other in celebration.

It was to our delighted surprise that, just days later, a publisher made an offer to bring out Emma's book. The upturn in fortune this time gave Emily an opportunity to toast her friend's success.

And, before Emma's novel was even launched, the chance would come to share in a truly joint achievement when we sold the rights to this book too. Our early fears that the success of one before the other might threaten our bond founded on writerly equality had ultimately proven unfounded.

But while collaborating on *A Secret Sisterhood* would bring us much happiness, it would also create new stresses and strains. Leisurely conversations over coffee or glasses of wine were replaced by rushed updates, snatched in library corners, and nights out together sacrificed for evenings writing in our homes, working into the early hours. Ultimately, though, we would be drawn closer still through our discoveries, and the experience of writing as a pair.

Of all the many examples of literary sisterhood that we'd glean through our joint research, the most unexpected came towards the end of writing this book. Knowing that Emma would be attending one of Margaret Atwood's public lectures, Emily persuaded her to slip the great author a handwritten note about our work. We could hardly believe it when Margaret replied, asking to read some sample chapters, and later letting us know that she'd be willing to write a foreword for this book.

Someone whose work needs no introduction, Margaret is known for her encouragement of younger writers as well as those closer to her in age. Her bond with fellow Canadian literary star Alice Munro began in 1969 – when they were both near the beginning of their careers – a time during which Margaret recalls sleeping on Alice's floor on a visit to Victoria. Looking back on that period, the pair would formulate a theory to explain why their home country had produced such a successful generation of female writers. According to them, literary endeavour was permissible for women, whereas men had to conform to rigid ideals of masculinity. Writing fiction was deemed a harmless feminine pursuit, and, since most men were hardly likely to read books by women, authors such as Alice and Margaret were free to pursue their craft without interference.

When Alice won a Nobel Prize for her short stories in 2013, Margaret joined her, once again in Victoria, this time in the grander surroundings of the Empress Hotel. A heart-warming photograph, which Alice would later display on her bookcase, offers a glimpse of the pair's private celebration, their arms around each other, glasses of champagne close by.

Margaret's would be one of the most prominent voices to lead tributes in the press to her longstanding friend. Female writers of the past, however, had fewer chances to publicly praise the women who helped, cajoled and influenced them. Opportunities to converse were largely restricted to the parlour rather than amplified on the national stage. But there are other, more significant, reasons why these relationships have failed to find their place in literary lore.

Again and again, such creative collaborations have been neglected, with attention being trained instead on the influence of men. Closeness with other family members has been celebrated too, while friendships women sought outside the home were regarded as a threat to the conventional roles of devoted daughter, mother and wife. Creative alliances between women, therefore, have come to be seen as subversive or a source of shame.

And so, misleading myths of isolation have long attached themselves to women who write: a cottage-dwelling spinster; an impassioned roamer of the moors; a fallen woman, shunned; a melancholic genius. Over the years, a conspiracy of silence has obscured the friendships of female authors, past and present. But now it is time to break the silence and celebrate this literary sisterhood – a glimmering web of interwoven threads that still has the power to unsettle, to challenge, to inspire.

ACKNOWLEDGEMENTS

In keeping with the theme of this book, during our years of research and writing, a great many individuals and organisations have extended the hand of friendship to us.

Margaret Atwood, so long an inspiration, took us entirely by surprise when she agreed to write the foreword for *A Secret Sisterhood*. This, at a time when we were still editing the manuscript, did so much to encourage us.

Authors and experts – Lindsey Ashford, Diana Athill, Jennifer Cognard-Black, Joan D. Hedrick, Nancy Henry, Deirdre Le Faye, Rebecca Lilley, Kathleen McCormack, Laurel Ann Nattress and Jude Piesse, all gave generously of their time and vast knowledge of several of the writers in this book.

Our research was also greatly aided by the help of the following people: Morex Arai at the Huntington Library (San Marino, California); Keith Arscott and Gillian Dow at Chawton House Library; Lyndsi Barnes, Isaac Gewirtz and Joshua McKeon at the New York Public Library's Henry W. and Albert A. Berg Collection; Sarah Baxter at the Society of Authors; Beth Burgess and staff at the Harriet Beecher Stowe Center; John Burton of the George Eliot Fellowship, Chris Coleby and staff at Hollybank School; Rhian Dolby and Sarah Lewkin at the Hampshire Record Office; Mary Guyatt at the Jane Austen House Museum; Becky Harvey at the Nuneaton Museum & Art Gallery; Maria Isabel Molestina-Kurlat at the Morgan Library

& Museum; Sarah Laycock and staff at the Brontë Parsonage Museum; Helen MacEwan and Jones Hayden of the Brussels Brontë Group; staff at the Nuneaton Heritage Centre; staff of the former Red House Museum (Gomersal); Moira Rudolf of Regency Walking Tours; Ali Wells at the Herbert Art Gallery & Museum; Stephen R. Young at Yale University Library's Beinecke Rare Book & Manuscript Library; and Helen Wicker at the Kent History and Library Centre.

We are very grateful to Jonathan G. Ouvry, for granting us permission to quote from the letters and diaries of George Eliot and George Henry Lewes; to Cambridge University Press for permission to quote from *The Journals of George Eliot* edited by Margaret Harris and Judith Johnston; to Hampshire Record Office (on behalf of the depositor) for allowing us to quote from some of the Austen-Leigh Papers; to the Harriet Beecher Stowe Center for permission to quote from an unpublished letter from Calvin Ellis Stowe to Harriet Beecher Stowe; to Manchester University Press for allowing us to quote from *The Letters of Mrs Gaskell* edited by J.A.V. Chapple and Arthur Pollard; to the New York Public Library for permission to quote from the originals of letters and diaries by Katherine Mansfield, Harriet Beecher Stowe, Mary Taylor and Virginia Woolf held in their collections; to Oxford University Press for permission to quote from *Jane Austen's Letters* (fourth edition) collected and edited by Deirdre Le Faye, *The Letters of Charlotte Brontë* (volumes I–III) edited by Margaret Smith, and *The Collected Letters of Katherine Mansfield* (volumes I–IV) edited by Vincent O'Sullivan and Margaret Scott; and to the Society of Authors as the Literary Representative of the Estates of Katherine Mansfield, John Middleton Murry and Virginia Woolf for permission to quote from letters and diaries.

We also owe debts of gratitude to Keely Charlick, Catherine Cho, Leslie Frankel, Tony Gilbertson, Penny Gore, Patricia McVeigh and Sarah Moore, all of whom helped us in important practical ways.

We were both very fortunate that Arts Council England awarded us Grants for the Arts, using public funding.

And, though most of the words within these covers were written sitting at our own writing desks, between us we benefited from periods of intense creative focus at the following retreats: the Bread Matters Residency near Lisbon (Thank you to Will and Inês Amado), Circle of Missé in the Loire (Thank you to Aaron Tighe and Wayne Milstead), Mill House Retreat in Devon (Thank you to all the staff).

Just as Charlotte Brontë benefited from the – sometimes stern, sometimes nurturing – wisdom of her school teacher Margaret Wooler, and Fanny Austen would retain fond memories of her inspiring governess Anne Sharp, we are grateful to the many writing tutors and mentors who have guided us, in particular: Linda Anderson, Jane A. Adams, Pat Borthwick, Andrew Cowan, Jill Dawson, Louise Doughty, Karen Maitland, Derek Neale, Gill Nuttall and Michèle Roberts. We've also learnt so much from our colleagues and students at City, University of London, and New York University London, as well as those we have worked with elsewhere over the years.

We couldn't ask for better literary agents than Veronique Baxter at David Higham Associates and Ariella Feiner at United Agents in the UK, and Michelle Tessler at the Tessler Agency in the USA. Your tireless work on our behalves has changed our lives in so many ways. We would also like to thank Max Edwards, Nikoline Eriksen, Sophie Scard and Laura West.

A Secret Sisterhood has benefited enormously from the insightful editing of Nicole Angeloro at Houghton Mifflin Harcourt and Jennifer Barr at Aurum Press, who believed from the start that there was a story here worth telling.

Many thanks also to Susanna Brougham and Alison Moss for their careful copy editing. Also to Jessica Axe, Ann Barrett, Caroline Curtis, Richard Green, Liz Somers, Jessie Sullivan and all at Aurum. And to Liz Anderson, Lisa Glover and all at Houghton Mifflin Harcourt.

Thank you to all the guest bloggers and interviewees whose work has enriched our website SomethingRhymed.com, where we first began to write regularly about female literary friendship. Early on, we were also encouraged by the confidence of the readers of SomethingRhymed.com that this subject deserved to be explored in a full-length book. Particular mentions must go to: Sarah Emsley, Naomi Frisby, Rohan Maitzen and Andrea Stephenson.

Our writer and academic friends kept us going too, especially: Sarah Butler, Susan Barker, Michael Caines, Michelle Carriger, Samantha Ellis, Miranda El-Rayess, Lauren Frankel, Edward Hogan, Antonia Honeywell, Ann Morgan, Irenosen Okojie, Julia Pascal, Emily Pedder, Elizabeth L. Silver, J.C. Sutcliffe and Wendy Vaizey – some of whom commented on early drafts, and all of whom believed in us long before our words made it into print.

To our extended families, the Blanchards, the Prouts and the Ruppins: we thank you for your good humour and unwavering support. To our first friends, our sisters, Erica, Louise and Sarah, and to our parents, Elaine and Phil Sweeney and to both the late John Crump and Taeko Midorikawa Crump: we thank you for teaching us the enduring value of friendship and sisterhood.

Finally, to Jack Blanchard and Jonathan Ruppin – partners, allies and friends – we thank you for always lending a sympathetic ear; for reading and rereading our multiple drafts; for keeping us well fed during long stints in our studies, and, most of all, never failing to be there when we emerged.

SELECT BIBLIOGRAPHY

In addition to the manuscript sources consulted (detailed in the Notes), the following publications were those most helpful to our research.

~

JANE AUSTEN AND ANNE SHARP

Amy, Helen (ed.), *The Jane Austen Files: A Complete Anthology of Letters and Family Recollections*, Amberley, 2015

Austen, Jane, *Emma*, Penguin Classics, 1996

–, *Lady Susan/The Watsons/Sanditon*, Penguin Classics, 1974

–, *Mansfield Park*, Penguin Classics, 1996

–, *Northanger Abbey*, Penguin Classics, 1995

–, *Persuasion*, Penguin Classics, 1985

–, *Pride and Prejudice*, Penguin Classics, 1996

–, *Sense and Sensibility*, Penguin Classics, 1995

Austen-Leigh, James Edward, *A Memoir of Jane Austen*, Richard Bentley and Son (second edition), 1871

Bugg, John, *Five Long Winters: The Trials of British Romanticism*, Stanford University Press, 2013

Butler, Marilyn, *Jane Austen and the War of Ideas*, Oxford University Press, 2006

Byrne, Paula, *The Real Jane Austen: A Life in Small Things*, HarperPress, 2013

Harman, Claire, *Jane's Fame: How Jane Austen Conquered the World*, Canongate, 2010

Hickman, Peggy, *A Jane Austen Household Book with Martha Lloyd's Recipes*, Readers Union, 1978

Hill, Constance, *Jane Austen: Her Homes & Her Friends*, John Lane, 1902

Honan, Park, *Jane Austen: Her Life*, Weidenfeld & Nicolson, 1987

Kelly, Helena, *Jane Austen: The Secret Radical*, Icon Books, 2016

Lane, Maggie, *Jane Austen and Food*, Endeavour Press, 2013

Le Faye, Deirdre, *A Chronology of Jane Austen and Her Family*, Cambridge University Press (second edition), 2013

–, *Fanny Knight's Diaries: Jane Austen Through Her Niece's Eyes*, The Jane Austen Society, 2000

–, *Jane Austen: A Family Record*, Cambridge University Press (second edition), 2003

– (ed.), *Jane Austen's Letters*, Oxford University Press (fourth edition), 2014

Nicolson, Nigel, *Godmersham Park: Before, During and After Jane Austen's Time*, Jane Austen Society, 1996

Renton, Alice, *Tyrant or Victim: A History of the British Governess*, Weidenfeld & Nicolson, 1991

Sutherland, Kathryn (ed.), *J. E. Austen Leigh: A Memoir of Jane Austen and Other Family Recollections*, Oxford University Press, 2002

Tomalin, Claire, *Jane Austen: A Life*, Penguin Books, 2012

Uglow, Jenny, *In These Times: Living in Britain Through Napoleon's Wars 1793–1815*, Faber & Faber, 2014

~

CHARLOTTE BRONTË AND MARY TAYLOR

Alexander, Christine (ed.), *Tales of Glass Town, Angria and Gondal: Selected Writings*, Oxford University Press, 2010

Bellamy, Joan, *'More Precious than Rubies': Mary Taylor, friend of Charlotte Brontë, strong-minded woman*, Highgate Publications, 2002

Barker, Juliet, *The Brontës*, Abacus, 2010

Brontë, Charlotte, *Jane Eyre*, Penguin Classics, 2006

–, *Shirley*, Penguin Classics, 2006

–, *The Professor*, Penguin Classics, 1989

–, *Villette*, Penguin Classics, 1985

Chapple, J.A.V. and Arthur Pollard (eds.), *The Letters of Mrs Gaskell*, Manchester University Press, 1966

Fraser, Rebecca, *Charlotte Brontë*, Methuen, 1988

Gaskell, Elizabeth, *The Life of Charlotte Brontë*, Penguin Classics, 1997 [based on the text of the first edition]

–, *The Life of Charlotte Brontë*, Oxford University Press, 2009 [based on the text of the third edition]

Gérin, Winifred, *Charlotte Brontë: The Evolution of Genius*, Clarendon Press, 1967

Gordon, Lyndall, *Charlotte Brontë: A Passionate Life*, Chatto & Windus, 1994

Harman, Claire, *Charlotte Brontë: A Life*, Viking, 2015

Macdonald, Frederika, *The Secret of Charlotte Brontë: Followed by Some Reminiscences of the Real Monsieur and Madame Heger*, T.C. and E.C. Jack, 1914

MacEwan, Helen, *The Brontës in Brussels*, Peter Owen, 2014

Shorter, Clement K., *Charlotte Brontë and Her Circle*, Dodd Mead and Company, 1896

Smith, Margaret (ed.), *The Letters of Charlotte Brontë with a selection of letters by family and friends*, Clarendon Press, vols. I–III, 1995-2004

Stevens, Joan (ed.), *Mary Taylor, Friend of Charlotte Brontë: Letters from New Zealand and Elsewhere*, Auckland University Press, 1972

Taylor, Mary, *The First Duty of Women. A series of articles repr. from the Victoria magazine, 1865 to 1870*, General Books, 2012

–, *Miss Miles or A Tale of Yorkshire Life 60 Years Ago*, Oxford University Press, 1990

–, *Swiss Notes by Five Ladies*, Inchbold & Beck, 1875

Whitehead, Barbara, *Charlotte Brontë and her 'dearest Nell': The story of a friendship*, Smith Settle, 1993

Wise, Thomas James and John Alexander Symington, *The Shakespeare Head Brontë, The Brontës: Their Lives, Friendships & Correspondence in Four Volumes*, Shakespeare Head Press, 1932

~

GEORGE ELIOT AND HARRIET BEECHER STOWE

Ashton, Rosemary, *George Eliot: A Life*, Hamish Hamilton, 1996

Belasco, Susan (ed.), *Stowe in Her Own Time: A Biographical Chronicle of Her Life, Drawn from Recollections, Interviews, and Memoirs by Family, Friends, and Associates*, University of Iowa Press, 2009

Blind, Mathilde, *George Eliot*, W. H. Allen, 1888

Bodenheimer, Rosemarie, *The Real Life of Mary Ann Evans: George Eliot, her Letters and Fiction*, Cornell University Press, 1994

Cognard-Black, Jennifer, *Narrative in the Professional Age: Transatlantic Readings of Harriet Beecher Stowe, George Eliot, and Elizabeth Stuart Phelps*, Taylor & Francis, 2004

–, and Elizabeth MacLeod Walls (eds.), *Kindred Hands: Letters on Writing by British and American Women Authors, 1865-1935*, University of Iowa Press, 2006

Cross, J.W. (ed.), *George Eliot's Life as Related in Her Letters and Journals*, vols. I–III, William Blackwood and Sons, 1885

Edel, Leon (ed.), *Henry James Letters*, vol. I, 1843–1875, Macmillan, 1974

Eliot, George, *Adam Bede*, Penguin Classics, 2008

–, *Daniel Deronda*, Penguin Classics, 1995

–, *Middlemarch*, Penguin Classics, 2003

–, *Romola*, Penguin Classics, 1997

–, *Silly Novels by Lady Novelists*, Penguin Books, 2010

–, *The Spanish Gypsy*, Pickering & Chatto, 2008

Fields, Annie (ed.), *Life and Letters of Harriet Beecher Stowe*, Houghton Mifflin and Company, 1898

Haight, Gordon S., *George Eliot: A Biography*, Oxford University Press, 1969

– (ed.), *George Eliot & John Chapman: with Chapman's Diaries* (second edition), Archon Books, 1969

– (ed.), *The George Eliot Letters*, Yale University Press, vols. I–VIII, 1954–78

Harris, Margaret and Judith Johnston, *The Journals of George Eliot*, Cambridge University Press, 1998

Hedrick, Joan D., *Harriet Beecher Stowe: A Life*, Oxford University Press, 1994

Henry, Nancy, *The Life of George Eliot: A Critical Biography*, Wiley-Blackwell, 2012

Hughes, Kathryn, *George Eliot: The Last Victorian*, Fourth Estate, 1999

James, Henry, *The Middle Years*, W. Collins Sons & Co., 1917

Kohn, Denise, Sarah Meer and Emily B. Todd, *Transatlantic Stowe: Harriet Beecher Stowe and European Culture*, University of Iowa Press, 2006

McCormack, Kathleen, *George Eliot in Society: Travels Abroad and Sundays at the Priory*, Ohio State University Press, 2013

Spencer, Herbert, *An Autobiography*, vol. I, Williams and Norgate, 1904

Stowe, Charles Edward, *The Life of Harriet Beecher Stowe: Compiled from her Letters and Journals*, Sampson Low, Marston, Searle & Rivington, 1889

Stowe, Harriet Beecher, *A Key to Uncle Tom's Cabin; presenting the original facts and documents upon which the story is founded together with collaborative statements verifying the truth of the work* (second edition), Sampson Low, Son & Co., 1853

–, *Lady Byron Vindicated*, Sampson Low, Son & Marston, 1870

–, *Oldtown Folks*, Harvard University Press, 1966

–, *Sunny Memories of Foreign Lands*, Routledge, 1854

–, *Uncle Tom's Cabin, Or, Life Among the Lowly*, Penguin Classics, 1981

Uglow, Jenny, *George Eliot*, Virago Press, 2011

Wilson, Forest, *Crusader in Crinoline: The Life of Harriet Beecher Stowe*, J. B. Lippincott, 1941

~

KATHERINE MANSFIELD AND VIRGINIA WOOLF

Baker, Ida, *Katherine Mansfield: The Memories of LM*, Michael Joseph, 1971

Bell, Anne Olivier (ed.), *The Diary of Virginia Woolf*, vol. I, 1915–19, The Hogarth Press, 1983

–, with Andrew McNeillie, *The Diary of Virginia Woolf*, vols. II–V, 1920–41, The Hogarth Press, 1978–84

Dubino, Jeanne, *Virginia Woolf and the Literary Marketplace*, Palgrave Macmillan, 2010

Hankin, Cherry A. (ed.), *Letters Between Katherine Mansfield and John Middleton Murry*, Virago Press, 1988

–, *The Letters of John Middleton Murry to Katherine Mansfield*, Constable, 1983

Jones, Kathleen, *Katherine Mansfield: The Story-Teller*, The Book Mill, 2012

Kimber, Gerri and Vincent O'Sullivan (eds.), *The Collected Works, Volume 2: The Collected Fiction of Katherine Mansfield, 1916–1922*, Edinburgh University Press, 2012

–, and Angela Smith (eds.), *The Collected Works, Volume 3: The Poetry and Critical Writings of Katherine Mansfield*, Edinburgh University Press, 2014

–, and Claire Davison with Anna Plumridge (eds.), *The Collected Works, Volume 4: The Diaries of Katherine Mansfield including Miscellaneous Works*, Edinburgh University Press, 2016.

Lea, F.A., *The Life of John Middleton Murry*, Methuen, 1959

Lee, Hermione, *Virginia Woolf*, Vintage, 1997

Levy, Paul (ed.), *The Letters of Lytton Strachey*, Viking, 2005

Light, Alison, *Mrs Woolf and the Servants*, Penguin Books, 2008

Love, Jean O., *Virginia Woolf: Sources of Madness and Art*, University of California Press, 1978

Mansfield, Katherine, *The Collected Stories of Katherine Mansfield*, Penguin Classics, 2007

Meyers, Jeffrey, *Katherine Mansfield: A Darker View*, Cooper Square, 2002

Middleton Murry, John (ed.), *Journal of Katherine Mansfield*, Persephone Books, 2006

Morrell, Ottoline, *Ottoline at Garsington: Memoirs of Lady Ottoline Morrell 1915–1918*, Faber & Faber, 1974

Newman, Hilary, *Virginia Woolf and Katherine Mansfield: A Creative Rivalry*, Cecil Woolf, 2004

Nicolson, Nigel with Joanne Trautmann, *The Letters of Virginia Woolf*, vols. II–IV, 1912–31, The Hogarth Press, 1976–78

Noble, Joan Russell (ed.), *Recollections of Virginia Woolf*, Peter Owen, 1972

Norburn, Roger, *A Katherine Mansfield Chronology*, Palgrave Macmillan, 2008

Orton, William, *The Last Romantic*, Cassell & Co., 1937

O'Sullivan, Vincent and Margaret Scott (eds.), *The Collected Letters of Katherine Mansfield*, vols. I–IV, Clarendon Press, 1984–2008

Schulkind, Jeanne (ed.), *Moments of Being*, Pimlico, 2002

Tomalin, Claire, *Katherine Mansfield: A Secret Life*, Penguin, 2003

Woolf, Leonard, *Beginning Again: An Autobiography of the Years 1911 to 1918*, Harvest/Harcourt Brace Jovanovich, 1975

Woolf, Virginia, *Mrs Dalloway*, Penguin Classics, 2000

–, *Jacob's Room*, Penguin Classics, 1992

–, *Night and Day*, Penguin Classics, 1992

–, *Selected Short Stories*, Penguin Classics, 2000

–, *To the Lighthouse*, Penguin Classics, 2000

A WEB OF LITERARY CONNECTIONS

Angelou, Maya, *The Collected Autobiographies of Maya Angelou*, Virago, 2007

Angier, Carol, *Jean Rhys: Life and Work*, Faber & Faber, 2011

Boyd, Valerie, *Wrapped in Rainbows: The Life of Zora Neale Hurston*, Scribner, 2003

Brittain, Vera, *Testament of Friendship: The Story of Winifred Holtby*, Virago, 2012

–, *Testament of Youth: An Autobiographical Study of the Years 1900–1925*, Virago, 2004

Grayling, A. C., *Friendship*, Yale University Press, 2013

Hurston, Zora Neale, *Their Eyes Were Watching God*, Virago, 1992

Kaplin, Carla (ed.), *Zora Neale Hurston: A Life in Letters*, Doubleday, 2002

Kennard, Jean E., *Vera Brittain and Winifred Holtby: A Working Partnership*, University of New Hampshire by University Press of New England, 1989

Lillios, Anna, *Crossing the Creek: The Literary Friendship of Zora Neale Hurston and Marjorie Kinnan Rawlings*, University of Florida Press, 2011

Morrison, Toni, *Beloved*, Vintage, 1997

Rhys, Jean, *Wide Sargasso Sea*, Penguin Modern Classics, 2000

Woolf, Virginia, *A Room of One's Own*, Penguin Books, 2012

Yalom, Marilyn with Theresa Donovan Brown, *The Social Sex: A History of Female Friendship*, Harper Perennial, 2015

NOTES

Authors' original spelling and punctuation have been retained in quotations, even when they have made errors.

We have usually referred to the book's central biographical subjects by first name. In the case of individuals not personally known to these central characters, we have most often referred to them by surname. Exceptions to these rules include teachers and doctors, referred to by their honorifics; George Henry Lewes, referred to as Lewes to avoid confusion with George Eliot; and John Middleton Murry, referred to as Murry, the name by which he was commonly known.

When we are quoting from an original manuscript, we have included in the notes the institution where it is held. For ease of reference for future researchers, we have also included publication details where possible.

IN SEARCH OF A SECRET SISTERHOOD

Page 18
• *'in a fit of caution'*: Mary Taylor to Charlotte Brontë, June to 24 July 1848, The Morgan Library & Museum, Joan Stevens (ed.), *Mary Taylor, Friend of Charlotte Brontë: Letters from New Zealand and Elsewhere*, Auckland University Press, 1972, p.75.

~

JANE AUSTEN AND ANNE SHARP

The details included in this section are most often drawn from the letters and diaries of Fanny Knight, the letters of Jane Austen and *A Memoir of Jane Austen* (1871) by James Edward Austen-Leigh. We consulted extant letters and other documents by Jane and Cassandra Austen at the Morgan Library and Museum. Manuscript sources were also consulted at Kent History and Library Centre, Hampshire Record Office and the British Library. We also made substantial use of *The Jane Austen Files: A Complete Anthology of Letters and Family Recollections* (edited by Helen Amy) and *Jane Austen's Letters* (collected and edited by Deirdre Le Faye). We are indebted to Deirdre Le Faye for the painstaking work she undertook on the exhaustive *Chronology of Jane Austen and Her Family*. The biographies of Paula Byrne and Claire Tomalin were of regular assistance too.

ABBREVIATIONS

AS	Anne Sharp
BL	British Library
Byrne	Paula Byrne, *The Real Jane Austen*, HarperPress, 2013
CEA	Cassandra Elizabeth Austen
Chronology	Deirdre Le Faye, *A Chronology of Jane Austen and Her Family*, Cambridge University Press (second edition), 2013
DC	Dorothy Chapman
DLF	Deirdre Le Faye
FCK	Fanny Catherine Knight (née Austen)

Files	Helen Amy (ed.), *The Jane Austen Files: A Complete Anthology of Letters and Family Recollections*, Amberley, 2015
Household	Peggy Hickman, *A Jane Austen Household Book: with Martha Lloyd's Recipes*, Readers Union, 1978
HRO	Hampshire Record Office
JA	Jane Austen
JEAL	James Edward Austen-Leigh
KHLC	Kent History and Library Centre
Letters	Deirdre Le Faye (ed.), *Jane Austen's Letters*, Oxford University Press (fourth edition), 2014 (© Deirdre Le Faye, 2011)
LMA	London Metropolitan Archives
Memoir	James Edward Austen-Leigh, *A Memoir of Jane Austen*, Richard Bentley and Son, 1871
ML	Martha Lloyd
Morgan	Department of Literary and Historical Manuscripts, The Morgan Library and Museum
pb	Fanny Catherine Knight (née Austen), Pocketbook, Kent History and Library Centre
Tomalin	Claire Tomalin, *Jane Austen: A Life*, Penguin, 2012
Uglow	Jenny Uglow, *In These Times: Living in Britain Through Napoleon's Wars 1793–1815*, Faber & Faber, 2014

A CIRCLE OF SINGLE WOMEN

Page 23

• *scoured Jane's personality*: JEAL, *Memoir*, p.55.

Page 24

• *In the 1840s*: Caroline Austen, 'My Aunt Jane Austen: A Memoir', 1867, *Files*, Helen Amy (ed.), p.39.
• *She refused to collaborate*: Helen Amy (ed.), *Files*, p.558; Lord Brabourne, 'Letters of Jane Austen Edited with an Introduction and Critical Remarks', 1884, *Files*, Helen Amy (ed.), p.426.
• *Subtitled 'Devoted Friends'*: 'Jane Austen's Last Days: An Unpublished Letter', *The Times*, 1 February 1926, pp.13–4.
• *'my dearest Anne'*: JA to AS, 22 May 1817, Morgan, *Letters*, p.355.

Page 25

• *'constituted the very class…'*: JEAL, *Memoir*, p.9.
• *The uptight tone*: CEA to AS, 28 July 1817, Morgan, *Letters*, p.362.
• *But unpublished papers*: FCK pb and letters to DC are all held at KHLC and have never been published in full.
• *Anne was a writer*: FCK to DC, 12 January 1806, KHLC.
• *The child's entry*: FCK, 21 January 1806, pb, KHLC.

Page 26

• *thirty-one years earlier…*: Her age has been calculated according to her death certificate, rather than the less reliable census returns. AS's birthday is recorded in FCK pb as 15 January. This is further supported by a baptismal certificate for Ann Sharp, daughter of Elizabeth and John in the St Paul, Deptford, Composite register, LMA, dated February 1773.
• *kindly condescension*: Evident in the tone of FCK's letters to former governess DC.
• *reached Godmersham Park…*: Details of Godmersham Park are drawn from FCK pb and letters; Historic England, Godmersham Park, List Entry number: 1000290; tour of Godmersham Park and materials supplied by Godmersham Park Heritage Centre; DLF, *A Chronology of Jane Austen and Her Family*, Cambridge University Press (second edition), 2013; Nigel Nicolson, *Godmersham Park: Before, During and After Jane Austen's Time*, Jane Austen Society, 1996.
• *a woman who penned theatricals*: FCK to DC, 12 January 1806, KHLC.

Page 27

• *were often paid little more*: Alice Renton, *Tyrant or Victim: A History of the British Governess*, Weidenfeld & Nicolson, 1991, p.38.

• '*a kind of shuttlecock…*': 'Jane Austen's Last Days: An Unpublished Letter', *The Times*, 1 February 1926, p.13.

• *Jane's unfashionable attire*: FCK to Marianne Austen, 23 August 1869, quoted in DLF, *Fanny Knight's Diaries: Jane Austen Through Her Niece's Eyes*, The Jane Austen Society, 2000, pp.38–9.

• *Fanny recorded…*: Details of AS's arrival and first days at Godmersham Park, including quotations, are drawn from FCK to DC, 25 January 1804, KHLC.

• *casual disregard for consistent spelling*: JA's royalty cheque of 1816, for example, was made out to 'Miss Jane Austin'.

Page 28

• *Elizabeth Sharpe*: Elizabeth Sharpe, 20 April 1803, burial record, St James Piccadilly, LMA.

• *dangerous bout of ill health*: FCK to DC, 8 January 1804, KHLC.

• *delay her departure*: FCK to DC, 27 November 1803, KHLC; FCK to DC, 8 January 1804, KHLC.

• *noisy newborn*: FCK to DC, 13 December 1804, KHLC.

• *entrance hall forever rang*: JA to Francis Austen, 25 September 1813, p.240.

Page 29

• *Edward enjoyed his fortune…*: JA to CEA, 2 June 1799, *Letters*, 44-5; JA to CEA, 30 June–1 July 1808, *Letters*, p.144; JA to CEA, 17 May 1799, p.41; FCK to Francis Austen, 25 September 1813, *Letters*, p.240; FCK, 10 October 1805, pb, KHLC.

• *lady of the house invited…*: Details about Fanny's birthday are drawn from JA to DC, 25 January 1804, KHLC.

• *at ten o'clock*: JA to CEA, 15–17 June 1808, *Letters*, p.131.

• *fine china*: JA to CEA, 16 September 1813, *Letters*, p.233.

• '*à la Godmersham*': JA to CEA, 15–17 June 1808, *Letters*, p.132.

• '*happy Indifference…*': JA to Francis Austen, 25 September 1813, *Letters*, p.239.

Page 30

• *just such a decorative object*: In vol. II, chapter XI of *Sense and Sensibility*, the Dashwood sisters are snubbed by a snobbish man examining decorative toothpick cases. He turns out to be the brother of their sister-in-law – a woman who has convinced her husband, their own brother, to neglect them. JA, *Sense and Sensibility*, Penguin Classics, 1995, pp.186–7.

• *Elizabeth did not take kindly…*: Details of Elizabeth Austen's interests are drawn from FCK to DC, 27 November 1804, KHLC; FCK, 11 December 1805, pb, KHLC. Elizabeth Austen's attitude to intellectual conversation, including the quotation, is drawn from Anna Lefroy, 'Recollections of Aunt Jane', 1864, *Files*, Helen Amy (ed.), p.28.

• *volunteer soldiers*: FCK, 17 September 1804, pb, KHLC; Claire Tomalin, *Tomalin*, pp.131–5.

Page 31

• *the younger children…*: Most descriptions of the children are drawn from FCK to DC, 28 July 1805, KHLC.

• *breakfasting à deux*: FCK, 1 December 1805, pb, KHLC.

• *The governess then heard*: FCK to DC, 15 April 1806, KHLC; FCK, 5 July 1805, pb, KHLC.

• *the child's great-aunt*: References to taking tea in Eggarton with AS appear throughout FCK's pb. For more information on 'Mrs' Elizabeth Knight of Eggarton, see DLF, *Letters*, p.599.

• *lured from their studies*: FCK, 28 June 1804, pb, KHLC.

Page 32

• *sharing her bed*: FCK, 29 September 1805, pb, KHLC.

• *vast, empty room*: JA to CEA, 3 November 1813, Morgan, *Letters*, p.260.

Page 33

• *criticised the status quo*: In 1793 Wordsworth's brother urged him to 'be cautious in writing or expressing your political Opinions', reminding him that by 'the suspension of the Habeas

Corpus Acts, the Ministers have great powers'. Quoted in John Bugg, *Five Long Winters: The Trials of British Romanticism*, Stanford University Press, 2013, p.145.

• *a sum with which*: According to the historical UK inflation rates calculator, £10 in 1803 equals about £893 in 2017. JA wrote of using £10 for winter clothing in JA to CEA, 18–19 December 1798, *Letters*, p.26: 'I shall keep *my* ten pounds to wrap myself up in next winter'.

Page 34

• '*...putrid fevers*': JA to CEA, 21–2 May 1801, Morgan, *Letters*, p.90.

• *On 19 June...*: Anne's collapse, the lead-up and its aftermath, including quotations, are drawn from FCK, 19–24 June 1804, pb, KHLC.

Page 35

• *high turnover of household staff*: FCK, Memorandums at the Beginning of the Year 1805, pb, KHLC.

• *financial trouble*: Thomas Keymer, '*Northanger Abbey* and *Sense and Sensibility*', Edward Copeland and Juliet McMaster (eds.), *The Cambridge Companion to Jane Austen*, Cambridge University Press, 2011, pp.21–38.

Page 36

• Sense and Sensibility *would later portray*: The Dashwood women in *Sense and Sensibility* were left to cope on £500 per year – more than the £460 household income that the Austen brothers considered sufficient for their mother and sisters.

Page 37

• *25 Gay Street*: DLF, 25 March 1805, *Chronology*, p.308.

• *first crops up*: JA to CEA, 21–3 April 1805, *Letters*, p.109.

• *an annotation tucked away*: In *Letters*, p.571, DLF claims: 'The Miss Sharp whom JA mentions as being in Bath in 1805 is clearly not the same as this Miss Anne Sharp'.

• *away from home*: 'Papa, Anny and Henry set off at 8 in the morning for Town', FCK, 18 March 1805, pb, KHLC; 'Papa, Edwd, George & Henry came home', FCK, 6 April 1805, pb, KHLC; 'Miss Sharpe came home', FCK, 13 April 1805, pb, KHLC.

• *work outside the schoolroom*: FCK, 13 August 1804, pb, KHLC; FCK, 4 September 1804, pb, KHLC.

Page 38

• *about her eyes*: FCK to DC, 9 April 1805, KHLC.

• *outwardly reserved*: Both Anna Lefroy and Caroline Austen remember JA as the more fun-loving of the sisters. Anna Lefroy, 'Recollections of Aunt Jane', 1864, Helen Amy (ed.), *Files*, p.27; Caroline Austen, 'My Aunt Jane Austen: A Memoir', Helen Amy (ed.), *Files*, p.35.

• *Maria Edgeworth and Frances Burney*: In vol. I, chapter V of *Northanger Abbey*, novels by Frances Burney and Maria Edgeworth are singled out for praise. JA, *Northanger Abbey*, Penguin Classics, 1995, vol. I, chapter V, 34.

• *her new novel*: JA's unfinished manuscript of *The Watsons* is written on paper watermarked 1803, and appears to have been started and abandoned in 1804–5. Like *Sense and Sensibility*, the novel is about a young woman left woefully unprovided for after the death of a family patriarch.

• *on 9 April 1805...*: Details of JA's return to Gay Street and Miss Colbourne's visit are drawn from JA to CEA, 8–11 April 1805, *Letters*, 103-7.

Page 39

• '*reduce her establishment...*': Henry Thomas Austen to Frank Austen, 28 January 1805, HRO.

Page 40

• *Martha to join their new household*: JA to CEA: 'I am quite of your opinion as to the folly of concealing any longer our intended partnership with Martha...', 21–3 April 1805, *Letters*, p.109.

• *amateur cook and apothecary*: Peggy Hickman, *Household*, passim.

• '*to take lessons of...*': JA to CEA, 21–3 April 1805, 109. AS had returned to Godmersham Park by this stage, but 'to take' suggests that this is a plan for a future date.

REBELLION BEHIND CLOSED DOORS

Page 41

• *six o'clock in the evening...*: Details of the Austen women's 1805 stay at Godmersham Park, including quotations, are drawn from FCK, 18 June to 15 September 1805, pb, KHLC; FCK to DC, 28 July 1805, KHLC.

Page 42

• *keep quiet about her past*: In response to *The Times*'s 1 February publication of JA and CEA letters to AS, Mrs Creaghe-Haward wrote: 'My aunt Miss Middleton (1817–94) knew her well and often spoke of her... From what she said I gather that Miss Sharp was a clever, rather dominant woman, much thought of in Everton society of her day. She was very reticent about her early life before coming to Liverpool, and also made a mystery of her age': Mrs Creaghe-Howard, 'Points from Letters', *The Times*, 12 February 1926, p.8. In her Will, Anne Sharp left: 'To Miss Mary Middleton ten pounds and Scotts bible. To Robina Middleton ten pounds and Milner's Church History. To Caroline Middleton ten pounds and four volumes of D'Aubigné on the Reformation'. The Last Will and Testament of Anne Sharp, 11 January 1851.

• *baptismal ledger*: St Paul, Deptford, Baptismal Record, February 1773, LMA.

Page 43

• *As a writer herself*: FCK to DC, 12 Jan 1806, KHLC.

Page 44

• *Scotch reels*: JA's love of dancing is evidenced in JA to FCK, 20–1 February 1817, 345; Henry Austen, 'Biographical Notice of the Author', 1818, Helen Amy (ed.), *Files*, p.16.

• *satirical bent*: For an example of Mrs Austen's playful streak, see the letter and poem she wrote to a pupil, encouraging him to return to 'the Mansion of Learning' where 'we study all day, Except when we play', quoted in Claire Tomalin, Tomalin, 26. For more on Mrs Austen, see Claire Tomalin, Tomalin, pp.143–55.

• *secretly penned...*: The play described in FCK, 26 June 1805, pb, KHLC is not attributed to AS. However, it includes several of the same characters as those in AS's play described in FCK to DC, 12 January 1806, KHLC. This suggests that AS did not own up to being its creator when it was first put on, redrafted the play during the intervening period, and then told the Godmersham Austens about her authorship when they staged the play 'with a few more additions', as FCK put it, on 4 January 1806.

Page 46

• *great animation*: JA to CEA, 15–17 June 1808, *Letters*, p.132.

• *ailing relatives*: JA to CEA, 24 August 1805, *Letters*, p.112.

• *'pretty but not strikingly so'*: FCK, 25 January 1804, pb, KHLC.

• *'Pray say everything kind...'*: JA to CEA, 30 August 1805, *Letters*, p.117.

Page 47

• *A plan was already afoot*: JA to CEA, 30 August 1805, *Letters*, p.117.

• *holiday plans...*: Details of the Worthing trip are drawn from FCK to DC, 15 September 1805, KHLC; FCK, 17–22 September 1805, pb, KHLC.

Page 48

• *'horridly affected... rather amusing'*: JEAL to Anna Lefroy, September 1820, HRO.

• *an all-time high*: William Playfair, 'Price of Wheat: 1565–1821'.

Page 49

• *a cheery woman*: Peggy Hickman, *Household*, p.34.

• *into the night*: JA to CEA, 8 January 1799, *Letters*, p.35.

• *as many four-pound loaves*: Earl of Suffolk, 25 April 1805, House of Lords debate, Hansard, vol. 4, cc.374–5.

Page 50

• *for a sojourn…*: Details of DC's return to Godmersham Park are drawn from FCK to DC, 15 September 1805, KHLC; FCK, 25 September to 10 October 1805, pb, KHLC.

• *upon her return…*: Details of AS's return to Godmersham Park, including quotations, are drawn from FCK, 1 November 1805, pb, KHLC, and FCK to DC, 2 November 1805, KHLC.

Page 51

• *attack by France*: FCK, 30 September 1805, pb, KHLC; FCK, 11 December 1805, pb, KHLC.

• *a Gallic invasion*: Jenny Uglow, *Uglow*, Loc 7407.

• *rose before the rest of her household*: JEAL, *Memoir*, 50; Caroline Austen, 'My Aunt Jane Austen: A Memoir', Helen Amy (ed.), *Files*, p.36.

• *'paintress'…*: Details of the portraiture, including quotations, are drawn from FCK, 5 November 1805, pb, KHLC; FCK, 14 December 1805, pb, KHLC; FCK to DC, 22 February 1806, KHLC.

Page 52

• *one of Anne's headaches…*: Details of AS's operation and its aftermath, including quotations, are drawn from FCK, 15 November to 13 December 1805, pb, KHLC; FCK to DC, 22 November 1805, KHLC. The scene was also informed by William Lewis and John Aikin, *An Experimental History of the Materia Medica: Or of the Natural and Artificial Substances Made Use of in Medicine*, Johnson, 1784, pp.188–9; Coriann Convertito, *The Health of British Seamen in the West Indies 1770–1806*, University of Exeter PhD, 2011, p.44.

Page 52–3

• *Trim Street in Bath*: In 1801, JA wrote to CEA that Mrs Austen 'will do everything in her power to avoid Trim St'; *The New Bath Directory* of 1805 shows that Trim Street was a commercial street.

Page 54

• *snow and melt…*: Details of the festive games and theatricals, including quotations, are drawn from FCK, 18 December 1805 to 2 January 1806, pb, KHLC; FCK, 20 December 1805, pb appendix, KHLC; FCK, 4 January 1806, pb appendix, KHLC; FCK to DC, 12 January 1806, KHLC.

• Evenings at Home: John Aikin and Anna Letitia Barbauld, *Evenings at home; or, the juvenile budget opened: Consisting of a variety of miscellaneous pieces*, vol. I, J. Johnson, 1792–6.

Page 55

• Mansfield Park: JA, *Mansfield Park*, Penguin Classics, 1996, vol. I, chapter XIV, p.110.

• *poetry annuals*: *The Poetical Register and Repository of Fugitive Poetry for 1803*, Rivington, 1805.

• *Anny*: It is clear that 'Anny' refers to AS because in FCK's pocketbook she mentions 'Anny's birthday' on 15 January 1806, which accords with her 15 January 1805 entry: 'Miss Sharpe's birthday'.

• Pride and Prejudice: *Cecilia* by Frances Burney, 1782, ends with a paragraph in which the capitalised phrase 'PRIDE and PREJUDICE' recurs three times. It is likely that this also informed JA's renaming of *Pride and Prejudice*.

Page 56

• *come to an end*: FCK, 18 January 1806, pb, KHLC.

• *'I assure you…'*: FCK, 12 January 1806, pb, KHLC.

• *family friend Martha*: DLF, *Chronology*, p.327.

• *to offer opinions*: Various authors, 'Opinions by various people of Jane Austen's work', BL manuscript.

CLOSING RANKS

Page 59

• *putting pen to paper*: Evidence of lost correspondence between JA and AS appears regularly in JA's letters. For an example during this period, see JA to CEA, 1–2 October 1808, *Letters*, p.147.

Page 60

• *'Panegyric on the Departed'*: JA to CEA, 13 October 1808, *Letters*, p.152.

• *state of the corpse*: JA to CEA, 15–16 October 1808, *Letters*, p.155.

• *Mrs Austen enjoyed*…: Details of life at Chawton Cottage are drawn from Constance Hill, *Jane Austen: Her Homes & Her Friends*, John Lane, 1902, pp.169–85.

Page 61

• *household chores*: Caroline Austen, 'My Aunt Jane Austen: A Memoir', 1867, Helen Amy (ed.), *Files*, p.36.

• *She confided in Jane*: JA to CEA, 30 January 1809, *Letters*, p.180.

• *'eyes have been…'*: FCK to DC, 15 March 1807, KHLC.

Page 62

• *'I can no more forget…'*: JA to CEA, 25 April 1811, *Letters*, p.190.

• *'magnificent project'*: JA to CEA, 31 May 1811, Morgan, *Letters*, pp.198–200.

Page 63

• *'I have given up…'*: JA to CEA, 6 June 1811, Morgan, *Letters*, p.201.

• *August of 1811*: Mary Lloyd Austen, 29 August 1811, pocketbook, HRO.

• *Collyer's public stagecoach*: Caroline Austen, 'My Aunt Jane Austen: A Memoir', 1867, Helen Amy (ed.), *Files*, p.32.

Page 64

• *'the characters are…'*: Unsigned review, *Critical Review*, vol. IV, 1 February 1812, pp.149–57.

• *trip to London*…: Details of this trip, including quotations, are drawn from JA to CEA, 20 May 1813, *Letters*, pp.218–20; JA to CEA, 24 May 1813, Morgan, *Letters*, pp.220–23.

Page 65

• *'as delightful a creature…'*: JA to CEA, 29 January 1813, *Letters*, p.210.

• *'very superior…'*: Unsigned review, *Critical Review*, March 1813, pp.318–24.

• *'one of the cleverest things'*: Richard Sheridan, quoted in Park Honan, *Jane Austen: Her Life*, Weidenfeld & Nicolson, 1987, p.318.

Page 66

• *share her children*: JA to CEA, 29 January 1813, *Letters*, p.210.

Page 67

• *'– Oh! I have…'*: JA to CEA, 3 November 1813, Morgan, *Letters*, p.260.

• *'Oh! Sir Wm…'*: JA to CEA, 23 June 1814, *Letters*, p.277. The full quotation raises questions about AS's relations with men: 'She writes highly of Sir Wm – I do so want him to marry her! – There is a Dow: Lady P. presiding there, to make it all right. – The Man is the same; but she does not mention what he is by Profession or Trade. – She does not think that Lady P. was privy to his scheme on her; but on being in his power, yielded. – Oh! Sir Wm – Sir Wm – how I will love you, if you will love Miss Sharp!'.

• *'I know your starched Notions…'*: JA to CEA, 4 February 1813, *Letters*, p.212.

• *wife of an Irish judge*: JA to CEA, 3 November 1813, Morgan, *Letters*, p.260.

Page 68

• *'its good sense & moral Tendency…'*: AS, 'Opinions by various people of Jane Austen's work', BL manuscript.

• *'fame nor profit'*: Henry Austen, 'A Biographical Notice', 1818, Helen Amy (ed.), *Files*, p.17.

Page 69

• *James Stanier Clarke*…: Details about JA's visit to Carlton House and its aftermath, including quotations, are drawn from the following exchange of letters: JA to James Stanier Clarke, 15 November 1815, HRO, *Letters*, p.308; James Stanier Clarke to JA, 16 November 1815, Morgan, *Letters*, p.309; JA to John Murray, 11 December 1815, *Letters*, pp.317–18; JA to John Murray, 11 December 1815, *Letters*, p.318; JA to James Stanier Clarke, 11 December 1815, *Letters*, p.319; James Stanier Clarke to JA, ?21 December 1815, *Letters*, p.320.

• *Friendship Book*: There is debate about whether this anonymous portrait is of Jane Austen. The President of the Jane Austen Society of North America makes a case for its authenticity: Joan Kingel Ray & Richard James Wheeler, 'James Stanier Clarke's Portrait of Jane Austen', *Persuasions*, vol. XXVII, 2005.

• *presentation copies of* Emma: DLF, *Letters*, p.571.

• *plush Persian carpets*: Jane Fawcett, *Historic Floors: Their History and Conservation*, Butterworth-Heinemann, 1998, p.160.

• *crystal chandeliers overhead*: W.H. Pyne, *The History of the Royal Residences*, vol. III, A. Dry, 1819.

Page 70

• *'because she* is *a woman…'*: JA to ML, 16 February 1813, Morgan, *Letters*, p.217.

• *each of his residences*: JEAL, *Memoir*, p.66.

• *elegant double staircase*: John B. Papworth, *Select Views of London; with Historical and Descriptive Sketches of Some of the Most Interesting of its Public Buildings*, R. Ackermann, 1816.

• *the direction of the library*: Augustus Pugin, plan of Carlton Palace, J. Taylor, 1826.

Page 71

• *library at Carlton House*: The presentation copy of *Emma* given by JA to the Prince Regent is now housed in the Royal Collection.

• *her dozen copies*: DLF, *Chronology*, p.525.

• *literary acclaim and financial success*: JA to FCK, 30 November 1814, *Letters*, p.299: 'tho' I like praise as well as anybody, I like what Edward calls *Pewter* too'.

• *'The authoress…'*: Augustus Hare, *Life and Letters of Maria Edgeworth*, Houghton Mifflin and Company, 1895, p.249, p.260.

Page 72

• *'best-chosen language…'*: JA, *Northanger Abbey*, Penguin Classics, 1995, vol. I, chapter V, 34.

• *twelve recipients*: John Murray's Archives record that presentation copies were sent to the following recipients: two to Hans Place (presumably for JA and Henry Austen); the Prince Regent's librarian; J. Leigh Perrot (the author's uncle); two for Mrs Austen; Captain Austen (presumed to be JA's brother Charles); James Austen; H.F. Austen (presumed to be Frank); FCK; AS; Maria Edgeworth. A further two copies were given by the publisher to the Countess of Morley and Augusta Leigh. Augusta Leigh was the half-sister of Lord Byron, who, rumour had it, was having an incestuous affair with him. Augusta brought her copy of *Emma* with her when she went to stay at Byron's house to offer assistance during the confinement of his wife, who had her suspicions about the true nature of the siblings' relationship. But they did have something rather less inflammatory in common too. Lady Byron was also a great admirer of Jane Austen.

• *marbled card*: AS's presentation copy of *Emma*, 24 June 2008, Bonhams, Lot 107.

Page 73

• *'better than M.P.…'*: AS, *Opinions of Emma*, BL.

• *'human intellect…'*: JA, *Emma*, Penguin Classics, 1996, vol. II, chapter XVII, p.247.

• *'quite one of her Letters…'*: JA to CEA, 8–9 September 1816, Morgan, *Letters*, p.335.

• *'nursing myself…'*: JA to CEA, 8–9 September 1816, Morgan, *Letters*, p.335.

Page 74

• *resolved to write a letter*: JA to AS, 22 May 1817, Morgan, *Letters*, p.355–6.

• *lock of Jane's hair…*: All details about JA and CEA's interactions immediately following JA's death, including quotations, are drawn from CEA to JA, 28 July 1817, Morgan, *Letters*, p.362.

Page 75

• *'starched Notions'*: JA to CEA, 4 February 1813, *Letters*, p.212.

• *Anne returned to Chawton Cottage*: Mary Lloyd Austen, 31 August 1820, pocket book, HRO.

• *£30 in her Will*: Claire Tomalin, Tomalin, p.284.

Page 76

• *her own boarding school*: DLF, *Letters*, p.571; UK Census, Everton, 1841 and 1851.

• 'She was very reticent...': Mrs Creaghe-Howard, 'Points from Letters', *The Times*, 12 February 1926, p.8.
• *far greater wealth*: This is evidenced by the Last Will and Testament of Anne Sharp, 11 January 1851.

~

CHARLOTTE BRONTË AND MARY TAYLOR

The details included in this section are most often drawn from the letters of Charlotte Brontë and Mary Taylor, and Elizabeth Gaskell's *Life of Charlotte Brontë* – particularly the two letters sent to her by Mary Taylor, sections of which are interspersed within the text of that book. Where possible (despite some of the factual inaccuracies mentioned in our notes), we have been guided by Mary Taylor's belief that the first edition of the *Life* was the truest one and have relied on that version where possible. When we have drawn on new information included in the revised third edition, we have stated this in our notes. The two letters from Mary Taylor to Elizabeth Gaskell no longer exist in their original form. We consulted original letters and other writings by Charlotte Brontë and Mary Taylor in the collections of the Brontë Parsonage Museum, the New York Public Library's Henry W. and Albert A. Berg Collection and the Morgan Library and Museum. We made substantial use, too, of the published *Letters of Charlotte Brontë* (edited by Margaret Smith) and *Mary Taylor: Letters from New Zealand and Elsewhere* (edited by Joan Stevens). Juliet Barker's exhaustive biography, *The Brontës*, was also indispensable.

ABBREVIATIONS

Alexander	Christine Alexander (ed.), *Tales of Glass Town, Angria and Gondal: Selected Writings*, Oxford University Press, 2010
Barker	Juliet Barker, *The Brontës*, Abacus, 2010
Bellamy	Joan Bellamy, *'More Precious than Rubies' Mary Taylor: friend of Charlotte Brontë, strong-minded woman*, Highgate Publications, 2002
Berg	The Henry W. and Albert A. Berg Collection of English and American Literature, The New York Public Library, Astor, Lennox and Tilden Foundations
BPM	Brontë Parsonage Museum
CB	Charlotte Brontë
EN	Ellen Nussey
EG	Elizabeth Gaskell
LCB	Margaret Smith (ed.), *The Letters of Charlotte Brontë with a selection of letters by family and friends*, Clarendon Press, vols. I–III, 1995–2004 (© Margaret Smith 1995, 2000, 2004)
Life (first)	Elizabeth Gaskell, *The Life of Charlotte Brontë* Penguin, 1997 [based on the text of the first edition]
LMG	J.A.V. Chapple and Arthur Pollard (eds.), *The Letters of Mrs Gaskell*, Manchester University Press, 1966
Morgan	Department of Literary and Historical Manuscripts, The Morgan Library and Museum
MT	Mary Taylor
Reminiscences	Ellen Nussey, 'Reminiscences of Charlotte Brontë', *Scribners Monthly*, May 1871, II.i
RHJ	Roe Head Journal
SHB LL	T.J. Wise and J.A. Symington, *The Shakespeare Head Brontë, The Brontës: Their Lives, Friendships & Correspondence in Four Volumes*, Shakespeare Head Press, 1932
Shorter	Clement K. Shorter, *Charlotte Brontë and Her Circle*, Dodd, Mead and Company, 1896
Taylor	Joan Stevens (ed.), *Mary Taylor, Friend of Charlotte Brontë: Letters from New Zealand and Elsewhere*, Auckland University Press, 1972

THREE'S A CROWD

Page 80-1
• *ten or so pupils*: Juliet Barker, Barker, p.199.

• *blue cloth coats they wore…*: All details about the Taylor sisters' clothing in this paragraph were drawn from an account by EN included in Clement K. Shorter, Shorter, p.235.

• *'a little old woman'*: EG, *Life* (first), p.78.

• *rosy cheeks*: This detail is drawn from CB's description of Rose Yorke, the character based (in personality and appearance) on MT. CB, *Shirley*, Penguin Classics, 2006, chapter IX, p.143.

• *'too pretty to live'*: From EN's account in Clement K. Shorter, Shorter, p.234.

• *other students assumed*: From EN's account in Clement K. Shorter, Shorter, p.235.

• *the airy schoolroom…*: This schoolroom scene is drawn from a description by MT in a letter to EG, included in EG, *Life* (first), p.78.

• *reminiscent of an abbess*: Juliet Barker, Barker, p.199.

Page 83

• *'You are very ugly.'*: This incident is related in one of MT's letters to EG: 'I told her she was very ugly'. EG, *Life* (first), p.79.

• *…untamed frizz of hair:* EN, Reminiscences, p.19.

• *bony frame*: EN, Reminiscences, p.19.

Page 84

• *'a great deal of good'*: EG is quoting directly from one of MT's letters in EG, *Life* (first), p.80.

• *'yield pleasure to Mary Taylor…'*: CB to Mary Dixon, early 1843, *LCB* I, p.313.

• *Ellen Nussey arrived*: The following first encounter, including the quotation, is drawn from an account in EN, *Reminiscences*, pp.18–19.

Page 85

• *she would deride*: In this letter to her publisher, CB outlines what she believes are EN's strengths and weaknesses. CB to W.S. Williams, 3 January 1850, *LCB* II, p.323.

• *Epistolary evidence suggests:* In a letter from Martha Taylor to EN, after MT and CB had left the school, she asks if she may now sleep with EN – suggesting they are both without sleeping partners after their sister and friend have finished their schooling. Martha Taylor to EN, 17 May 1832, *SHB* I, p.102.

Page 86

• *vied for first place*: From EN's account in Clement K. Shorter, Shorter, p.234.

• *most coveted prizes*: Martha Taylor to EN, 17 May 1832, *SHB* I, p.102. This letter strongly suggests that EN won the prize.

• *savagely split apart*: EN, Reminiscences, p.24. Chapter 23 of *Jane Eyre* ends with the chestnut tree in the grounds of Thornfield being struck by lightning and split. CB, *Jane Eyre*, Penguin Classics, 2006, chapter 23, p.296.

Page 88

• *none the wiser*: Clement K. Shorter, Shorter, p.234.

Page 89

• *'bed-fellow…calm sleep'*: CB to EN, ?26 October 1852, *LCB* III, p.73. When EN transcribed this letter for publication, she replaced 'bed-fellow' with 'companion'. *LCB* III, p.74 (n5).

• *romantic friendships*: Marilyn Yalom with Theresa Donovan Brown, *The Social Sex: A History of Female Friendship*, Harper Perennial, 2015, pp.143–4.

• *'My darling…'*: CB to EN, ?October / November 1836, *LCB* I, pp.154–5.

• *'I wish I could live with you always…'*: CB to EN, 26 September 1836, *LCB* I, p.152.

Page 90-1

• *'Am I to spend…'*: CB, RHJ III, 11 August 1836, Bonnell Collection, BPM, Alexander, p.162. Six individual pieces written by CB during her time as a teacher at Roe Head are known collectively as the Roe Head Journal.

Page 91

• *At one such private hour…*: This scene, including quotations, is drawn from the first of the pieces that make up the RHJ. CB, 4 February 1836, RHJ I, Morgan, Alexander, pp.158–60.

Page 92

• *Mary had been known to arrange:* Joan Bellamy, Bellamy, p.10.

• *'How can you give so much of yourself…':* The dialogue within this scene is reconstructed from an extract from one of MT's letters to EG, included in the *Life*. MT wrote: 'I went to see her, and asked how she could give so much for so little money… She confessed it was not brilliant, but what could she do?'. EG, *Life* (first), p.106.

Page 93

• *she broke the red sealing wax…:* This scene, including quotations, is drawn from Robert Southey to CB, 12 March 1837, BPM, *LCB* I, pp.165–7.

Page 94

• *'I must thank you…':* CB to Robert Southey, 16 March 1837, *LCB* I, pp.168–9.

• *…heartily approve:* In reply to CB, Southey would write that 'You have received admonition as considerately & kindly as it was given'. Robert Southey to CB, 22 March 1837, *LCB* I, p.170.

TWO ADVENTUROUS SPIRITS

Page 97

• *who had become reliant:* Barbara Whitehead, *Charlotte Brontë and her 'dearest Nell': The story of a friendship*, Smith Settle, 1993, p.85.

• *exacerbating existing tensions:* Joan Bellamy, Bellamy, p.25.

Page 98

• *a package she would receive…:* MT's letter to CB has not survived, but CB recounted its contents in EN, 7 August 1841, *LCB* I, p.266. Most of the details in the following scene, including quotations, are drawn from this letter, written while CB was working for the White family at Upperwood House in Rawdon.

Page 99

• *'cast oil on the flames':* CB to EN, 2 November 1841, *LCB* I, p.272.

• *jokingly offering:* EN, Reminiscences, p.26.

• *insisted on paying him:* Rebecca Fraser, *Charlotte Brontë*, Methuen, 1988, p.180.

• *an astute investment:* Claire Harman, *Charlotte Brontë: A Life*, Viking, 2015, p.156.

• *Charlotte told her aunt…:* All the following details and quotations are drawn from CB to Elizabeth Branwell, 29 September 1841, *LCB* I, pp.268–9.

Page 100

• *£150:* Claire Harman, *Charlotte Brontë: A Life*, Viking, 2015, p.135.

Page 101

• *The pair had quarrelled:* CB to EN, 2 November 1841, *LCB* I, p.271.

• *'quite enter':* CB to EN, 20 January 1842, *LCB* I, p.278.

• *willowy Emily:* All these details about Emily Brontë's appearance are drawn from EN, Reminiscences, pp.26–7.

Page 102

• *her clever older brother Joe:* Joan Bellamy, Bellamy, p.23, p.28.

• *eleven-hour journey:* Juliet Barker, Barker, p.442.

• *Like Lucy Snowe:* CB, *Villette*, Penguin Classics, 1985, chapter VI, p.108.

• *St Paul's was the one landmark…:* EG, *The Life of Charlotte Brontë* (third edition), Oxford University Press, 2009, p.172. MT's account of the group's stay in London and arrival in Brussels, given in one of her letters to EG, does not appear in the original version of the *Life*.

• *gamely volunteered himself:* Joan Bellamy, Bellamy, p.29.

• *arduous journey by stagecoach:* Juliet Barker, Barker, p.444.

Page 103

• *the British chaplain of Brussels:* Helen MacEwan, *The Brontës in Brussels*, Peter Owen, 2014, p.21.

- *female porter:* Helen MacEwan, *The Brontës in Brussels*, Peter Owen, 2014, p.35.
- *dark, brooding mass of foliage:* Juliet Barker, Barker, p.446.
- *A decade later:* CB, *Villette*, Penguin Classics, 1985, chapter XII, p.174.
- *Claire Zoë Heger:* Helen MacEwan, *The Brontës in Brussels*, Peter Owen, 2014, p.45.

Page 104

- *stronger impression on Charlotte:* CB to EN, May 1842, *LCB* I, p.284.
- *permission of Madame and Monsieur Heger:* Juliet Barker, Barker, p.447.
- *a newsy letter to Ellen…*: The following scene, including quotations, is drawn from CB, MT and Martha Taylor to EN, March-April 1842, Morgan, *Taylor*, pp.28–30.

Page 106

- *When Martha returned home:* Joan Bellamy, Bellamy, pp.30–1.
- *allowing the director:* Claire Harman, *Charlotte Brontë: A Life*, Viking, 2015, p.150.

Page 108

- *a strong constitution:* Juliet Barker, Barker, p.474.
- *like Elizabeth Gaskell:* EG, *Life* (first), pp.182–3.

Page 109

- *given them a letter…*: Constantin Heger to CB (Margaret Smith's translation), 5 November 1842, *LCB* I, pp.299–300.
- *not be the security…*: This account, including quoted dialogue, covering CB's departure from Haworth and arrival in London, is drawn from what CB related to EG during the period of their friendship – EG later including the story in EG, *Life* (first), p.184.

Page 110

- *In a letter to Ellen…*: CB to EN, ?late June 1843, *LCB* I, p.325.

Page 111

- *later destroy almost all:* MT to CB, June to 24 July 1848, Morgan, *Taylor*, 75. Just one of CB's letters to MT (4 September 1848, *LCB* II, pp.111–15) survives.

Page 112

- *an extant letter:* MT to EN, 16 February 1843, *Taylor*, pp.42–4.
- *Charlotte begged Ellen…*: CB to EN, 6 August 1843, *LCB* I, p.327.
- *Another missive…*: This account of CB's walk and visit to the cathedral, including quotations, is drawn from CB to Emily Brontë, 2 September 1843, *LCB* I, pp.329–30. The dialogue is adapted from this passage: 'The priest asked if I was a Protestant then. I somehow could not tell a lie and said "yes".'

Page 114

- *had been discontinued:* The stopping of lessons, and limiting of contact between CB and Monsieur Heger, is suggested both by CB's letters of the time and the account of a former pupil at the pensionnat in Frederika Macdonald, *The Secret of Charlotte Brontë: Followed by Some Reminiscences of the Real Monsieur and Madame Heger*, T.C. and E.C. Jack, 1914, p.61.
- *Mary… sent a letter:* This letter from MT has not survived, but CB describes its contents in CB to Mary Dixon, 16 October 1843, *LCB* I, p.336.

Page 115

- *'it is odd in a woman…':* MT to EN, winter 1843, *Taylor*, p.50.
- *a mournful letter to Ellen…*: CB to EN, 23 January 1844, *LCB* I, pp.340–1.

Page 116

- *Ellen would recall her feelings…*: This scene, including the quotation, is drawn from EN to Mary Gorham, 21 May 1844, *LCB* I, pp.347–8.

Page 117

- *'a great planet':* CB to EN, c. 26 October 1844, *LCB* I, p.372.

ONE GREAT MYTH

Page 119

• *On a mild winter's day*…: Details about the likely date of Mary's climb, the local geography and arrival in Wellington are drawn from Joan Stevens, *Taylor*, 57, pp.66–7, p.73 (n2).

Page 120

• *The last time they'd met*: EG, *Life* (first), p.206. EG gives the date of this meeting as January 1845, but it was in fact February. MT set sail on 18 March and arrived in Wellington on 24 July 1845.

Page 121

• *been afflicted by*: CB to Constantin Heger, 18 November 1845, *LCB* I, p.437.

• *this distant outpost*…: MT to CB, June to 24 July 1848, Morgan, *Taylor*, pp.73–7. The letter was finished on 24 July 1848, but written over a period of several weeks, most likely beginning in June (second part of letter held at Berg).

• *an eighteen-gun sloop*: Joan Stevens, *Taylor*, p.73 (n2).

Page 122

• *Charlotte read the letter through*: CB to EN, 10 December 1848, *LCB* II, p.153 and p.153 (n6), CB to EN, ?22 January 1849, *LCB* I, 172. In mid-December, a few days after the first of these two letters, Charlotte heard from Mary.

• *'much shattered'*: CB to EN, 28 July 1848, *LCB* II, p.93.

Page 122–3

• *'we could not tell him of our efforts…'*: CB to W.S. Williams, 2 October 1848, *LCB* II, p.123.

Page 123

• *biggest disappointments came*: All details about the letter, including quotations, are drawn from MT to CB, June to 24 July 1848, Morgan, *Taylor*, pp.73–6.

Page 124

• Quarterly Review *attacked*…: Elizabeth Rigby, 'Vanity Fair – and Jane Eyre', *Littel's Living Age*, March 1849, 20, pp.503–7. The review was published in the *Quarterly Review* in December 1848, and subsequently reprinted in this American magazine.

Page 125

• *sink if she failed him*: CB to W.S. Williams, 25 December 1848, *LCB* II, p.159.

Page 126

• *By the time Charlotte confided*: CB to EN, c. 12, 14 May 1849, *LCB* II, p.208.

• *Written in April 1849*…: MT to CB, 10 April 1849, *Taylor*, p.86 and p.86 (n4).

Page 127

• *'writing it has been a boon…'*: CB to W. S. Williams, 29 August 1849, *LCB* II, p.241.

• *'Why do you like Miss Austen so very much?...'*: CB to George Henry Lewes, 12 January 1848, *LCB* II, p.10.

Page 128

• *Charlotte's missive had not*: CB to EG, 17 November 1849, *LCB* II, p.288.

• *'Boys! I have been dining with "Jane Eyre"'*: Leonard Huxley, *The House of Smith Elder*, William Clowes & Sons, 1923, p.68.

Page 129

• *It was dark*…: This scene, including quotations and EG's depiction of Patrick Brontë, is drawn from EG to Catherine Winkworth, 25 August 1850, *LMG*, pp.123–5.

Page 130

• *The consignment*…: Details, including quotations, are drawn from MT's half of MT and Ellen Taylor to CB, 13 August 1850, Berg, *Taylor*, pp.96–8.

• *an unenthusiastic assessment*: George Henry Lewes, 'Shirley: A Tale. by Currer Bell, Author of "Jane Eyre". Smith, Elder, and Co. 1849', *Edinburgh Review*, January 1850, pp.153–73.

Page 131

• *comment to Ellen Nussey*: CB to EN, 26 February 1851, *LCB* II, p.579.

• *by the time Charlotte voiced*: CB to EN, 6 January 1852, *LCB* III, p.5.

• *In the early months of 1852*…: This scene, including the quotation, is drawn from MT to CB, 1852, Berg, *Taylor*, pp.107–10. The letter was most likely sent in the spring of 1852. The library record dates it to April 1852.

• *Charlotte had joked*: CB to Margaret Wooler, 21 October 1851, *LCB* II, p.705.

Page 132

• *feel that it would be best*: CB to EN, 31 October 1852, *LCB* III, p.76.

• *persuading her publisher*: CB to Elizabeth Smith, 30 December 1852, *LCB* III, p.96.

• *'not the serious, grave, cool-headed individual'*: CB to Henry Nussey, 5 March 1839, *LCB* I, p.185.

Page 132–3

• *'Could I ever feel…'*: CB to EN, 9 April 1851, *LCB* II, p.599.

Page 133

• *came to understand*…: This scene, including quotations, drawn from CB to EN, 15 December 1852, *LCB* III, p.93. The dialogue is adapted from CB's description: 'I asked if he had spoken to Papa. He said – he dared not'.

Page 134

• *six sad letters*: Juliet Barker, Barker, p.867.

Page 135

• *'bearing' her current position*…: The following details, including quotations, are drawn from MT to EN, 24 February to 3 March 1854, *Taylor*, p.120.

• *'very stern & bigoted'*: EG to John Forster, 23 April 1854, *LMG*, p.280.

Page 136

• *'narrow'*: EG to John Forster, 8-14? May 1854, *LMG*, p.282.

• *persuaded her father to relent*: EG to John Forster, 17 May 1854, *LMG*, p.289.

• *Florence Nightingale*: Juliet Barker, Barker, p.900.

• *beginning of January 1855*: EG to Catherine Winkworth, 1 January 1855, *LMG*, p.327.

• *'some beef-tea…'*: CB to EN, ?early March 1855, *LCB* III, p.328.

• *courageous and dignified*: Patrick Brontë to EN, 30 March 1855, *LCB* III, pp.329–30.

Page 137

• *he contacted Elizabeth himself*: Patrick Brontë to EG, 5 April 1855, *LCB* III, p.335.

• *Here, at last*…: The following details about MT's thoughts, including the quotation, are drawn from MT to EN, 19 April to 10 May 1856, pp.126–8.

• *a letter that would be delayed*: Joan Stevens, *Taylor*, p.125.

Page 138

• *'bright little minds'*: EG, *Life* (first), p.70.

• *'a vivid picture of a life…'*: George Henry Lewes to EG, 15 April 1857, Gordon S. Haight (ed.), *The George Eliot Letters* II, Yale University Press, 1954, p.315.

• *'learn to rejoice that his wife…'* This comment by Sir James Kay-Shuttleworth is related in William Gaskell to EN, 15 April 1857, *SHB* IV, p.222.

• *In July 1857*…: MT to EG, 30 July 1857, *Taylor*, pp.132–3.

Page 139

• *'hasty, impulsive person…'*: MT to EN, 28 January 1858, *Taylor*, p.134.

• *decidedly odd*: Joan Bellamy, Bellamy, p.116.

• *Mary, on the other hand*: Barbara Whitehead, *Charlotte Brontë and her 'dearest Nell': The story of a friendship*, Smith Settle, 1993, pp.221–2. In 1878, for instance, Mary answered questions from the clergyman Altheus Wilkes, who wanted to write a book about the Brontës.

~

GEORGE ELIOT AND HARRIET BEECHER STOWE

The details included in this section are most often drawn from the letters of George Eliot and Harriet Beecher Stowe, and the journal entries of George Eliot (in *The Journals of George Eliot*, edited by Margaret Harris and Judith Johnston). Whenever possible, we have viewed the pair's correspondence in its original form, in the collections of the New York Public Library's Henry W. and Albert A. Berg Collection, Harvard University's Houghton Library and Schlesinger Library, and the Huntington Library. We also relied on the published *George Eliot Letters* (edited by Gordon S. Haight) and Jennifer Cognard-Black's transcriptions of four letters by Harriet Beecher Stowe in *Kindred Hands: Letters on Writing by British and American Women Authors, 1865–1935* (edited by Jennifer Cognard-Black and Elizabeth Macleod Walls). Joan D. Hedrick's illuminating biography, *Harriet Beecher Stowe: A Life*, was another invaluable resource. Marlene Springer's essay 'Stowe and Eliot: An Epistolary Friendship' (*Biography*, 9.1, winter 1986, pp.59–81) provided an interesting introduction to the pair's relationship.

ABBREVIATIONS

Berg	The Henry W. and Albert A. Berg Collection of English and American Literature, The New York Public Library, Astor, Lennox and Tilden Foundations
GE	George Eliot (Marian Lewes)
GE Biography	Gordon S. Haight, *George Eliot: A Biography*, Oxford University Press, 1969
GE & JC	Gordon S. Haight (ed.), *George Eliot & John Chapman: with Chapman's Diaries* (second edition), Archon Books, 1969
GEL	Gordon S. Haight (ed.), *The George Eliot Letters*, Yale University Press, vols. I–VIII, 1954–78
GHL	George Henry Lewes
GHLD	George Henry Lewes Diary
HBS	Harriet Beecher Stowe
Hedrick	Joan D. Hedrick, *Harriet Beecher Stowe: A Life*, Oxford University Press, 1994
Henry	Nancy Henry, *The Life of George Eliot: A Critical Biography*, Blackwell, 2012
JC	John Chapman
JGE	Margaret Harris and Judith Johnston (eds.), *The Journals of George Eliot*, Cambridge University Press, 1998
Kindred Hands	Jennifer Cognard-Black and Elizabeth Macleod Walls (eds.), *Kindred Hands: Letters on Writing by British and American Women Authors, 1865–1935*, University of Iowa Press, 2006
LMG	J.A.V. Chapple and Arthur Pollard (eds.), *The Letters of Mrs Gaskell*, Manchester University Press, 1966
McCormack	Kathleen McCormack, *George Eliot in Society: Travels Abroad and Sundays at the Priory*, Ohio State University Press, 2013
Schlesinger	Beecher-Stowe family papers, Schlesinger Library, Radcliffe Institute, Harvard University

THE STUFF OF LEGEND

Page 143

• *A wonderful surprise…*: In GE, 5 May 1869, *JGE*, p.135, the author refers to the letter she received from HBS as 'delightful', but she also mentions the bad health she has suffered on her travels, and it is clear that she is glad to be home.

• *known off the page*: Even in the 1871 UK Census, GE's surname was recorded as Lewes and she was listed as the wife of GHL.

• *As the carriage reached the end…*: Kathleen McCormack, McCormack p.27 (figure 7) and p.31. Most details about GE's home are drawn from this book.

Page 144

• *high surrounding wall*: This mention of the wall is included in Charles Eliot Norton's snobbish account of a visit to the Priory. Charles Eliot Norton, 29 January 1869, *GEL* V, p.8.

• *Amelia and Grace Lee*: UK Census, 1871.

• *custom-made wallpaper*: GHL, 13 November 1863, GHLD, *GEL* IV, p.112.

Page 145

• *Marian had long admired*: George Eliot, 'Harriet Beecher Stowe's *Dred*, Charles Reade's *It is Never too Late to Mend* and Frederika Bremer's *Hertha'*, *Silly Novels by Lady Novelists*, Penguin Books, 2010, pp.93–4. In this anonymous review of HBS's latest novel, GE praised HBS's writing – especially with regard to her earlier book, *Uncle Tom's Cabin*.

• *'Is this the little woman who made this great war?'*: Annie Fields (ed.), *Life and Letters of Harriet Beecher Stowe*, Houghton Mifflin and Company, 1898, p.269.

• *crowds turned up in their droves*: Joan Hedrick, Hedrick, p.240.

• *hosted by the Lord Mayor…*: Harry Stone, 'Charles Dickens and Harriet Beecher Stowe', *Nineteenth-Century Fiction*, December 1957, 12.3, pp.197–9.

Page 146

• *a supposedly chance rendezvous*: Stanley Weintraub, *Victorian Yankees at Queen Victoria's Court: American Encounters with Victoria and Albert*, University of Delaware Press, 2011, pp.61–2.

• *Edward Henry Corbould*: These pictures form part of the Royal Collection.

• *sold the exclusive serial rights*: 'Appendix I: GE's Literary Earnings', *GEL* VII, p.361.

• *Decades later, long after her death*: Gordon S. Haight states that HBS wrote 'Out of the blue' in Gordon S. Haight, *GE Biography*, p.412.

• *a kindly message*: HBS to GE, 15 April 1869, Berg, *Kindred Hands*, 25. HBS mentioned having received this message in her first letter.

• *Elizabeth Gaskell, for instance…*: EG to Grace Schwabe, 19 June 1853, *LMG*, p.237; EG to George Smith, 2 November 1859, *LMG*, p.587; EG to GE, 10 November 1859, *LMG*, p.592. In the first of these letters, Elizabeth talks of meeting with Harriet twice on her first European tour.

Page 147

• *'soiled' morals*: EG to Harriet Martineau, 29 October 1859, *LMG*, p.587.

• *intended initially…*: This background and the scene that follows, including the quotations, is drawn from HBS to GE, 15 April 1869, Berg, *Kindred Hands*, pp.25–7. HBS refers to GHL as GE's husband in the same sentence in which she introduces her own husband.

• *and future tourists would pay*: Bill Belleville, *River of Lakes: A Journey on Florida's St John's River*, University of Georgia Press, 2000, p.173.

Page 148

• *a hit with the literary establishment*: Gordon S. Haight, *GE Biography*, pp.404–5.

Page 149

• *'heart soul & life blood…'*: HBS to GE, 25 May 1869, Berg.

• *Worried that delivering her story*: Joan D. Hedrick, Hedrick, p.332.

• *'so intensely American'*: HBS to GE, 15 April 1869, Berg, *Kindred Hands*, p.25.

• *'My dear Friend'…*: GE to HBS, 8 May 1869, Schlesinger, *GEL* V, p.29, p.31.

Page 150

• *hunting big game*: Nancy Henry, Henry, p.159.

• *written a pitiful letter*: GHL to John Blackwood, 9 January 1869, *GEL* V, p.4.

• *fast and loose with the truth*: Kathryn Hughes, *George Eliot: The Last Victorian*, Fourth Estate, 1999, p.388.

• *When, that day…*: GE to John Blackwood, 11 May 1869, *GEL* V, p.34.

Page 151

• *Later, he would sit down*: GHL, 8 May 1869, GHLD, *GEL* V, p.33.

• *with two American friends*: Grace Norton and Sara Sedgwick accompanied Henry James that day. Rosemary Ashton, *George Eliot: A Life*, Hamish Hamilton, 1996, p.299.

• *subsequent letter to his father…*: Unless otherwise stated, details, including quotations, in the following scene are drawn from Henry James to Henry James Sr., 10 May 1869, Leon Edel (ed.), *Henry James Letters, Volume I, 1843–1875*, Macmillan, 1974, pp.116–7.

• *artfully decorated drawing room*: J. W. Cross, *George Eliot's Life as Related in Her Letters and Journals,* vol. III, William Blackwood and Sons, 1885, frontispiece illustration.

• *the armchairs carefully arranged*: Kathleen McCormack, McCormack, p.32.

• *written three reviews*: Kathryn Hughes, *George Eliot: The Last Victorian*, Fourth Estate, 1999, p.388. Henry James's verdict on *The Spanish Gypsy* appeared in the *North American Review* (Henry James, 'The Spanish Gypsy. A Poem', *North American Review*, October 1868, 107.221, pp.620–35).

Page 152

• *During the gap in years…*: Henry James, *The Middle Years*, W. Collins Sons & Co., 1917, pp.64–5.

Page 153

• *four times in the night*: GHL, 9 May 1869, GHLD, *GEL* V, p.33.

• *Harriet's description*: HBS to GE, 25 May 1869, Berg.

Page 153–4

• *a Boston bookshop*: Forest Wilson, *Crusader in Crinoline: The Life of Harriet Beecher Stowe*, J.B. Lippincott, 1941, p.534.

Page 154

• *'sacred veil of silence'*: HBS to Anne Isabella Byron, 17 December 1856, Charles Edward Stowe, *The Life of Harriet Beecher Stowe compiled from her Letters and Journals*, Sampson Low, Marston, Searle & Rivington, 1889, p.451.

• *Over three weeks in June*: Joan D. Hedrick, Hedrick, p.356.

Page 155

• *As she made clear in her letter*: HBS to Oliver Wendell Holmes, June 1869, Charles Edward Stowe, *The Life of Harriet Beecher Stowe compiled from her Letters and Journals*, Sampson Low, Marston, Searle & Rivington, 1889, pp.453–4.

• *when the doctor returned it*: Joan D. Hedrick, Hedrick, p.357.

• *unsurprisingly been drawn…*: GE to HBS, 11 July 1869, Schlesinger, *GEL* V, p.48.

Page 156

• *published simultaneously*: 'The True Story of Lady Byron's Life' was published in the September issues of the *Atlantic Monthly* (24.143) and *Macmillan's* (20.119).

• *remains unpublished*: All of GE's known correspondence to HBS is published in *GEL*. A portion of these letters appears, in a less rigorously edited form, in *George Eliot's Life as Related in Her Letters and Journals*, edited by J.W. Cross. Three of HBS's letters to GE are published in *Kindred Hands*. Partial and at times inaccurate versions of the letters also appear in *Life and Letters of Harriet Beecher Stowe*, edited by Annie Fields, and *The Life of Harriet Beecher Stowe*, edited by Charles Edward Stowe. One letter (viewable online) is held in the Amy Lowell Autograph Collection of the Houghton Library, Harvard University. The unpublished remainder of HBS's correspondence to GE (and also from Calvin Ellis Stowe to GE) is held in the collections of the Berg.

• *Her letter goes on…*: Most details in this scene, including quotations, are drawn from HBS to GE, 3 August 1869, Berg.

• *an alcohol addiction*: Joan D. Hedrick, Hedrick, p.140.

Page 157

• *Harriet too had been suffering*: Joan D. Hedrick, Hedrick, p.362.

• *significant number of his poems*: GE to Cara Bray, 23 August 1869, p.54.

• *'the novel of "Romola"'…*: HBS, 'The True Story of Lady Byron's Life', *Atlantic Monthly*, September 1869, 24.143, p.305.

Page 158

- *wrote to other close friends*: GE to Cara Bray, 23 August 1869, *GEL* V, p.54; GE to Sara Sophia Hennell, 21 September 1869, *GEL* V, p.56.
- *the poems… were now finished*: GE, 1 August 1869, *JGE*, p.137.
- '*This was always one of my best loved subjects…*': GE to John Blackwood, 21 April 1873, *GEL* V, p.403.

THE SPECTRE OF SCANDAL

Page 161

- '*distressingly haggard*': GE, 17 September 1869, *JGE*, p.138.
- *The new nurse*: This refers to Thornton Lewes's second nurse. The first had left on 18 August 1869. GE, 19 August 1869, *JGE*, p.137.
- *On at least one afternoon*: GHL, 18 May 1869, GHLD, *GEL* V, p.40 (n7).

Page 162

- *Back on 1 January*: GE, 1 January 1869, *JGE*, p.134.
- '*I do not feel very confident…*': GE, 11 September 1869, *JGE*, p.138.
- *In mid-October, she recorded*: GE, 13 October 1869, *JGE*, p.139.
- *sometimes felt frustrated*: Nancy Henry, Henry, p.178.
- '*This death seems to me the beginning of our own*': GE, 19 October 1869, *JGE*, p.139.

Page 163

- *scale of the scandal…*: Joan D. Hedrick, Hedrick, pp.364–5.
- A Key to Uncle Tom's Cabin – *a bestseller*: Claire Parfait, *The Publishing History of Uncle Tom's Cabin, 1852–2002*, Ashgate, 2007, p.109.
- *cherry-picking*: Joan D. Hedrick, Hedrick, p.231.

Page 164

- '*war to the knife*': HBS to J. R. Osgood, n.d., Joan D. Hedrick, Hedrick, p.366. The letter from which Joan D. Hedrick quotes is in the collections of the Huntington Library (HBS to J.R. Osgood, n.d., Fields Papers, HL).
- *usual heartfelt greeting…*: Most details in this scene, including quotations, are drawn from GE to HBS, 10 December 1869, *GEL* V, pp.71–2. The original of this letter appears to be lost. Gordon S. Haight reproduces the copy from the Tinker Collection at Yale University Library.
- '*silent blue eyed golden haired boy…*': HBS to GE, 25 May 1869, Berg.

Page 165

- *New York clinic of George Taylor*: Joan D. Hedrick, Hedrick, p.367.
- '*clear as the sun fair as the moon…*': HBS to Hattie and Eliza Stowe, November to December 1869, Schlesinger.
- *sheep grazing on the Green*: Roy Rosenzweig and Elizabeth Blackmar, *The Park and the People: A History of Central Park*, Cornell University Press, 1992, p.252.

Page 166

- '*ribbed & stretched & otherwise operated on*': HBS to Hattie and Eliza Stowe, November to December 1869, Schlesinger.
- '*paralysis of the sciatic nerve…*': HBS to GE, 3 August 1869, Berg.

Page 167

- *obliged with a long letter*: This letter no longer exists in its original form. Susan Belasco reproduces a copy from Dr Williams's London Library. Most details in this scene, including quotations, are drawn from HBS to Eliza Lee Cabot Follen, 16 December 1852, Susan Belasco (ed.), *Stowe in Her Own Time: A Biographical Chronicle of Her Life, Drawn from Recollections, Interviews, and Memoirs by Family, Friends, and Associates*, University of Iowa Press, 2009, pp.62–9.
- *treated…to a reading of the letter*: GE recalled her first impressions of HBS in GE to HBS, 8 May 1869, Schlesinger, *GEL* V, pp.29–30.

Page 169

• *'I am a little bit of a woman…'*: The wording of GE's letter, in which she also expresses her initial impressions of HBS, is slightly different from that which appears in the copy of the letter from Dr Williams's London Library. GE to Cara and Charles Bray, 12 March 1853, *GEL* II, p.92.

• *fearing that his daughter…*: Kathryn Hughes, *George Eliot: The Last Victorian*, Fourth Estate, 1999, p.29.

• *German and Italian, Greek and Latin*: Nancy Henry, Henry, p.31.

Page 170

• *schoolmistress's job stimulating…*: Joan D. Hedrick, Hedrick, pp.54–7.

• *helping one of her brothers*: Joan D. Hedrick, Hedrick, p.89.

• *'too great a sacrifice…'*: Cara Bray to Sara Sophia Hennell, 30 March 1845, *GEL* I, p.184.

• *laughing at him in her sleeve*: GE to Sara Sophia Hennell, 5 November 1846, *GEL* I, p.225.

Page 171

• *began to feel faint*: GE to Cara Bray, 24 November 1843, *GEL* I, p.166.

• *one he would never finish*: Gordon S. Haight, *GE Biography*, pp.50-1. Gordon S. Haight quotes the words of Eliza Lynn Linton, writing about Dr Brabant in her 1899 book, *My Literary Life*.

• *'in a little heaven here…'*: GE to Cara Bray, 20 November 1843, *GEL* I, p.165.

• *who grew suspicious*: JC, 27 June 1851, GE & JC, p.186.

• *John Chapman…*: Details about GE's relationship with JC, including the quotation, come from JC, 18-19 January 1851; 18–19 February 1851; 24 March 1851, *GE & JC*, p.142, pp.133–4.

Page 172

• *leading many to assume*: Herbert Spencer, *An Autobiography*, vol. I, Williams and Norgate, 1904, p.399.

• *Marian wrote to confess*: GE to Herbert Spencer, 16? July 1852, *GEL* VIII, pp.56–7.

• *enclosed a photograph*: HBS to GE, 8 February 1872, Berg.

• *Unable to bear*: GE to HBS, 24 June 1872, *GEL* V, p.281.

• *she'd seen the results…*: Both the sketch and a copy of the photograph (the latter produced much later, after GE's death) are part of the collections of the Herbert Art Gallery & Museum in Coventry. The sketch, by GE's friend, Cara Bray, was drawn during a tour of Europe in 1849. The exact date of the original photograph is unknown.

Page 173

• *first declared his affection*: Joan D. Hedrick, Hedrick, p.97.

• *Prussian school system…*: Details about Calvin Ellis Stowe's trip, HBS's pregnancy and the birth of their twins are drawn from Joan D. Hedrick, Hedrick, pp.98–100, p.112. The quotation is from a letter by Calvin Ellis Stowe, written on 7 June 1836, prior to his departure (held in the collections of the Harriet Beecher Stowe Center, Hartford, CT).

Page 174

• *introduced her to Lewes in 1851*: JC, 6 October 1851, *GE & JC*, 217; GE to Charles Bray, 8 October 1851, *GEL* I, p.367.

Page 175

• *much later, in 1857*: GE to Isaac Pearson Evans, 26 May 1857, *GEL* II, pp.331-2.

• *just about possible*: Unlike earlier biographers, such as Gordon S. Haight, who suggests that it would have been out of the question for GE and GHL to marry, Nancy Henry makes the convincing case that such a union would not have been impossible. Nancy Henry, Henry, pp.98–101.

• *Unlike Arthur Bell Nicholls*: CB to EN, ?20 October 1854, Margaret Smith (ed.), *The Letters of Charlotte Brontë with a selection of letters by her family and friends*, vol. III, Clarendon Press, 2004, p.295.

• *…and the skull-cap*: Forest Wilson, *Crusader in Crinoline: The Life of Harriet Beecher Stowe*, J. B. Lippincott, 1941, p.166.

Page 176

• *With a twinkling sense of humour…*: CES to GE, 30 May 1869, Berg.

• *'a Christ in dwelling'*: CES to GE, 31 July 1872, Berg.

Page 177

• *several séances*: Joan D. Hedrick, Hedrick, p.367.

• *ghost of a famed female author…*: This scene, including quotations, is drawn from HBS to GE, 25 May 1869, Berg; HBS to GE, 11 May 1872, Berg.

Page 178

• *must have gratified Harriet*: EG, *Life* (first), 1997, p.410, p.413.

Page 179

• *'deeply interested…'*: GE to HBS, 11 July 1869, Schlesinger, *GEL* V, pp.48–9.

• *brought up the Charlotte Brontë episode again*: HBS to GE, 11 May 1872, Berg.

• *'whether rightly or not…'*: GE to HBS, 24 June 1872, *GEL* V, p.280.

Page 180

• *'comfort through love and care'*: GE to HBS, 10 December 1869, *GEL* V, p.71.

AN ACT OF BETRAYAL

Page 181

• *had not forgotten Harriet Beecher Stowe*: GE to Cara Bray, 3 August 1871, *GEL* V, p.173.

Page 182

• *'Dear Friend'…*: Details of this letter from HBS, including quotations, are drawn from HBS to GE, 8 February 1872, Berg. When mentioning the magazine, *Harpers Weekly* (as it was then), Harriet refers to it as 'Harpers Monthly'.

• *'be so unreasonable as to expect…'*: GE to HBS, 10 December 1869, *GEL* V, p.72.

• *sent off promptly within days…*: GE to HBS, 4 March 1872, Schlesinger, *GEL* V, p.252. Following the pattern of earlier letters between the pair, it is likely that HBS's letter of 8 February arrived at the Priory within a period of two-and-a-half weeks.

Page 183

• *'without any very serious intention…'*: GE, 2 December 1870, *JGE*, p.141.

Page 184

• *'bits will be published right and left…'*: Gordon S. Haight quotes from a letter by John Blackwood, written on 4 September 1871. Gordon S. Haight, *GE Biography*, p.437.

• *As usual, Harriet had travelled*: Details about HBS's travel arrangements and Fred's disappearance are drawn from Joan D. Hedrick, Hedrick, pp.382–3.

Page 185

• *'drawing-room scandal'*: 'The Week', *Nation*, 6 January 1870, 10.236, p.2.

• *'weak and trashy production'*: *Charleston Daily News*, 7 January 1870, p.1.

• *'a turning over again…'*: *Richmond Dispatch*, 6 January 1870, p.2.

• *would have arrived*: Both GE and HBS agree that there had been a gap of approximately two years since GE's letter of December 1869 (GE to HBS, 10 December 1869, *GEL* V, pp.71–2). HBS had already answered GE's previous letter sent over two-and-a-half years earlier (GE to HBS, 11 July 1869, Schlesinger, *GEL* V, pp.47–9).

Page 185–6

• *about halfway through*: GE, n.d. 1872, *JGE*, p.142.

Page 186

• *With a frostiness…*: GE to HBS, 4 March 1872, Schlesinger, *GEL* V, pp.252–3.

• *Treading carefully for now…*: HBS to GE, 11 May 1872, Berg.

Page 187

• *Since the revival…*: Most of this background plus the scene that follows, including quotations, is drawn from HBS to GE, 23 September 1872, Berg, *Kindred Hands*, p.27.

• *first staying at a resort*: Joan D. Hedrick, Hedrick, pp.383–4.

• *presumably still mid-tour*: The address written at the top of the letter (seemingly in HBS's hand) reads 'Hartford', but, as she was in Salem, Massachusetts, on 17 September and in Boston, Massachusetts, by 26 September, it seems unlikely that she returned to her home in Connecticut between those dates. HBS writes that she is 'away from my papers', which further suggests that whoever wrote 'Hartford' at the top of the letter was mistaken. Joan D. Hedrick lists some of HBS's tour dates in the section mentioned in the previous note.

Page 188

• *in no uncertain terms*: The original of this letter appears to be lost. Gordon S. Haight reproduces a fragment copy, which forms part of the Tinker Collection at Yale University Library. GE to HBS, October? 1872, *GEL* V, p.322.

Page 189

• *'shadow of old Casaubon'*: GHL to John Blackwood, 13 July 1872, *GEL* V, p.291.
• *On receipt of this second letter*: This background and the scene that follows, including quotations, is drawn from HBS to GE, 26 September 1872, Berg, *Kindred Hands*, pp.29–30.

Page 190

• *'Dear Love, did you think…'*: The letter has been incorrectly marked with the date 1831. From the context of its contents, it should be 1873. HBS to GE, 20 April 1873(?), Berg.

Page 191

• *'rare genius'…*: George Eliot, 'Harriet Beecher Stowe's *Dred*, Charles Reade's *It is Never too Late to Mend* and Frederika Bremer's *Hertha*', *Silly Novels by Lady Novelists*, Penguin Books, 2010, p.94.
• *desired her friend's thoughts*: The subject of anti-Semitism is one that GE talks of at some length in this letter. GE to HBS, 29 October 1876, Schlesinger, *GEL* VI, pp.301–2.
• *When Daniel Deronda came out…*: This background and the following scene, including quotations, are drawn from HBS to GE, 18 March 1876, Berg.

Page 192

• *'a splendid success'*: HBS to GE, 25 September 1876, Berg, *Kindred Hands*, p.33.
• *'the Jewish element'*: GE to HBS, 29 October 1876, *GEL* VI, p.301.
• *her editor had expressed concern*: John Blackwood to GE, 24 February 1876, *GEL* VI, pp.221–2.

Page 193

• *'no existence outside of the author's study'*: Henry James, 'Daniel Deronda: A Conversation', *Atlantic Monthly*, December 1876, 38.230, p.686.
• *'warm appreciation…'*: GE to John Blackwood, 2 September 1876, *GEL* VI, p.275.
• *Marian's subconscious prejudices*: George Eliot, *Daniel Deronda*, Penguin Classics, 1995, chapter 33, pp.383–4.
• *Harriet sent her friend the gift*: The letter that accompanied this gift is held in the collections of the Amy Lowell Autograph Collection of the Houghton Library, Harvard University.
• *'had been gnawed by the rats – and left'*: Gordon S. Haight quotes the words of Frances Anne (Fanny) Kemble. Gordon S. Haight, *GE Biography*, p.512.

Page 194

• *'a thickening of the mucous membrane'*: Gordon S. Haight, *GE Biography*, p.514.
• *her anguished cries*: Gordon S. Haight, *GE Biography*, p.516.
• *When, in April 1879*: GE to HBS, 10 April 1879, *GEL* VII, p.132.
• *This time, though, her letter…*: HBS to GE, 6 May 1880, Berg.

Page 195

• *'so fine and noble…'*: HBS to Annie Fields, 1 January 1881, Huntington Library, San Marino, California.

Page 196

• *'like falling stars'*: Extract from Hattie Stowe's letter quoted in Susan T. Howard to Annie Fields, January 1890, Huntington Library, San Marino, California.

• *'most delightful'*: Charles Edward Stowe, *The Life of Harriet Beecher Stowe Compiled from her Letters and Journals*, Sampson Low, Marston, Searle & Rivington, 1889, p.459.

~

KATHERINE MANSFIELD AND VIRGINIA WOOLF

The details included in this section are most often drawn from the letters, diaries and journals of Katherine Mansfield and Virginia Woolf. Ida Baker's *Katherine Mansfield: The Memories of LM* is another chief source. We consulted Virginia Woolf's diaries and extant letters from Katherine Mansfield to Virginia Woolf in the New York Public Library's Henry W. and Albert A. Berg Collection. An unpublished letter from Virginia Woolf to Katherine Mansfield has been made available to view online by the Mortimer Rare Book Room, Smith College. We also made substantial use of the *Collected Letters of Katherine Mansfield* (edited by Vincent O'Sullivan and Margaret Scott); *The Letters of Virginia Woolf* (edited by Nigel Nicolson with Joanne Trautmann); *The Diary of Virginia Woolf* (edited by Anne Olivier Bell with Andrew McNeillie); and *The Collected Works of Katherine Mansfield, vol. IV: The Diaries of Katherine Mansfield including Miscellaneous Works* (edited by Gerri Kimber and Claire Davison with Anna Plumridge). The biographies of Kathleen Jones, Hermione Lee and Claire Tomalin were of regular assistance too.

ABBREVIATIONS

Beginning	Leonard Woolf, *Beginning Again: An Autobiography of the Years 1911 to 1918*, Harvest/Harcourt Brace Jovanovich, 1975
Berg	The Henry W. and Albert A. Berg Collection of English and American Literature, The New York Public Library, Astor, Lennox and Tilden Foundations
CWKM	Katherine Mansfield, *The Collected Works of Katherine Mansfield*, vols. II–IV, Edinburgh University Press, 2012–16 [See Select Bibliography for editors.]
DVW	Anne Olivier Bell with Andrew McNeillie (eds.), *The Diary of Virginia Woolf*, vols. I–IV, The Hogarth Press, 1978–84
Garsington	Ottoline Morrell, *Ottoline at Garsington: Memoirs of Lady Ottoline Morrell 1915–1918*, Faber & Faber, 1974
IB	Ida Baker
JMM	John Middleton Murry
Journal	John Middleton Murry (ed.), *Journal of Katherine Mansfield*, Persephone Books, 2006
KM	Katherine Mansfield
Lee	Hermione Lee, *Virginia Woolf*, Vintage, 1997
LJMMKM	Cherry A. Hankin (ed.), *The Letters of John Middleton Murry to Katherine Mansfield*, Constable, 1983
LKM	*The Collected Letters of Katherine Mansfield*, vols. I–V, Vincent O'Sullivan and Margaret Scott (eds.), Clarendon Press, 1984–2008 (© The Estate of Katherine Mansfield 1984, 1987, 1993, 1996, 2008)
LM	Ida Baker, *Katherine Mansfield: The Memories of LM*, Michael Joseph, 1971
LVW	Nigel Nicolson with Joanne Trautmann (eds.), *The Letters of Virginia Woolf*, vols. II–IV, 1976–8
LW	Leonard Woolf
Morgan	Department of Literary and Historical Manuscripts, The Morgan Library and Museum
OM	Ottoline Morrell
Smith	Frances Hooper Collection, Mortimer Rare Book Room, Smith College
Stories	Katherine Mansfield, *The Collected Stories of Katherine Mansfield*, Penguin Classics, 2007
Tomalin	Claire Tomalin, *Katherine Mansfield: A Secret Life*, Penguin, 2003
VB	Vanessa Bell
VW	Virginia Woolf

FRIENDS OR FOES?

Page 199
• *without feeling assured of success*: VW to VB, 26 April 1917, *LVW* II, p.150.
• *'utterly unscrupulous character'*: VW to VB, 11 February 1917, *LVW* II, p.144.

Page 200
• *'an ugly impassive…'*: Lytton Strachey to VW, 17 July 1916, Paul Levy (ed.), *The Letters of Lytton Strachey*, Viking, 2005, p.310.
• *'Katherine Mansfield has dogged…'*: VW to Lytton Strachey, 25 July 1916, *LVW* II, p.107.
• *meet at Garsington…*: Details of the early days of KM's friendship with VW are drawn from LW, *Beginning*, pp.203–4.
• *any significant new work*: JMM, *Journal*, p.ix.

Page 201
• *Women's Co-operative Guild*: VW to Margaret Llewelyn Davies, 22 February 1915, *LVW* II, p.59.
• *Since the arrival of the machine…*: VW to VB, 26 April 1917, *LVW* II, p.150.
• *Four years earlier…*: Details of VW's mental health and its treatment during this period are drawn from LW, *Beginning*, pp.148–70.
• *As the train trundled eastbound*: VW's habitual mode of transport into London was by rail.

Page 202
• *Zeppelin raids*: Zeppelin raids in the area are detailed in John Hook, *London Air Raid Incidents*, 1990, London Metropolitan Archives.
• *On arriving at Katherine's studio flat…*: Descriptions of KM's living conditions and situation during this period are drawn from IB, *LM*, pp.101–5; KM to OM, 15 August 1917, *LKM* I, p.325.
• *Lottie Hope, and Nellie Boxall*: Alison Light, *Mrs Woolf and the Servants*, Penguin, 2008, pp.167–8. Although Virginia Woolf referred to her as 'Nelly', Alison Light has confirmed that her name was spelt 'Nellie' on her birth and death certificates, and that she always referred to herself as 'Nellie', p.xiii.

Page 203
• *outsider in literary London*: OM, *Garsington*, p.150.

Page 204
• *The evening left…*: Details of this evening are drawn from KM to VW, ?24 June 1917, *LKM* I, p.313; VW to VB, 27 June 1917, *LVW* II, p.159.
• *under the table*: Barbara Bagenal, *Recollections of Virginia Woolf*, Joan Russell Noble (ed.), Peter Owen, 1972, p.150. Barbara Bagenal recalls LW lying on the kitchen table while her bed was made up beneath it. Ordinarily, however, she would not have been with the Woolfs, so we've assumed that LW would more usually occupy the safer spot beneath the table.

Page 205
• *earliest sexual experience…*: Details of VW's early experience of sexual abuse are drawn from VW, 'Sketch of the Past', *Moments of Being*, Pimlico, 2002, p.81.
• *'…every sort of hog…'*: VW to VB, 27 June 1917, *LVW* II, p.159.
• *'My God, I love…'*: KM to VW, ?24 June 1917, *LKM* I, p.313.

Page 206
• *'consider how rare…'*: KM to VW, ?24 June 1917, *LKM* I, p.313.
• *The first blow…*: VW to Clive Bell, 17 September 1917, *LVW* II, p.179 (n2).
• *gather at the home*: VW, 'Sketch of the Past', *Moments of Being*, Pimlico, 2002, p.50.
• *In early August 1917*: VW to OM, 15 August 1917, *LVW* II, p.174.
• *But the particular incident*: VW, 10 October 1917, *DVW* I, p.57; VW, 11 October 1917, Berg, *DVW* I, p.58; VW, 27 October 1917, *DVW* I, p.67 (n42); KM to VW, c. 23 August 1917, Berg, *LKM* I, p.327.

Page 207
• *Bertrand Russell*: For more information on KM's interactions with Bertrand Russell, see Claire Tomalin, Tomalin, Loc 3022.

- *accusing Katherine of*: OM, *Garsington*, p.150, p.167. See also pp.185–92 for details of JMM's accusation that OM had fallen in love with him, and the fallout this caused between KM and OM.
- *Among her old friends*: LW, *Beginning*, pp.30–1.
- *'Chaste & the Unchaste'*: VW, 11 October 1917, Berg, *DVW* I, p.58.

Page 208

- *each guest's every whim*: OM, *Garsington*, p.167.
- *through Garsington's host herself…*: KM and OM were in regular correspondence during August 1917, and KM knew of VW's gossip by c. 23 August 1917.
- *'I do like her…'*: KM to OM, 3 July 1917, *LKM* I, p.315.
- *On Katherine's return to London…*: the probable influence of KM on 'Kew Gardens' by VW is drawn from VW to OM, 15 August 1917, *LVW* II, p.174; KM to OM, 15 August 1917, *LKM* I, p.325. For further analysis, see Katie Macnamara, 'How to Strike a Contemporary: Woolf, Mansfield, and Marketing Gossip', Jeanne Dubino (ed.), *Virginia Woolf and the Literary Marketplace*, Palgrave Macmillan, 2010.
- *'Katherine Mansfield describes…'*: VW to OM, 15 August 1917, *LVW* II, p.174.

Page 209

- *'…write about that flower garden'*: KM to OM, 15 August 1917, *LKM* I, p.325.
- *'The golden oranges…'*: Most descriptions, including quotations, in this paragraph are taken from KM to OM, 15 August 1917, *LKM* I, p.325.

Page 210

- *a few nights at Asheham*: VW's preferred spelling of Asheham rather than Asham has been used throughout
- *The invitation arrived*: KM to VW, mid-August 1917, Berg, *LKM* I, p.324.
- *gonorrhoea*: For further detail on KM's likely contraction of gonorrhoea, see Claire Tomalin, Tomalin, Loc 1426.
- *The lengthy delays…*: Details of this visit are drawn from VW, 18 August 1917, *DVW* I, p.43; VW, 19 August 1917, *DVW* I, p.43; VW, 21 August 1917, *DVW* I, p.44; VW, 22 August 1917, *DVW* I, p.44; KM to VW, c. 23 August 1917, Berg, *LKM* I, p.327.
- *behaviour was guarded*: LW, *Beginning*, p.204.

Page 211

- *recurrent rheumatism*: KM to VW, mid-August 1917, Berg, *LKM* I, p.324.
- *'Night-Scented Stock'*: KM, *CWKM* III, pp.110–12.
- *After a promising start…*: JMM, *Journal*, pp.viii–ix.
- *Katherine mulled over*: KM to VW, c. 23 August 1917, Berg, *LKM* I, p.327.
- *quite a tendency*: OM, *Garsington*, pp.148–50.

Page 212

- *'make our undiscovered…'*: KM, *CWKM* IV, p.191.
- *late August 1917…*: Quotations in the following three paragraphs are taken from KM to VW, c. 23 August 1917, Berg, *LKM* I, p.327.

Page 213

- *And so, Virginia tore up*: VW to Clive Bell, 17 September 1917, *LVW* II, p.179.
- *'many delicate things fall…'*: VW, 10 October 1917, *DVW* I, p.58.
- *first page of* Prelude: VW, 9 October 1917, *DVW* I, p.56.
- *the meal came around…*: Details of this visit are drawn from VW, 10 October 1917, *DVW* I, p.57; VW, 11 October 1917, Berg, *DVW* I, p.58; KM to Dorothy Brett, 11 October 1917, *LKM* I, pp.330–1.
- *show of impassivity*: OM, *Garsington*, p.149.
- *'the living power…'*: VW, 12 July 1918, *DVW* I, p.167.
- *The change of title*: Georgina Joysmith, editorial note, IB, *LM*, p.103.

Page 214

- *'Chaste & the Unchaste'*: VW, 11 October 1917, Berg, *DVW* I, p.58.

• *Burma and later Rhodesia*: Georgina Joysmith, editorial note, IB, *LM*, p.21 and IB, *LM*, p.88.
• *minstrels' gallery*: IB, *LM*, p.102.
• *Aldous Huxley*: Jeffrey Meyers, *Katherine Mansfield: A Darker View*, Cooper Square, 2002, p.151.

Page 215
• *'formally buried'*: VW to OM, 25 October 1917, *LVW* II, p.190.
• *'I am sorry…'*: KM to Dorothy Brett, 19 November 1917, *LKM* I, p.334.
• *laboriously set the type*: LW, *Beginning*, p.237.

Page 216
• *To Hell with other people's presses!'*: KM to JMM, 29 May 1918, *LKM* I, p.203.
• *Virginia holed herself away…*: Descriptions of the Woolfs' work on *Prelude* are drawn from VW, 9 July 1918, *DVW* I, p.164; VW, 10 July 1918, *DVW* I, p.165; LW, *Beginning*, p.237.
• *'…sell it on a barrow…'*: KM to VW, 29 May 1918, Berg, *LKM* II, p.200.

Page 217
• *pronounced it unremarkable*: JMM, 'Introduction', KM, *Journal*, p.x.
• *She defended* Prelude: VW to Clive Bell, 16 July 1918, *LVW* II, p.262.
• *'Doesn't set the Thames on fire'*: VW, 16 July 1918, *DVW* I, p.168.
• *'…one fine but very modest example'*: VW to Duncan Grant, 15 May 1918, *LVW* II, p.241.
• *'afflicted with jealousy…'*: VW to Roger Fry, 1 August 1920, *LVW* II, p.438.

CAT AND MOUSE

Page 219
• *'marmoreal…'*: VW, 28 May 1918, *DVW* I, p.150.

Page 220
• *On 7 January…*: Details of KM's journey and arrival are drawn from IB, *LM*, p.106.
• *no longer alone…*: Details of IB's arrival and stay with KM are drawn from IB, *LM*, pp.107–8; KM to JMM, 12 January 1918, *LKM* II, p.9; KM to JMM, 16 February 1918, *LKM* II, p.74; 19 February 1918, *LKM* II, p.79; KM to JMM, 24 May 1918, *LKM* II, p.190.

Page 221
• *'state of work…'*: KM to JMM, February 1918, quoted in IB, *LM*, p.107.
• *'abject slave'*: JMM to KM, 15 February 1918, *LJMMKM*, p.122.
• *contrarian kind of love*: KM to JMM, 24 May 1918, *LKM* II, p.190.
• *'use her as a walking stick'*: KM to JMM, 16 February 1918, *LKM* II, p.74.
• *purchase of a handpress…*: JMM to KM, 3 February 1918, Cherry A. Hankin (ed.), *Letters Between Katherine Mansfield and John Middleton Murry*, Virago, 1988, p.106.

Page 222
• *hardly a sum to sniff at*: Kathleen Jones, *Katherine Mansfield: The Story-Teller*, The Book Mill, 2012, Loc 5195.
• *'It's the soberest…'*: JMM to KM, 11 February 1918, *LJMMKM*, p.119.
• *'her roof over her…'*: KM to JMM, 30 November 1919, *LKM* III, pp.127–8.
• *a spot of exercise…*: Details of this walk and its aftermath are drawn from KM to JMM, 15 February 1918, *LKM* II, p.73; *CWKM* IV, 19 February 1918, p.421; IB, *LM*, p.108.

Page 223
• *already regarded 'Bliss'*: KM to JMM, 26 February 1918, *LKM* II, p.94; KM to JMM, 27 February 1918, *LKM* II, p.98.
• The English Review: British literary magazine 1908 to 1937.
• *Its readers would be treated…*: All quotations from 'Bliss' are taken from KM, *Stories*, pp.91–105.
• *sentimentally so*: VW to Janet Case, 20 March 1922, *LVW* II, pp514–15.

Page 224
• *Now that she had returned*: VW, 3 August 1918, *DVW* I, p.177.
• *'marriage is of no more importance…'*: VW to OM, 24 May 1918, *LVW* II, p.243.

Page 225

• *'get down to what is true rock'*: VW, 28 May 1918, *DVW* I, p.150.

• *ahead of their guests*: VW, 3 August 1918, *DVW* I, p.177.

• *the Woolfs had travelled…*: Details of the train journey are drawn from VW, 31 July 1918, *DVW* I, p.176.

• *opening up Asheham for their guests…*: Details of VW's arrival at Asheham are drawn from VW, 31 July 1918, *DVW* I, p.176; VW to OM, ?1 August 1918, *LVW* II, p.263. This date information is repeated as published in *LVW* II. However, 2 August 1918 is more probable since VW wrote of expecting the Murrys tomorrow and KM wrote to OM on 3 August 1918 saying that they were supposed to go to the Woolfs' today.

• *But the warm spell*: VW, 3 August 1918, *DVW* I, p.177.

• *'beastly attack…'*: KM's words in this and the subsequent paragraph are taken from KM to VW, 2 August 1918, *LKM* II, p.263.

Page 226

• *'may be rather hopelessly ill'*: VW, 3 August 1918, *DVW* I, p.177.

• *'We are supposed to have fought…'*: KM to OM, 3 August 1918, *LKM* II, p.264.

• *rented bedsit in Chelsea*: IB, *LM*, p.111.

Page 227

• *'merely greases…'*: VW to Barbara Bagenal, 20 September 1918, *LVW* II, p.277.

• *True, Virginia's inheritance…*: For further detail on the Woolfs' financial arrangements, see Hermione Lee, Lee, pp.325–6 and p.560; for further detail on the Murrys' financial arrangements, see Kathleen Jones, *Katherine Mansfield: The Story-Teller*, The Book Mill, 2012, Loc 6294.

• *In August 1918…*: Descriptions of the weekend are drawn from VW, 3 August 1918, *DVW* I, p.178.

• *But an intrusion…*: See KM to VW, mid-August 1917, Berg, *LKM* I, p.324, for KM's depiction of VW's icy aloofness. See KM to VW, ?24 June 1917, *LKM* I, p.313, for KM's portrayal of VW's air of mystery and for the gesture also accorded to Pearl in 'Bliss'. For further analysis of the possible influence of VW on 'Bliss' by KM, see Macnamara, Katie, 'How to Strike a Contemporary: Woolf, Mansfield, and Marketing Gossip', Jeanne Dubino (ed.), *Virginia Woolf and the Literary Marketplace*, Palgrave Macmillan, 2010.

• *As she would recount…*: Details of VW's reaction to 'Bliss', including quotations, are drawn from VW, 7 August 1918, *DVW* I, pp.179–80; VW, 8 August 1918, *DVW* I, p.180; VW to Janet Case, 20 March 1922, *LVW* II, pp.514–15.

Page 229

• *'fish out of the Garsington pond…'*: KM to JMM, 28 February 1918, *LKM* II, p.98.

• *'a little disturbed…'*: VW to VB, 9 August 1918, *LVW* II, p.266.

• *'one of those Dostoievsky…'*: KM to OM, 3 July 1917, *LKM* I, p.315.

Page 229–30

• *take Virginia until 1921…*: Hermione Lee, 'Introduction', *Moments of Being*, Jeanne Schulkind (ed.), Pimlico, 2002, p.xi.

Page 230

• *A period of almost a decade*: Love, Jean O., *Virginia Woolf: Sources of Madness and Art*, University of California Press, 1977, pp.200–1.

• *'cuddling and kissing…'*: VW, 'Old Bloomsbury', *Moments of Being*, Jeanne Schulkind (ed.), Pimlico, 2002, p.44.

• *'sitting on the green…'*: Quotations about VW's marriage in this paragraph are taken from VW, 14 June 1925, *DVW* III, p.30; VW, 29 February 1936, *DVW* V, p.13.

• *Not so very long into their marriage*: VW to VB, 11 April 1920, *LVW* II, p.428.

• *'never had understood…'*: VB to Clive Bell, 27 December 1912, quoted in Hermione Lee, Lee, p.331.

• *'fucks her once a week…'*: Clive Bell to Mary Hutchinson, 7 May 1919, quoted in Hermione Lee, Lee, p.331.

• *Like Bertha*: VW to LW, 1 May 1912, *LVW* I, p.615.

Page 231

• *'made love to her'*: Lea, F.A., *The Life of John Middleton Murry*, Methuen, 1959, p.31.
• *Her infatuation...*: KM, 29 June 1907, *CWKM* IV, p.52.
• *'more powerfully...'*: KM, 1 June 1907, *CWKM* IV, pp.47–8.

Page 232

• *their unwise friendship*: IB, *LM*, p.49.
• *a supposed lesbian affair*: IB, *LM*, p.54.
• *'every bit as sacred...'*: KM to IB, 7 September 1921, *LKM* IV, p.277.
• *'the Monster'*: VW, 9 November 1918, *DVW* I, p.216.
• *Here, Virginia wrote of Ida*: VW, 11 October 1917, Berg, *DVW* I, p.58.
• *She recalled waiting...*: Details of KM and IB's visit to VW are drawn from IB, *LM*, pp.132–3.
• *After the War Office*: JMM to KM, 20 May 1918, *LJMMKM*, p.150; 2 June 1918, *LJMMKM*, p.166.

Page 233

• *took out a lease...*: Details of the household in Hampstead are drawn from IB, *LM*, pp121–30.
• *'mine beyond words...'*: KM to IB, 1 August 1918, *LKM* II, p.262.
• *'were there for pleasure...'*: KM to VW, 1 November 1918, Berg, *LKM* II, p.286.
• *When Virginia paid her first visit...*: Details of this visit are drawn from VW, 16 January 1923, Berg, *DVW* II, p.226.

Page 234

• *On 10 December...*: Details of this visit are drawn from VW, 10 December 1918, *DVW* I, pp.226–7.

Page 235

• *'there's room for everyone...'*: VW to Roger Fry, 1 August 1920, *LVW* II, p.438.
• *'a pale shell'*: KM to IB, 8 March 1921, *LKM* IV, p.188.

Page 236

• *'lacerated feelings'*: VW, 24 April 1919, *DVW* I, p.268.
• *she cared for her...*: VW, 16 January 1923, Berg, *DVW* II, p.226.

LIFE AND DEATH

Page 237

• *Amid all this activity*: VW, 17 December 1918, *DVW* I, p.228; VW, 22 January 1919, *DVW* I, p.235.
• *cheerful presents*: VW, 18 February 1919, *DVW* I, p.243.
• *wine-fuelled fun*: KM to Dorothy Brett, 1 January 1919, *LKM* II, pp.298–9.

Page 238

• *no word of thanks...*: Details of VW's foiled attempt to see KM are drawn from VW, 18 February 1919, *DVW* I, p.243.
• *'quicksands'*: VW, 18 February 1919, *DVW* I, p.243.
• *'brittle as barley sugar'*: VW to VB, 16 February 1919, *LVW* II, p.331.

Page 239

• *'...sailing on tropic seas –'...*: KM to VW, 20 February 1919, Berg, *LKM* II, p.301.
• *feeling rather foolish*: VW, 21 February 1919, *DVW* I, p.243.
• *laden with gifts*: Details of most of these gifts are drawn from KM to VW, 12 May 1919, *LKM* II, p.318; KM to VW, 4 June 1919, *LKM* II, p.323.
• *The pair plunged...*: Details of VW's visits and KM's situation are drawn from VW, 22 March 1919, *DVW* I, p.257.

Page 240

• *'that no one else has ever...'*: VW to Lady Robert Cecil, 26 ?January 1919, *LVW* II, p.321.
• *'a sense of ease...'*: VW, 22 March 1919, *DVW* I, p.258.
• *'apologies, or sense...'*: VW, 22 March 1919, *DVW* I, p.257.
• *By Easter Monday 1919...*: Details of this Easter Monday walk are drawn from VW, 24 April 1919, *DVW* I, p.268.

• *faintly ridiculous*: LW, *Beginning*, p.28–9.

Page 241

• *'haggard & powdered'*: VW, 24 April 1919, *DVW* I, p.268.

• *not attract many readers...*: Details of the success of *Kew Gardens* are drawn from LW, *Beginning*, p.241; VW, 9 June 1919, *DVW* I, p.278; VW, 10 June 1919, *DVW* I, p.280.

• *'a thing of original and therefore strange beauty'*: Harold Child, 'Kew Gardens: Unsigned Review', 29 May 1919, *Times Literary Supplement*.

Page 242

• *These sold at such a rate*: LW, *Beginning*, p.253.

• *'Night-Scented Stock'*: KM sent a copy of this poem to OM but it remained unpublished until 1923. Gerry Kimber & Angela Smith, *CWKM* III, p.112.

• *William Heinemann with a rejection*: VW, 17 April 1919, *DVW* I, p.265.

• *'You must forgive...'*: KM to VW, 4 June 1919, *LKM* II, p.324.

• *Wrapped up...*: VW to VB, 6 June 1919, *LVW* II, p.366.

Page 243

• *The note-books...'*: Quotations from KM's review of *Kew Gardens* are taken from: KM, 'A Short Story', *Athenaeum*, 13 June 1919, 4650, p.459.

• *on 14 June 1919...*: Details of VW's visit, including quotations, are drawn from VW, 14 June 1919, *DVW* I, pp.281–2.

Page 244

• *During the autumn of 1919*: Details of VW's busy autumn are drawn from VW, 28 November 1919, *DVW* I, p.313.

• *The review...*: Quotations from KM's review of 'Night and Day' are taken from KM, 'A Ship Comes into the Harbour', *Athenaeum*, 21 November 1919, 4673, p.1227.

Page 245

• *'secret friend'*: KM, 'Friends and Foes', *Athenaeum*, 3 December 1920, 4727, p.759.

• *feeling desolate*: VW, 28 November 1919, *DVW* I, p.314.

• *'We have no right...'*: JMM to KM, 14 November 1919, *LJMMKM*, p.212.

• *'something hard...'*: JMM to KM, 23 November 1919, *LJMMKM*, p.223.

• *the review's publication...*: All details of JMM's visit to VW are drawn from JMM to KM, 23 November 1919, *LJMMKM*, p.223. Dialogue is reconstructed from the reported speech contained in this letter.

Page 246

• *Just seven months earlier*: VW, 17 April 1919, *DVW* I, p.265.

• *'Virginia's cry...'*: KM to JMM, 26-7 November 1919, *LKM* III, p.122.

• *'a lie in the soul'*: KM to JMM, 10 November 1919, *LKM* III, p.82.

Page 247

• *Detecting anger*: KM to JMM, 26-7 November 1919, *LKM* III, p.122.

• *'scrupulously truthful'*: KM to VW, ?24 June 1917, *LKM* I, p.313.

• *works of George Eliot*: VW, 5 December 1919, *DVW* I, pp.315–16.

• *'a decorous elderly dullard'*: VW, 28 November 1919, *DVW* I, p.314.

• *she now shuddered*: VW, 10 April 1920, *DVW* II, p.28.

• *She vowed to wait*: VW, 5 May 1920, *DVW* II, p.34.

• *within a fortnight*: VW, 20 May 1920, *DVW* II, p.41.

• *'I am grown very dull'*: KM to VW, 25 May 1920, *LKM* IV, p.14.

Page 248

• *stiff and formal*: VW, 26 May 1920, *DVW* II, p.43.

• *On a cool day...*: Details of this visit, including quotations, are drawn from VW, 31 May 1920, *DVW* II, pp.43–5. Dialogue is repeated from it verbatim and reconstructed from its reported speech.

Page 249

• *she had become haunted*: KM to JMM, 17 November 1919, *LKM* III, p.100.

• *early June day in 1920*: Details of this visit, including quotations, are drawn from VW, 5 June 1920, *DVW* II, pp.45–6. Dialogue is repeated from it verbatim and reconstructed from its reported speech.

Page 250

• Times Literary Supplement: Harold Child, 'Two Stories', *Times Literary Supplement*, 29 January 1920, 941, p.63.

• *'nothing but hate'*: VW, 9 November 1920, *DVW* I, p.216.

• *Constable & Co.*: JMM to KM, 2 February 1920, *LJMMKM*, p.261.

• *a war novel*: VW, 26 January 1920, *DVW* II, p.13.

Page 251

• *other writer friends*: VW, 26 September 1920, *DVW* II, p.68.

• *a luncheon hosted*: VW, 6 July 1920, *DVW* II, p.52.

• *Katherine's Hampstead home*: VW, 2 August 1920, *DVW* II, p.61.

• *consider reviewing it*: VW, 2 August 1920, *DVW* II, p.55.

• *'If she's good then I'm not'*: VW, 28 November 1919, *DVW* I, p.315.

Page 252

• *In late August 1920…*: Details of this visit, including quotations, are drawn from VW to VB, 24 August 1920, *LVW* II, p.441; VW, 25 August 1920, Berg, *DVW* II, p.61; as well as from descriptions more generally of visits during this period from VW, 16 January 1923, Berg, *DVW* II, p.226. Dialogue is reconstructed from reported speech.

Page 253

• *'insincere-sincere'*: Details and quotations from this message are taken from VW, 19 December 1920, Berg, *DVW* II, p.80.

• *whether, like her, Katherine ever doubted*: VW, 25 August 1920, Berg, *DVW* II, p.62.

• *Katherine replied swiftly…*: Details from this letter, including quotations, are taken from KM to VW, 27 December 1920, *LKM* IV, p.154.

Page 254

• *The pair talked about Katherine…*: Details of this conversation are drawn from VW, 16 February 1921, *DVW* II, p.91.

• *Katherine had already learnt*: IB, *LM*, p.154.

• *she put pen to paper*: Details of this letter, including quotations, are drawn from VW to KM, 13 February 1921, Smith.

Page 255

• *Katherine was finally…*: Details of KM's situation during this period are drawn from Georgina Joysmith, editorial note, IB, *LM*, p.172; IB, *LM*, pp.206–9; KM to IB, 5 June 1922, *LKM* V, p.193; KM to IB, 14 June 1922, *LKM* V, p.201.

• *'the small lies…'*: VW, 16 January 1923, Berg, *DVW* II, p.227.

• *the drafting of* Jacob's Room: VW, 20 May 1920, *DVW* II, p.40.

• *'sterile acrobatics'*: VW, 14 February 1922, *DVW* II, p.161.

• *'soars in the newspapers…'*: VW, 12 March 1922, Berg, *DVW* II, pp.170–1.

Page 256

• *By mid-August…*: Details in this paragraph are drawn from IB, *LM*, p.209.

• *a mutual friend*: Sydney Waterlow to VW, 21 August 1922, quoted in VW, 23 August 1922, *DVW* II, p.194, and VW, 22 August 1922, *DVW* II, p.192.

• *Virginia agonised…*: VW's attitude towards attending the salon, including quotations, are drawn from VW, 22 August 1922, *DVW* II, p.192, and VW to Sydney Waterlow, 24 August 1922, *LVW* II, p.553.

Page 257

• *could start afresh*: VW, 16 January 1923, Berg, *DVW* II, p.227.

• *But the opinions…*: Details of KM's life at Le Prieuré are largely drawn from IB, *LM*, pp.211–26.

Page 258

• *'Mrs Murry's dead!'*…: VW's immediate reaction to KM's death is drawn from VW, 16 January 1923, Berg, *DVW* II, pp.225–7.
• *Katherine's obituary*: 'Death of Katherine Mansfield: A Career of Great Literary Promise', *The Times*, 12 January 1923, p.6.

Page 259

• *'There's no competitor…'*: VW, 28 January 1923, Berg, *DVW* II, p.228.
• *would have made of them*: VW, 17 October 1924, Berg, *DVW* II, p.317; VW to Dorothy Brett, 8 March 1929, *LVW* IV, p.32.
• *so deeply influenced*: For further analysis of KM's influence on VW, see Hilary Newman, *Virginia Woolf and Katherine Mansfield: A Creative Rivalry*, Cecil Woolf, 2004.

Page 260

• *'What odd friends…'*: VW to Vita Sackville-West, 5 August 1927, *LVW* III, p.408.
• *a matchless genius*: JMM, *Journal*, Introduction; JMM, *The Letters of Katherine Mansfield*, vol. I, Introductory note, Constable & Co., 1928.
• *Eight years after Katherine's death…*: Descriptions of this dream, including quotations, are drawn from VW, 8 June 1931, *DVW* IV, p.29.

A WEB OF LITERARY CONNECTIONS

Page 261

• *George Eliot read*: George Henry Lewes, [11]–18 May 1857, George Henry Lewes diary, Gordon S. Haight (ed.), *The George Eliot Letters*, vol. II, Yale University Press, 1954, p.326. This entry mentions George Eliot reading *Emma* and *Sense and Sensibility* to George Henry Lewes while the couple was away from home during the spring of that year. George Eliot's travel journal, written some time after her trip – published in Margaret Harris and Judith Johnston (eds.), *The Journals of George Eliot*, Cambridge University Press 1998, p.279 – also mentions her reading *Persuasion* and *Northanger Abbey*.
• A Room of One's Own: Virginia Woolf, *A Room of One's Own*, Penguin Books, 2012, pp.75–76, pp.81–82, p.78.

Page 263

• *'Villette – Villette…?'*: George Eliot to Cara and Charles Bray, 12 March 1853, Gordon S. Haight (ed.), *The George Eliot Letters*, vol. II, Yale University Press, p.92.
• *marked by mutual distrust*: Vera Brittain, *Testament of Friendship: The Story of Winifred Holtby*, Virago, 2012, p.106.
• *would be repaired*: Vera Brittain, *Testament of Youth: An Autobiographical Study of the Years 1900–1925*, Virago, 2004, p.452.

Page 264

• *'travelling companion'*: Vera Brittain, *Testament of Friendship: The Story of Winifred Holtby*, Virago, 2012, p.130.
• *person who 'made me'*: Jean E. Kennard, *Vera Brittain and Winifred Holtby: A Working Partnership*, University of New Hampshire by University Press of New England, 1989, p.xiv. Kennard is quoting from a letter from Winifred to Vera, written on 26 September 1935.
• *During the summer of 1937…*: Carol Angier, *Jean Rhys: Life and Work*, Faber & Faber, 2011, pp.361–2.
• *continued to write to each other*: All details about the pair's correspondence are drawn from Michela Calderaro, 'To be sexless, creedless, classless, free. Eliot Bliss: A Creole Writer', A Goodly Garlande. In onore di Sergio Perosa. Annali di Ca' Foscari, 42.4, 2003, pp.109–10.

Page 265

• *invited Zora to tea the next day…*: Valerie Boyd, *Wrapped in Rainbows: The Life of Zora Neale Hurston*, Scribner, 2003, 15, pp.350–1.
• *refer to Marjorie as a 'sister'*: Carla Kaplin (ed.), *Zora Neale Hurston: A Life in Letters*, Doubleday 2002, p.486.

- *When Zora visited…*: Anna Lillios, *Crossing the Creek: The Literary Friendship of Zora Neale Hurston and Marjorie Kinnan Rawlings*, University of Florida Press, 2011, pp.16–17.
- *Marjorie subjected herself*: Anna Lillios, *Crossing the Creek: The Literary Friendship of Zora Neale Hurston and Marjorie Kinnan Rawlings*, University of Florida Press, 2011, pp.27–8.

Page 266

- *against racial segregation*: Rebecca Sharpless, 'Neither Friends nor Peers: Idella Parker, Marjorie Kinnan Rawlings, and the Limits of Gender Solidarity at Cross Creek', *Journal of Southern History*, 1 May 2012, p.346.
- *putting in a good word*: Anna Lillios, *Crossing the Creek: The Literary Friendship of Zora Neale Hurston and Marjorie Kinnan Rawlings*, University of Florida Press, 2011, p.32.
- *Jane Austen and Charlotte Brontë*: Maya Angelou, *The Collected Autobiographies of Maya Angelou*, Virago, 2007, p.75, p.119, p.123, p.164.
- *find herself sharing the bill…*: Aisha I Jefferson, 'In Conversation: Nikki Giovanni and Maya Angelou on Sisterhood, and Their Friendship with Toni Morrison', *Essence*, 15 February 2013.
- *Maya threw her a party*: 'Maya Angelou, Joanne Gabbin and Nikki Giovanni', *Virginia Tech Videos* [audio], 16 October 2012.
- *Toni's tribute speech*: 'Ms. Toni Morrison presents the Literarian Award to Dr. Maya Angelou', *National Book Foundation* [video].

Page 269

- *sleeping on Alice's floor*: 'Writers on Munro', *The New Yorker*, 10 October 2013.
- *formulate a theory*: Lisa Allardice, 'Nobel prizewinner Alice Munro: "It's a wonderful thing for the short story"', *Guardian*, 6 December 2013.
- *heart-warming photograph*: This can be seen in the background behind Alice during the video of the pair's 'Google hangout', 22 January 2014.

INDEX

Writer friends Emily Midorikawa and Emma Claire Sweeney co-run Something Rhymed, a website that celebrates female literary friendship. They have written for the likes of the *Guardian*, the *Independent on Sunday* and *The Times*. Emily is a winner of the Lucy Cavendish Fiction Prize, Emma is author of the prize-winning novel *Owl Song at Dawn*, and they both teach at New York University London.